DEMOCRACY AND MORAL CONFLICT

ROBERT B. TALISSE

Vanderbilt University

CAMBRIDGE UNIVERSITY PRESS

CAMBRIDGE UNIVERSITY PRESS
Cambridge, New York, Melbourne, Madrid, Cape Town, Singapore, São Paulo, Delhi

Cambridge University Press
The Edinburgh Building, Cambridge CB2 8RU, UK

Published in the United States of America by Cambridge University Press, New York

www.cambridge.org
Information on this title: www.cambridge.org/9780521513548

First published 2009

Printed in the United Kingdom at the University Press, Cambridge

A catalogue record for this publication is available from the British Library

Library of Congress Cataloging in Publication data
Talisse, Robert B.
Democracy and moral conflict / Robert B. Talisse.
p.   cm.
Includes bibliographical references.
ISBN 978-0-521-51354-8
1. Democracy.   2. Democracy – Moral and ethical aspects.   I. Title.
JC423.T2745   2009
321.8–dc22
2009011370

ISBN 978-0-521-51354-8 hardback

For Joanne Billett

Contents

Acknowledgements   *page* viii

Introduction   1

1   The problem of deep politics   11
     I   The paradox of democratic justification   11
     II   A standard solution   23
     III Deep politics   35

2   Against the politics of omission   42
     I   The Rawlsian response   43
     II   Stout and immanent criticism   71
     III Conclusion   77

3   Folk epistemology   79
     I   The idea of a folk epistemology   80
     II   Principles of folk epistemology   87
     III An elaboration of folk epistemology   108
     IV   Conclusion   119

4   Justifying democracy   121
     I   Folk epistemology and the justification of democracy   121
     II   Folk epistemology and the problem of deep politics   139
     III Conclusion   154

5   Epistemic perfectionism   156
     I   Democracy and public ignorance   156
     II   Discourse failure   162
     III Epistemic perfectionism   170
     IV   Conclusion   185

Works cited   193
Index   201

Acknowledgements

The main idea for this book was developed in 2005, during the second half of a year in residence as a Fellow at the Center for Ethics and Public Affairs at Tulane University's Murphy Institute. I thank everyone at the Center – especially Meg Keenan and Rick Teichgraeber – for their warm hospitality and support. Work on the manuscript continued in the summer of 2007 with generous support from Vanderbilt University's Center for Ethics. The Center also helped to fund an interdisciplinary graduate seminar in the spring of 2007 that was focused on issues pertaining to democracy and religious conviction. I thank Charles Scott, director of the Center for Ethics for his support, as well as John Goldberg and John Weymark, with whom I co-taught the class. It was a very fulfilling experience to share instruction duties with such insightful colleagues. Discussions, both in the seminar room and out, with the visitors who participated in the seminar helped me to sharpen many of the arguments in this book; I thank Seyla Behnabib, Steve Macedo, Michael Perry, and Roger Scruton. The manuscript was completed in the summer of 2008 with the help of the incisive comments provided by two anonymous referees for Cambridge University Press.

Chapters of the present book draw from and develop arguments first advanced in articles published over the past several years. In particular, Chapter 2 develops material first presented in two papers: "Social Epistemology and the Politics of Omission," which appeared in 2006 in *Episteme* (2.2: 107–118), and "Stout on Public Reason," which was co-authored with Caleb Clanton and appeared in a 2005 special issue of *Soundings* (LXXXVII, 3–4; 349–368) devoted to Stout. Sections of Chapter 5 derive from my "From Pragmatism to Perfectionism," which appeared in 2007 in *Philosophy and Social Criticism* (33.3: 387–406) and my "Does Public Ignorance Defeat Deliberative Democracy," which appeared in 2005 in *Critical Review* (16.4: 455–463). I thank the publishers of these articles for permission to draw from them.

In writing this book and thinking about these issues I have benefited greatly from conversations with my friend and frequent collaborator Scott Aikin. In many respects, this book is an extension of our work together. My treatment of the epistemological issues discussed in Chapter 3 is much improved thanks to his good sense. I thank him for his philosophical camaraderie and generosity.

Thanks are also due to many friends and colleagues, all of whom provided various forms of assistance in the completion of this book: Brooke Ackerly, Jonathan Adler, Theano Apostolou, Guy Axtell, Jody Azzouni, Ken Baynes, James Bednar, James Bohman, William James Booth, Thom Brooks, Steve Cahn, Michael Calamari, Caleb Clanton, Allen Coates, Matthew Cotter, Josh Crites, Maureen Eckert, Bob Ehman, David Estlund, Matthew Festenstein, Jerry Gaus, Lenn Goodman, Dwight Goodyear, Michael Harbour, Nicole Heller, Micah Hester, Michael Hodges, Josh Houston, Gary Jaeger, Angelo Juffras, David Kaspar, Chris King, Steven Maloney, Pete Mandik, Mason Marshall, David McCullough, Mark Michael, Josh Miller, Cheryl Misak, Jonathan Neufeld, John O'Connor, John Peterman, John Post, Yvonne Raley, Walter Riker, Peter Simpson, Carol Swain, Henry Teloh, Robert Tempio, Ronald Tinnevelt, Jeffrey Tlumak, Katia Vanhemelryck, and Tyler Zimmer. Thanks are due additionally to Melinda Hall, who prepared the index. Joanne Billett once again proved an unflagging source of sustaining support, enthusiasm, and insight. This book is dedicated to her.

Introduction

Democracy is in crisis. So we are told by nearly every outlet of political comment, from politicians and pundits to academicians and ordinary citizens. This is not surprising, given that the new millennium seems to be off to a disconcerting and violent start: terrorism, genocide, torture, assassination, suicide bombings, civil war, human rights abuse, nuclear proliferation, religious extremism, poverty, climate change, environmental disaster, and strained international relations all forebode an uncertain tomorrow for democracy. Some hold that democracy is faltering because it has lost the moral clarity necessary to lead in a complicated world. Others hold that "moral clarity" means little more than moral blindness to the complexity of the contemporary world, and thus that what is needed is more reflection, self-criticism, and humility. Neither side thinks much of the other. Consequently our popular democratic politics is driven by insults, scandal, name-calling, fear-mongering, mistrust, charges of hypocrisy, and worse.

Political theorists who otherwise agree on very little share the sense that inherited categories of political analysis are no longer apt. Principles and premises that were widely accepted only a few years ago are now disparaged as part of a Cold War model that is wholly irrelevant to our post-9/11 context. An assortment of new paradigms for analysis are on offer, each promising to set matters straight and thus to ease the cognitive discomfort that comes with tumultuous times.

The diversity of approaches and methodologies tends to employ one of two general narrative strategies. On the one hand, there is the *clash of civilizations* account, which holds that the world is on the brink of, perhaps engaged in the early stages of, a global conflict between distinct and incompatible ways of life. On the other hand, there is the *democracy deficit* narrative, according to which democracy is in decline and steadily unraveling around us. Despite appearances, both narratives come in local and global versions. Although the clash of civilizations is primarily a global narrative, it manifests itself locally in the more extreme forms of identity politics and multiculturalism, in disquiet over immigration, and even in the anxiety that gay marriages pose a threat to traditional family values, if not to the traditional family itself. Likewise, whereas the democracy deficit analysis is a primarily local story, it manifests itself globally in anti-globalization and anti-corporate movements, which hold that international economic institutions are threatening self-government and self-determination around the world.

These narratives are not strictly incompatible (indeed, many theorists combine them); however, they are in tension. Whereas the clash of civilizations narrative is premised upon the claim that there is a distinctively Western way of life, the democracy deficit account laments the passing of common purposes and shared visions. Whereas the former encourages the aspiration for the institution of democracy throughout the world, the latter is far less confident that existing democracies should serve as a model for other countries to emulate. Finally, whereas the former points in the direction of a quasi-imperialist foreign policy of "nation building," the latter turns an introspective and critical eye on domestic issues.

Despite these differences, both narratives share a common premise: the old description of politics as simply a matter of "who gets what, when, and how" is obsolete; contemporary politics, both locally and globally, is driven by something deeper and more complicated than what has been variously called "interests," "incentives," or "preferences." We find ourselves ensconced in political contexts in which it seems that there is more at stake than the satisfaction of desire or the getting of what we want; increasingly we find that the political issues we must face unavoidably call into play our most fundamental moral commitments, our judgments concerning what is really important, what is ultimately valuable, what makes life worth living.[1] Such commitments not only specify our conceptions of the good life; they also provide us with our conception of politics itself – what the state is, from whence its authority derives, what liberty consists in, what forms of coercion should count as oppression, and who gets to decide. Consequently, these commitments also specify a conception of the *intolerable*, a view specifying the conditions under which morality requires resistance, even in the form of violent revolt, even at the expense of the other things that we hold dear.

---

[1] Some readers will recall the National Election Pool exit poll conducted in the 2004 presidential election in the United States which showed that an unusually large number of voters indicated that "moral values" determined how they voted. Although this poll has been widely criticized, Galston (2005: ch. 3) has proposed a convincing defense of its main findings.

A problem arises, however, once it is realized that we live under conditions of *moral pluralism*. We are *divided* over our most fundamental moral commitments. We disagree about moral basics, and accordingly disagree about the precise shape that our politics should take. Lacking a shared set of moral commitments, democratic citizens cannot resolve conflicts or justify collectively binding decisions by way of an appeal to concepts such as freedom, justice, dignity, autonomy, or even fairness. To be sure, values such as justice do enjoy a conceptual core upon which otherwise divided citizens tend to converge. Accordingly, we tend to agree that, for example, slavery was unjust and that the war against the Nazi regime was a just war. However, rapid changes in culture and technology have raised new kinds of dilemmas that seem to turn on the finer details of our moral concepts, including justice; with regard to these details we find ourselves fundamentally at odds with each other.[2] More importantly, since the values over which we are at odds are so *fundamental*, it is not clear how we should go about resolving our disputes. To what value can we appeal in deciding how to address disputes over *fundamental* values? We may say that in such cases, we ought to try to resolve our dispute in a way that is *fair*. But what if we are divided over the nature of fairness itself? Another reply might be that we ought to try to resolve such disputes by seeking a mutually acceptable *compromise*. But what if we disagree about the terms under which a compromise would be morally acceptable? Perhaps the only recourse is to try to maintain conditions of peaceful co-existence among incompatible moral worldviews. But even then, what if my moral worldview instructs me to value moral correctness over peace? Why should a truce with error be preferred to a fight for what is right? We may encapsulate these questions into one: is there a principled way to avoid Hobbes's war of all against all?

In this book, I offer what I take to be a principled alternative to the war of all against all. The alternative proposed in this book differs significantly from the standard views of democratic political philosophers. On standard views, the case for democracy derives from some decidedly *moral* commitment to, say, freedom, autonomy, dignity, liberty, or equality. Such views proceed from the assumption that there is already sufficient agreement, at least in principle, about the value and precise nature of such values among

---

[2] Consider the protests that resulted in England following Cabinet Minister Jack Straw's claim that the full veil or *niqab* constitutes a "visible statement of separation and of difference"; Muslim women protested with signs declaring that "the veil is women's liberation." *The Guardian* (October 6, 2006) at: www.guardian.co.uk/politics/2006/oct/06/immigrationpolicy.labour (accessed August 4, 2008).

citizens.[3] But there is good reason to think that, under current conditions, freedom, autonomy, dignity, liberty, and equality are *essentially controversial* – no elaboration of the details of their content can win widespread and sustainable agreement. By contrast, the case for democratic politics which I propose in this book draws from principles that are *epistemic* rather than *moral*. In the following chapters, I will try to convince you that *no matter what you believe about morality*, you have overriding epistemological reasons – reasons concerning how, what, and when one ought to believe something – to endorse democratic politics. Moreover, I aim to convince you that the epistemological reasons which lead to democratic politics are rooted in epistemic commitments that *you already endorse*. In other words, my project is not to show you that there is some view about how we should think and reason that entails that we should be democrats. Such a project would be easy, but question-begging. Instead, my project is to show you that the views that you already have about how we should think and reason commit you to a democratic political order. I hope that you find this a bold, perhaps outrageously bold, thesis. To modify a famous claim of Bertrand Russell's about the point of philosophy, my aim is to derive surprising and far-reaching conclusions from premises that are so modest as to seem undeniable.

As you will have already noticed, I sometimes write in a way that is addressed directly to you, the reader. Admittedly, this way of proceeding may prove to be awkward or strained at times, but please bear with me; this is not merely a quirk of style. It reflects a methodological strategy that I employ throughout much of the text, which I hope you will be willing to grant the aptness of, even if only provisionally or for the sake of argument. To explain: the epistemic case for democracy that I will develop is driven by what I shall call a *first-personal* epistemology. By this I mean that, in what follows, I will deliberately avoid an approach that has become standard in professional epistemology. This standard way of proceeding attempts to discern the necessary and sufficient conditions for knowledge by providing a proper analysis of the third-personal attribution of knowledge, that some subject, *S*, *knows* that some proposition, *p*. That I eschew this endeavor should not be taken to indicate some judgment on my part that it is misguided or a waste of time. The analysis of knowledge is centrally important to epistemology as a discipline, and there is good reason why

---

[3] Dworkin (2006) is a good example of this approach. Dworkin argues that a shared (but perhaps unacknowledged) commitment to human dignity underlies all of our moral conflicts. Some of the specifics of Dworkin's approach will be discussed in Chapter 5.

this task is best carried out by means of a third-personal analysis. Yet the analysis of knowledge is not the whole of epistemology, and my present purposes point in a different direction. As I said, I am interested in getting a fix on epistemic concepts other than knowledge. Specifically, I will ask you in these pages to scrutinize the function of certain epistemic concepts which are more basic than knowledge – concepts such as belief, truth, evidence, reasons, argument, and so on – in *your own case*.[4] The aim is to get a grip on the roles these concepts ordinarily play in our own lives as epistemic agents – our lives as creatures that form, examine, challenge, and revise beliefs – and to understand their interrelations. Accordingly, in addressing you in this book, I will have no need to appeal to the fanciful thought experiments and science-fictional hypothetical cases which are frequently employed by pro-fessional epistemologists. Again, the aim is to disclose the epistemology of us ordinary thinking creatures under ordinary epistemic conditions. I am interested in doing "no frills" epistemology here.

But the fact that I aim to uncover the epistemology we employ in our everyday lives does not entail that the project is strictly descriptive or without prescriptive import. What we will find, I contend, is that our ordinary epistemic practices embed a set of normative epistemic commitments – principles governing the activities by which we form, assert, defend, revise, challenge, and change beliefs. For example, I will argue that there is a tight conceptual connection between *believing* that Athens is the capital of Greece and *taking oneself to have sufficient evidence* that Athens is the capital of Greece. When this connection is breached – as when we discover that our evidence is insufficient – we feel the need to take epistemic action of some sort: we correct or revise our belief, we hedge, we self-deceive or rationalize in order to maintain the belief, or perhaps we suspend belief altogether. In any case, by taking epistemic action we reveal that we uphold the principle that beliefs *ought* to square with the evidence we have and that we as believers *ought* to track evidence. By uncovering our everyday epistemology in this way, we will also make explicit to ourselves the normative commitments implicit therein.

Given its obvious parallels with what is known as folk psychology, I call this general "no frills" first-personal epistemology *folk epistemology*. I will explain it in detail in Chapter 3. For now, it will suffice to say that in

---

[4] I say that these other concepts are more basic than knowledge because, on the standard analyses, knowledge is true justified belief, or true belief for which the believer has adequate reasons or evidence. There are several difficulties lurking in this intuitive account of knowledge that I will not engage in this book. The point is that the analysis of knowledge makes reference to the concepts of belief, truth, and evidence (among others); hence these concepts are more basic.

developing an epistemic case for democratic politics, I shall begin from what I take to be an intuitive grasp of what our ordinary concepts of belief, truth, reasons, argument, and evidence involve. Perhaps surprisingly, we will find that these folk concepts, when examined first-personally, imply a *social epistemology* according to which proper and responsible epistemic activity can be engaged only in cooperation with other epistemic agents and under certain specifiable social conditions.[5] The argument of the book is that the folk epistemology to which we are already committed entails a commitment to a certain social epistemology, which in turn requires a democratic political and social order. Thus, the folk epistemic commitments we – you and I – already endorse are sufficient to motivate an overriding commitment to democratic politics, in spite of our deep and serious disagreements over our most fundamental moral commitments.

It should be emphasized at this point (and I will emphasize this elsewhere) that the thesis is *not* that folk epistemic commitments entail specific claims about the nitty-gritty details of democratic government. The ambition is not to show that folk epistemology requires that one should take some particular view about term limits, electoral systems, taxation, or immigration policy. Rather, the claim is that folk epistemic norms entail a commitment to democratic norms in a broader sense: folk epistemology entails commitments to core democratic norms of freedom of speech, thought, and expression, freedom of conscience, political equality (including equality of participation), freedom of the press, protected dissent, political accountability, and so on. One might say, then, that the thesis of the book is that folk epistemic norms commit one to what Karl Popper (1971) characterized as the "open society," or to the broadly liberal and humanistic democratic vision defended in various ways by John Stuart Mill (1859), Bertrand Russell (1949), and John Dewey (1935), among many others. For reasons that I will specify later, I take it to be a virtue of the view that I shall be developing that it attaches to democratic norms in this broad sense and leaves open questions concerning the specific details of democratic governance. I will have occasion in Chapter 5 to say something about certain policies that have been proposed by Ronald Dworkin. Although I will support some of his proposals, I do not contend that the folk epistemic approach *requires* us to support them. Rather, the point is to

---

[5] By *social epistemology* I do not mean anything particularly fancy, such as the rejection of traditional or "individualist" methods of epistemology. I follow Goldman (1999: 4) in using the term to refer to the broad view that knowledge-seeking is in large part a social endeavor involving the coordination and collaboration of many individuals within various institutional contexts.

specify how the folk epistemic view frames issues concerning, for example, political campaign speech.

Another point is also worth raising at this juncture. The thesis that folk epistemic norms entail democratic political norms does *not* mean that the epistemological reasons you have to support democracy must be your actually *motivating* reasons. Like most readers of this book, you probably have a set of *moral* reasons for being a democrat which are sufficient to sustain your own day-to-day commitment to democracy, even in the light of what you see as serious moral failings of recent policy. For example, it is likely that your commitment to, say, equality, liberty, or autonomy is such that you take yourself to be morally obligated to support and uphold democracy under almost all non-extraordinary circumstances. If this is true of you, then consider the epistemic argument proposed in this book a *supplement* which may be appealed to when dealing with those who do not share your moral convictions regarding the overriding value of democracy. In any case, if my argument succeeds there will be nothing in the folk epistemic commitments that I identify that contradicts your moral convictions. However, it should also be noted that if my argument succeeds, you will discover that, although you may have moral reasons that, in fact, motivate your democratic commitments, you also have epistemic reasons that are *sufficient* to motivate those commitments.

But more importantly, if my folk epistemic argument succeeds, you will have a tool that will enable you to criticize existing democratic institutions and practices in a way that does not presuppose your own particular – perhaps unpopular and controversial – moral commitments. This is important because it is often suspected that criticisms of, say, standing democratic procedures are simply disguises or proxies for the substantive moral commitments of the critics. But where democratic citizens are divided over substantive moral commitments, any criticism of procedures and institutions that fits this characterization is doomed to impotence. For example, popular criticism in the United States of the handling of the 2000 Presidential election was frequently dismissed by Bush supporters as simply a strategic way of expressing dissatisfaction with the outcome; Gore supporters who objected to the process were charged with being insincere, unprincipled, or sore losers.[6] Of course, Gore supporters *were* dissatisfied with the outcome of the electoral process. But there were many who surely were driven primarily by concerns for the integrity of the democratic

---

[6] Recall the bumper stickers that emerged in the weeks following the 2000 election which mimicked the Gore–Lieberman campaign graphic but said instead "Sore Loserman."

process; for them, the process was objectionable *regardless* of the outcome. If the argument of this book succeeds, we will have specified a set of epistemic principles, common to citizens regardless of political affiliation, to which one may appeal in offering such criticism. Criticism that draws only from shared epistemic commitments deflects charges of insincerity and the like.

In identifying and explicating the commitments constitutive of our folk epistemology, I will frequently make reference to artifacts of our contemporary political culture (I did so in the previous paragraph). Examples are often drawn from sources of popular political discourse and commentary, including the work of popular pundits such as Al Franken, Ann Coulter, Michael Moore, Bill O'Reilly, and others. I suppose some may object to this, claiming that it is unfitting or worse for an academic to engage with this literature, which is, in the end, probably better characterized as entertainment and satire than political commentary. However, given that I aim in part to demonstrate that certain epistemic commitments are deeply entrenched in our everyday epistemic practices, the fact that popular political discourse is saturated with appeals to epistemic concepts such as "no spin zones," "straight talk," "inconvenient truths," and criticisms of "bias" and "lying liars" counts as crucial support for my case. I make no apology for this feature of the book.

Similarly, I make no apology for the fact that most of my examples draw from the popular political culture in the United States. After all, this is the political culture with which I am most familiar and am most qualified to discuss. But, as I shall argue in Chapter 3, the fact that the examples are drawn from a single political context does not entail that the folk epistemic principles which they elucidate are somehow provincial or culture-specific. Again, the aim is to identify a collection of epistemic principles that are entirely generic and basic to epistemic agency as such.

Finally, I should confess that I am in agreement with those who hold that our democracy faces a serious crisis. Importantly, though I do not deny that there are formidable threats to democracy posed from without in the form of international terrorism, rogue states with nuclear ambitions, and the like, I contend that there is also a serious crisis *within* contemporary democracy. To be sure, it is typically claimed that democracy is failing internally due to disunity or some moral unraveling of tradition; however, my worry is different. It is my view that the most serious internally posed crisis we face as democrats is not primarily moral, although it most commonly manifests itself in moral conflict. Perhaps it will come as no surprise that I think that the crisis we face is fundamentally epistemic in nature: we are losing our ability to *disagree* with one another; or, rather, we are losing our ability to see those with whom we disagree as *mistaken* or simply *wrong* rather than wicked, ignorant, dishonest, perverse, benighted, or foolish. Yet, it is one of the philosophical presuppositions of democracy that there can be disagreement – even deep, heated, and seemingly intractable disagreement – among reasonable, well-intentioned, well-informed, and sincere people doing their best to reason through an issue. Put otherwise, at the core of democracy is the belief that *reasoned argument* is possible, even among people who are very deeply divided over moral and religious doctrines. The most disturbing trends in contemporary democracy are those which attack this presupposition by encouraging us to lose sight of it.

And such trends are becoming increasingly prevalent. We are constantly encouraged in forums of popular political discussion to regard those with whom we disagree as *ipso facto* beyond the epistemic pale – incorrigible, silly, irrational, unintelligent, and, therefore, not worth engaging with or even regarding as fellow citizens.[7] Accordingly, public political debates provide occasion not for the exchange of reasons and arguments, but for the trading of insults; they are sophistical contests in which each participant tries to prove the most effective at making his opponent look silly. We shall note and examine these trends throughout the coming chapters. But the philosophical point is worth punctuating from the very start: if we lose our capacity to argue with each other, especially across deep moral divisions, we will lose our democracy.

I close these introductory remarks with a word about the kind of book I have tried to write. No doubt some readers will have detected from the foregoing that in this book I attempt an act of what is sometimes called *public philosophy*; that is, I aspire to present rigorous philosophical argumentation and analysis in a way that is, nonetheless, accessible to a non-academic readership. This aspiration is notoriously hazardous; the attempt to do respectable philosophy in a way that is suitable for public consumption invites simultaneous charges of simple-mindedness (from the academic readership) and over-demandingness (from the non-academic readership). The hazard seems heightened when the philosophical content which is to be made publicly palatable draws from an area as esoteric as epistemology. To further complicate matters, the very suggestion that the solution to a certain problem in democratic theory is to be found in epistemology is bound to aggravate some political theorists. In short, perils abound.

---

[7] Notice that Ann Coulter's recent book of popular political commentary is titled *If Democrats Had Any Brains, They'd Be Republicans* (2007).

I have had to deal with trade-offs between accessibility and thoroughness. To help make the points where accessibility trumps thoroughness more bearable for the academics, I have tried to flag the spots where crucial issues have been bracketed, and in some places I include in the footnotes some of the requisite detail. Where the discussion makes unavoidable the introduction of some nuance or complication that could test the patience of a non-academic reader, I try to slow down and raise a few examples. Unsurprisingly, neither of these strategies is perfect with respect to appeasing the incompatible demands of the different audiences that I am trying to address simultaneously, but this might be the best one can do. In any case, if this book stimulates reasoned criticism and counter-arguments from those who oppose my claims, I will have achieved some measure of success.

The problem of deep politics

In the Introduction, I characterized the problem to which this book is addressed as that of finding an alternative to a Hobbesian war of all against all under conditions of moral pluralism. This characterization of the problem is, of course, very rough and imprecise. In order to make headway in understanding, and hopefully solving, the problem that moral pluralism sets for democratic politics, we will need to begin from a more detailed and nuanced analysis of that problem. This is what I provide in this chapter.

I THE PARADOX OF DEMOCRATIC JUSTIFICATION

Framing the paradox

Imagine a society in which the legitimacy of the government – its institutions, procedures, laws, decisions, office-holders, and policies – is held to rest, at least indirectly, upon the consent of those it governs. Imagine further that action on the part of both the government and the citizenry is constrained by a set of rules specified in a public constitution. This constitution contains procedural provisions not only for holding regular elections, dividing political authority, checking political power, and punishing abuses, but also for its own criticism and revision. Additionally, let us say that the constitution specifies a set of protections for individuals from interference by the government, by foreign governments, and by other individuals, what is often referred to as a "menu" or "schedule" of rights and liberties. This menu specifies rights to hold and exchange property, to privacy, to equal protection under the law, to due process, and so on. In addition to these, the constitution also identifies rights of individual conscience. That is, individuals in our imagined society enjoy freedoms of thought, expression, assembly, petition, and religion, all within the constraint that each is entitled to as extensive a share of such liberties as is consistent with there being an equal share for all.

Under political conditions secured by such a constitution, it is natural to expect there to emerge a bustling and vibrant civil society of multiple organizations and groups directed to a diversity of ends. Accordingly, we may imagine that our citizens belong to, or participate in, a range of voluntary and affective associations, from religious groups, ethnic organizations, and political alliances to social clubs and cliques. One result of this is that a variety of moral doctrines will flourish in the society. We should expect that our imagined citizens will not share a common collection of moral commitments; instead, a diversity of such commitments should be expected to thrive among citizens.

It seems suitable to further suppose that citizens will generally take certain percepts among these commitments to be *basic*. That is, each citizen will take the core of his moral or religious doctrine to specify values, aims, and ends that are *fundamental* to living a proper life, both individually and in relation to others. Moreover, we should expect that the varied moral and religious doctrines that thrive among citizens do not form a consistent set. Accordingly, our imagined citizens will *disagree* over fundamental matters of right, obligation, duty, value, good, virtue, happiness, and justice. Of course, we should expect that many, if not all, of the doctrines endorsed by citizens will include a conception of toleration and will accordingly prescribe or require toleration with respect to a certain subset of opposing views. But we should also expect the notion of toleration to be interpreted differently by each doctrine, such that within every doctrine there will be a discrimination made between opposing doctrines that are acceptable objects of tolerance and those that are not.

A distinction is called for here. I have said that every doctrine which contains a conception of toleration will distinguish between opposing doctrines that deserve to be tolerated and those that do not. In this latter category there will be, on the one hand, opposing doctrines that, while not deserving of toleration, nonetheless may be tolerated under appropriate circumstances; on the other hand, there will be opposing doctrines that not only do not deserve toleration but must be *not tolerated*. In other words, every doctrine that contains a conception of toleration will nonetheless identify certain opposing doctrines as beyond the pale and, therefore, *intolerable*; in the case of intolerable opposing doctrines, what is morally required is *intolerance*.

Thus, it is possible to specify for each doctrine the *scope* of its conception of toleration. On some doctrines, toleration will be construed very broadly; very few opposing doctrines will be taken to be undeserving of tolerance and fewer still will be taken to require intolerance. Other doctrines will contain a narrow conception of toleration, extending tolerance only to those opposing doctrines that are very close relatives to themselves. There will, of course, be a wide variety of positions in between these two poles. Many doctrines will endorse the roughly Millian standard of toleration: one must tolerate anything that does not constitute harm to others. Others will draw the line between the tolerable and intolerable differently and on the basis of different considerations. And even among those that accept a roughly Millian standard, there will be considerable disagreement about the scope and nature of the concept of harm.

Accordingly, the citizens I have been asking you to imagine will differ not only at the level of their substantive doctrines of the good; they will also disagree about which sub-optimal moral and political arrangements are even tolerable. Given this, there will be not only *disagreements*, but *conflicts* among citizens holding different doctrines.

In addition to this, let us suppose that conditions of *moral pluralism* obtain. That is, let us suppose that there is a plurality of moral doctrines – religious, secular, what have you – that conflict with each other but nonetheless individually meet some rather loose conditions for minimal plausibility. Let us say that a doctrine is at least *minimally plausible* if it is internally coherent, is able to speak to the normal range of moral phenomena, seems based in a reasonable conception of human moral psychology, can proffer moral prescriptions that are able to guide action, and is supported by a range of considerations typically thought to be relevant to the justification of a moral doctrine. As I said, we need only a loose conception of plausibility here. The presumption of moral pluralism, then, comes to this: for every citizen holding a plausible doctrine, there are other citizens holding opposing but also plausible doctrines. We need not worry over different degrees of plausibility, or whether and when opposed doctrines are *equally* plausible. Further, we need not take a position concerning citizens holding implausible doctrines, or whether and when such doctrines deserve toleration. We are simply concerned to say that the fact of persistent and deep disagreement over fundamental moral doctrines is not in itself an indication of deeply entrenched irrationality; in other words, we are committed to the idea that sane, intelligent, sincere, and informed persons can come to hold different (and opposing) moral doctrines.

To be clear, moral pluralism in this sense is not moral relativism. In supposing that moral pluralism obtains, I am not thereby committing to the idea that all moral and religious doctrines are true (despite their being inconsistent with each other), or that their truth is relative to an agent's beliefs, interests, community, or culture. Moreover, moral pluralism is not skepticism. By accepting moral pluralism, one is not committed to the claim that all moral and religious doctrines are false, or nonsense, or non-cognitive, or unjustified. One can acknowledge moral pluralism while being committed to the final, objective, universal truth of one's own moral doctrine. All that moral pluralism requires is that one countenance the possibility of what might be called *honest moral error* – well-intentioned, sincere, informed, and rational agents doing their epistemic best can still wind up with false moral beliefs. This is simply the recognition that getting moral matters right is *difficult*. We can say, then, that moral pluralism, as the term is being employed here, is not itself a moral theory or a theory about morality; it is rather a claim about moral theories. More precisely, it is a claim about the travails of moral theorizing. And it is a rather mundane claim at that. Moral pluralism is the strictly descriptive claim that, at present, there are many minimally plausible moral doctrines, both secular and religious. To deny moral pluralism, then, is to assert that those who hold moral doctrines that are different from your own are not only mistaken, but necessarily inept, benighted, stupid, and perhaps insane. In other words, to deny moral pluralism is to deny that there is a distinction between being *wrong* and being out of one's mind. Only the most extreme fanatics take such a view.

I will have something further to say about fanatics below and in a later chapter. For now the point is this: given that moral pluralism obtains, conflict among citizens over fundamental commitments is not only inevitable, but many such conflicts are, at least at present and for practical purposes, rationally irresolvable. To repeat, the fact that citizens disagree at the level of plausible doctrines does *not* entail that at least some citizens are irrational, foolish, or benighted. Moral pluralism means instead that reasonable, intelligent, and sincere persons operating under favorable epistemic conditions can come to different but plausible conclusions about fundamental questions. Indeed, it is widespread consensus at fundamental moral levels, not moral disagreement, that is a symptom of irrationality, insincerity, or even, as John Rawls held, oppression (2005: 37).

Thus, we have before us an imaginary society. Let us say that the constitution I have asked you to imagine instantiates a kind of political and social order that can be called *constitutional democracy*, or just *democracy* for short.[1] If you are willing to allow that this imagined democracy resembles our own in the relevant respects, then we must confront a potentially

---

[1] I shall use the term *democracy* in this way throughout this book. Some would insist that I have described a *liberal* democracy. Depending on the details regarding what is meant by the term, I would

crushing dilemma: the core democratic idea that legitimacy of the democratic state rests upon the consent of those governed by it requires us to articulate principles that supply the justification for our government; however, the fact that citizens are deeply divided over fundamental commitments renders any such principles essentially contestable and, therefore, unlikely objects of widespread agreement. It seems, then, that the very liberties that constitute the core of democracy render the democracy's own conception of legitimacy unsatisfiable. This is the paradox of democratic justification.

It may appear that the paradox of democratic justification is a puzzle of merely academic interest and, therefore, of little consequence for the real world of democratic politics. But this is not the case. The paradox of democratic justification pervades our politics; contemporary democratic societies are plagued with controversies and clashes that emerge from the need for a democratic political order to justify itself to a morally and religiously conflicted citizenry. Let us consider briefly a few examples.

(1) *The science curriculum*
Throughout the United States, citizen groups and various religious organizations have fought to introduce referenda regarding the state-controlled science curriculum in public schools. According to many citizens, the theory of evolution, the cornerstone of modern biology by any reasonable measure, conflicts with their fundamental commitments concerning the origins, nature, and purpose of human life. In fact, according to some citizens, the theory of evolution is not simply *incorrect* in its account of life, but, in addition, is morally and intellectually corrupting. Given the compulsory nature of primary and secondary education, citizens demand that the curriculum of the public schools reflect – or at the very least not *undermine* – the values and commitments of the communities they serve.

Biologists and other science advocates contend that the evidence in favor of evolution is overwhelming, and that the duty of a science curriculum is to impart science's best understanding of the truth. Opponents have countered that the theory of evolution is in fact *not* the best understanding of biological life, and have contended that a competing theory, the theory of intelligent design, is a viable competitor; they have thus called for a curriculum that gives equal time to intelligent design theory, insisting that the biology curriculum should "teach the debate." Biologists have

not resist this. However, I think the terms *liberal* and *liberalism*, as they are employed in the academic literature (to say nothing of how they are used in popular discussion of politics), have become nearly useless, and so I avoid them when possible.

responded that intelligent design is *not* properly a scientific theory and hence *not* a viable alternative to the theory of evolution; hence, they contend, there is no debate to teach.

(2) Gay marriage

In 2004, twelve states in the United States placed on their election ballots referenda calling for amendments to their respective state constitutions to officially define marriage as a relationship between one man and one woman, thereby blocking marriage among same-sex couples. Much of the opposition to gay marriage is driven by the moral commitment, shared by many religious citizens, that homosexuality is a grave moral evil and, therefore, something that the state should not endorse. According to such citizens, extending marriage to same-sex couples is tantamount to *morally validating* homosexual relationships, something they feel morally compelled to oppose.[2]

Advocates of gay marriage contend that the issue has nothing to do with the morality of homosexuality, but is instead a simple question of justice. Advocates hold that legal equality demands that the same rights and privileges available to heterosexual couples by way of the institution of marriage must be available to all citizens, regardless of sexual orientation. To restrict marriage to heterosexual couples is to discriminate against homosexuals on the basis of a morally irrelevant characteristic, which is blatantly unjust.

(3) The jury and the Bible

In May 2003, Judge John E. Vigil of Adams County District Court in Colorado overturned the death sentence of a convicted rapist and murderer after discovering that jurors had consulted the Bible during deliberations. According to Vigil, "Jury resort to biblical code has no place in a constitutional death penalty proceeding."[3] Vigil's reasoning has it that since not all citizens accept the moral authority of the Bible, and are in fact not legally required to do so, the jury's appeal to the Bible in sentencing deliberations is tantamount to *imposing* a moral authority on the convicted. In March 2005,

---

[2] Compare the Vatican's 2003 statement, "Those who would move from tolerance to the legitimization of specific rights for cohabiting homosexual persons need to be reminded that approval or legalization of evil is something far different from the toleration of evil. In those situations where homosexual unions have been legally recognized or have been given the legal status and rights belonging to marriage, clear and emphatic opposition is a duty." *Considerations Regarding Proposals to Give Legal Recognition to Unions Between Homosexual Persons*, II.5 (www.vatican.va/roman_curia/congregations/cfaith/documents/rc_con_cfaith_doc_20030731_homosexual-unions_en.html (accessed May 5, 2008).

[3] *New York Times*, "Bible Reading Voids Death Sentence," May 24, 2003, p. A-13.

nonetheless supports other acts of disobedience, such as physically blocking entrances to abortion clinics. Explaining this posture, Dobson writes:

To those Christians who feel prohibited from stepping across a property line to save a baby, I would ask ... What would you have done as a citizen of Germany in World War II? The Nazi extermination camps were legal. Would you have broken your country's unjust laws in order to protect millions of people marked for death?[7]

Again, Dobson's envisioned analogy between abortion and the Holocaust is telling. His explicit claim is that standing abortion laws are illegitimate and, therefore, may be – perhaps, morally speaking, *must be* – disobeyed. This, of course, leaves one to wonder about the grounds upon which Dobson condemns violence against abortion doctors, but we will not investigate this here. Consider instead the further implications of Dobson's analogy. If, indeed, the system of legal abortion in the United States is analogous to the system of legal extermination in Nazi Germany, then those in the United States who seek to maintain or expand protections of a woman's right to choose to terminate her pregnancy are analogous to bona fide Nazis. Hence, on Dobson's view, individuals who are pro-choice are *not* fellow democratic citizens, but rather agents of an unjust, illegitimate, and anti-democratic political order. Accordingly, for members of Operation Rescue and Focus on the Family, pro-choice advocates are not proper democrats and thus, at the very least, do not deserve toleration.

The critic will next claim that my examples prove his point. He will say that organizations like Operation Rescue and Focus on the Family are *fringe* groups and thus are *not* representative of mainstream political sentiment in the United States. That I have drawn my examples from these organizations confirms that, in general, citizens are not as deeply divided as the paradox of democratic justification requires.

But the critic now seems to have misunderstood the nature and intended force of the paradox. The issue that I am confronting is not simply a sociological one regarding the number of citizens who take themselves to be deeply divided from other citizens regarding fundamental moral commitments.[8] The issue is rather that of *justifying* the democratic requirement that citizens must tolerate – or at least not judge *intolerable* – a wide range of moral and religious doctrines and be willing to accept democratic compromises in cases where their fundamental values conflict with standing

---

[7] "Why does Focus support the rescue movement?," family-topics.custhelp.com/cgi-bin/family_topics. cfg/php/enduser/std_adp.php?p_faqid=1240 (accessed July 29, 2005).

[8] I am inclined to think that the sociological data speak in favor of my view, but will not engage the issue here.

democratic outcomes. So, I can grant the critic's sociological point that, despite extremist rhetoric and other exaggerated portrayals on offer by fringe organizations, contemporary citizens are generally willing to accept democratic compromises. But the question that is central to our concern is this: *why should they?* What *reasons* can be offered for upholding democratic commitments at the expense of other, perhaps more important, values? That a great many citizens of contemporary democracies accept the necessity of political compromise as a matter of course and, therefore, do not demand such justifications is entirely beside the point. Whether demanded or not, democratic politics stands in need of justification.

Let us turn now to a second criticism that aims to dismiss the paradox of democratic justification. The second critic might pick up where the first critic left off and argue that there is an easy and obvious resolution to the paradox of democratic justification. Citizens have reason to uphold democratic commitments, even in cases in which those commitments clash with their more basic moral or religious doctrines, for the simple reason that the cost of defection is too high. Opponents of abortion could engage in acts of violence to promote the pro-life cause, and, from their point of view would be morally justified in doing so, but, alas, this course of action would be imprudent because the democratic state has the power to prosecute and severely punish those who break its laws. Thus, citizens have an obvious reason to uphold democratic commitments: if they do not uphold such commitments, they will be punished. Accordingly, the critic concludes, the paradox of democratic justification is resolved by power.

This criticism has the familiar, confident air of a Hobbesian political realism. However, it raises many problems, not all of which can be canvassed here. The most obvious difficulty with the criticism is that it requires us to understand political legitimacy as simple stability. Of course, stability is a desideratum of any political regime; however, the critic has construed stability simply as the power to force compliance. The difficulty with this view lies in the fact that there is a clear and intuitive difference between exercises of power that are *legitimate* and those that are merely *effective*. Likewise, one can easily cite historical examples about which it would be correct to say that power was *successfully* but *unjustly* wielded. Doubtless the critic will want to deny these distinctions. Yet if one follows the critic in relinquishing the distinction between legitimate and illegitimate (yet effective) power, one also relinquishes the normative ground which enables us to *criticize* power. Moreover, one relinquishes the normative ground which enables us to judge that a particular act of government – the desegregation of the public schools, for example – constitutes *moral progress* in the direction of justice. Hence the imagined response proposes to resolve the paradox of democratic justification by rejecting the idea of political justification altogether. This hardly seems an acceptable democratic response.

There is a further difficulty facing the political realist response to the paradox. Borrowing some nomenclature from Rawls which I shall appeal to more systematically in later chapters, one may say that the power-based resolution to the paradox makes political justification a matter of striking a mutually acceptable *modus vivendi*, or truce, among opposed parties (2005: 145). Where a political order is accepted as a *modus vivendi*, each contending party sees it as a less than optimal compromise to be tolerated only for as long as the relative balance of power among the contending parties precludes any one party from dominating the others. But as power relations are unstable and prone to fluctuation, so too is a social order whose justification lies exclusively in power. Under such conditions, it is reasonable to expect the contending parties to not acquiesce in the democratic status quo, but to attempt instead to manipulate the existing balance of power. Again, this seems an unpromising response to the paradox.

Thus, it seems that there is a strong *prima facie* reason to think that paradox of democratic justification stands, and lies, at the root of some of our most divisive political controversies. Given democracy's own conception of political legitimacy, a response to the paradox is called for. We turn, then, to an examination of a standard democratic resolution.

II A STANDARD SOLUTION

Democracy as procedure

On a standard account, the paradox of democratic justification is resolved by an appeal to the idea that democracy is essentially a *procedure* or *process*. The procedural account begins with an insight, well-captured by Rawls in a paraphrase of Isaiah Berlin, that there can be no social world without loss (2005: 197). That is, the procedural response begins with the claim that compromise is a condition of living with others in a political and social order. The next step is to draw the inference that since no one can get everything he wants by way of political decisions and outcomes, choice among political systems is essentially a choice concerning the terms under which compromises will be struck. Under some regimes, political decision is entirely in the hands of some sub-section of the population. In a monarchy, for instance, political rule rests entirely with the monarch. Accordingly, in a monarchy, compromise is a one-way street: the monarch gets his way, and the subjects compromise their way into compliance. Similarly, in an oligarchic regime, the few hold political power, and the many must compromise. In a theocracy, the priesthood gets its way, and the laypersons compromise. In a plutocracy, the rich make the rules and the poor compromise. And so on.

In a democracy, by contrast, political power is shared equally by the entire citizenry. Political decisions are made by means of a fair aggregative voting procedure in which each citizen has an equal voice and the majority rules (within certain constraints, as discussed below). Of course, contemporary democracy employs a variety of systems of representation, so democratic rule is not *direct*; nonetheless, the core idea is that, under democratic rule, the burden of political compromise is shared across the entire population. This means that no one can expect to get his way *all of the time*. The consolation is that since the democratic procedure fairly aggregates citizens' interests, as registered by votes, democracy can ensure that most people will get mostly what they want most of the time, or at least more often than they would under any of the viable alternate regimes.

This feature of democracy is supplemented by the range of constraints that are placed on majority rule. In other words, in a democracy, majority rule is constrained by a set of individual rights, specified in a constitution, that protect individuals from not only the unjust interference of the government and foreign governments, but also from the interference of the majority. In a democracy, there are certain things that a majority, no matter how numerous, cannot get (or at least cannot get easily). Accordingly, there are limits to the kind of compromises individuals are expected to endure at the hands of a democratic majority. The most extreme losses – losses of life, liberty, and property, for example – are precluded, except in certain special cases, as specified by law.

On the procedural account, then, the justification of any particular political decision lies in the fact that it was produced by a fair procedure that not only gives to all citizens an equal voice in decision-making, and protects individuals from unjust interference even by a democratic majority, but also guarantees to each citizen who finds himself in the minority on a specific issue the continuing opportunity to convince those holding the majority opinion that they are in error and should revise their view. So, even though there can be no social world without loss, in a democracy, no particular losses are by necessity *permanent*; decisions which seem to some citizen in the minority to be egregious and unacceptable errors can be, at least in principle, retrieved and corrected.

In short, the procedural view holds that the justification for democracy lies in the fact that it offers to citizens a process for making political decisions and effecting political change relatively efficiently and without violence. To employ a trope common among proceduralists, democracy replaces bullets with ballots. Hence, although democracy cannot guarantee to its citizens that they will always agree with its outcomes, it can guarantee a degree of peace, fairness, and stability that is not available under alternate regimes. And peace, fairness, and stability are crucial if one wants to change a regime non-violently from within. The proceduralist recognizes that democracy is not perfect, but will maintain, with Winston Churchill, that, even in light of its failings, democracy is better than its real-world competitors; even if it is not the best *simpliciter*, it is the best we can get.

Presuppositions of proceduralism

I shall not rehearse the most common criticisms that have been raised against the procedural view of democracy. Roughly, these criticisms attack democracy's aggregative mechanism, purporting to show that no achievable voting procedure can deliver results that can plausibly be held to represent the will of the majority; some go further to argue that the very concept of the will of the majority is incoherent. These are formidable criticisms, and they have given rise to a vast technical literature.[9] But they are not germane to our present concerns. I instead want to examine the question of whether or not the procedural response to the paradox of democratic justification is viable. This requires further elaboration of the procedural view.

Jane Mansbridge provides an accurate characterization of the workings of the procedural view in her description of what she calls "adversary democracy":

Voters pursue their individual interests by making demands on the political system in proportion to the intensity of their feelings. Politicians, also pursuing their own interests, adopt policies that buy them votes, thus ensuring accountability. In order to stay in office, politicians act like entrepreneurs and brokers, looking for formulas that satisfy as many, and alienate as few, interests as possible. From the interchange between self-interested votes and self-interested brokers emerge decisions that come as close as possible to a balanced aggregation of individual interests. (1983: 17)

We need not follow Mansbridge, and many other communitarians and participatory democrats, in lamenting the adversarial aspects of the

---

[9] For this kind of criticism, see especially Riker 1988. For a defense of democracy against this kind of critique, see Mackie 2003. Gaus 2003a: ch. 6, nicely surveys the issues.

procedural view.[10] After all, the commitment to moral pluralism entails that conflict among citizens is inevitable. Moreover, it should also be noted that even serious conflict need not involve incivility or hostility. For similar reasons, the central role of self-interest in the procedural system need not concern us here, for self-interest need not mean *selfishness*, or interest that is strictly *self-regarding* rather than altruistic or socially responsible. What is of interest is that the procedural view claims to have no deep moral aspirations or goals other than that of producing decisions in a way that treats all citizens' interests equally. On the procedural view, a democratic system is not in the business of evaluating the relative merits of citizens' interests, preferences, or opinions, nor does it aim to produce outcomes that represent the "common good." Rather, on the procedural view, democracy is essentially non-normative and "thin"; it aims only to arrive at decisions that accurately represent the aggregate of citizens' inputs. In this way, it aspires simply to give the people what they want.

The thin character of the procedural view is often considered to be its primary strength. Recall that the paradox of democratic justification arises precisely because citizens do not share a common set of normative commitments. When citizens are divided at the level of their conceptions of the good, an account of democracy that presupposes, or is explicitly aimed at realizing, some particular normative vision will fail to win widespread consent. By construing democracy non-normatively, the procedural view avoids this difficulty. Ian Shapiro formulates this aspect of the procedural view well:

Rather than think of democracy as a mechanism for institutionalizing the general will, we should recognize its claim to our allegiance as the best available system for managing power relations among people who disagree about the nature of the common good, among many other things, but who nonetheless are bound to live together. (2003: 146)

As he summarizes his point, Shapiro contends that the procedural view of democracy "embodies what those with an interest in avoiding domination share" (2003: 146). Since it is safe to assume that citizens who are deeply divided over basic moral and religious commitments share a common interest in avoiding being dominated by their moral opponents – those who are *ex hypothesi* committed to an inferior, false, or intolerable moral view – the procedural view seems a neat and clean resolution of the paradox.

---

[10] For this kind of criticism, see Etzioni 2001 and Barber 2004.

Yet there are serious difficulties with the procedural view understood as a response to the paradox of democratic justification. To be sure, the core of the proceduralist justification for democracy seems sound: when no one can get everything he wants, it makes sense for everyone to settle for the best arrangement he can get. But this justification presupposes that citizens are willing to conceive of their deepest moral commitments in a rather particular, perhaps peculiar, way. To be specific, the procedural view presupposes that we are able to regard our deepest moral and religious commitments as *wants*, *preferences*, and *interests*, entities or objects that can be individuated, quantified, and aggregated; moreover, it presumes that citizens are willing to view their commitments as *fungible* items that can be exchanged and bargained with. In this way, the procedural view emerges as a *quasi-economic* model, according to which "democracy is a kind of market" (Posner 2003: 166). This image is explicitly endorsed by Joseph Schumpeter in his description of the "democratic method" as "that institutional arrangement for arriving at political decisions in which individuals acquire the power to decide by means of a competitive struggle for the people's vote" (1942: 269).

The objection I want to raise against this aspect of the procedural view will not be that the market is an inadequate model for understanding the whole of democratic society.[11] Again, the target of the present analysis is *not* the procedural model of democracy as such, but rather the procedural model understood as a response to the paradox of democratic justification. The question, then, is whether the procedural view can provide a justification for democracy to citizens whose fundamental values lose out in the democratic process. The strength of the procedural view as a response to the paradox depends upon the aptness of the presupposition that citizens are able to treat their deepest moral and religious commitments as the kind of entities that can be entered into a market-like system of exchange, negotiation, and aggregation.

Is this presupposition justified? I think not. There is good reason to think that citizens are *unable* to regard their commitments in this way. Consider religious commitment. Many religious believers do not, indeed, *cannot*, regard their deepest value commitments as bargaining chips with which to attempt to strike the best political deal they can in light of their interests. Indeed, according to many religious believers, their commitments are not quite *interests* at all; they are instead more like *categorical commands* or inviolable directives from God or from some other source of ultimate moral authority. Accordingly, many religious believers see their most

---

[11] For this kind of criticism, see Sandel 1998b.

fundamental commitments as *non-negotiable, non-quantifiable,* and *not fungible.* Moreover, they are inclined to regard as unacceptable a procedure that simply aggregates citizens' interests, regardless of their normative merits. That is to say, many religious believers are inclined to see the proceduralist's thin vision of democratic politics as *itself* morally bankrupt: to treat all interests as equal is to treat good and evil, right and wrong, and virtue and vice as equal, which is morally corrupt as such and, therefore, unacceptable.

Here the proceduralist will rehearse the Berlinian consideration that there can be no social world without loss, and repeat Churchill's insight that democracy, warts and all, is the best we can get. But this response presumes that religiously committed citizens are willing to concede that engaging in real-world politics is more important than standing up for what is right, or for what God commands, come what may. Indeed, religiously committed citizens may concede the proceduralist's point that real-world politics necessarily involve dirty hands, but they may conclude from this that one ought to reject the terms and conditions of real-world politics, and instead stand for the Truth, unflinchingly and without apology, regardless of the real-world consequences. Indeed, the holy books of our most common religious traditions are filled with heroic portrayals of people who engage precisely in this kind of principled resistance to the norms of the real world. In many cases otherworldliness is precisely the point.

In response, the proceduralist may borrow from the realist strategy discussed earlier, and argue that the religious believer has misunderstood the procedural view. Adopting the procedural view does not require citizens to *morally endorse* the values and compromises embedded in the democratic process. That is, proceduralism does not require citizens to abandon the moral truth as they see it in favor of some version of moral neutrality or moral thinness. Indeed, proceduralism is consistent with the view that democracy is, as Alasdair MacIntyre has said, "civil war carried on by other means" (1984: 254). That is, the proceduralist can maintain that his view of democracy is compatible with the religious believer's fervor to stand up intrepidly for the Truth at all costs. According to the proceduralist, democracy provides the mechanism by which one can fight for the Truth without risking one's life.

But once the proceduralist has conceded that the political world is in the midst of a kind of civil war, the religiously committed citizen has an obvious rejoinder: what warrants the presumption that the democratic process, as understood by the proceduralist, is a suitable alternative framework for civil war? One wins a war by overcoming and destroying one's enemy; thus, in a war, power matters most. Why, then, should parties to a war over ultimate values agree to fight within a framework that aims to treat opposing points of view equally, and which, consequently, makes final victory unattainable? The point is that, according to the religiously committed citizen, there are many things that are at issue in contemporary politics, and among these is the appropriateness of the procedural model of democracy itself. And so the question of justification re-emerges.

The proceduralist will reply that the democratic process offers a *peaceful* alternative to conventional war; democracy is, again, war *by other means*. But this is to presuppose the principle that we should seek peace above all else. It is thus open to the religiously committed citizen to ask why peace should trump other important values, such as truth, or purity, or obedience to God's law. If, as the proceduralist concedes, democracy is indeed civil war by other means, why then should we not pursue civil war by the usual means? Why not engage in *real* civil war? The proceduralist will respond that civil war by the usual means involves great risks to one's life. From the point of view of the religiously committed citizen, this response reveals that the proceduralist model of democracy expects citizens to subordinate all values to that of self-preservation. Yet, according to many religiously committed citizens, nothing justifiably trumps obedience to God, not peace, not fairness, not civility, and not even self-preservation.[12] And so it will seem to the religiously committed citizen that the procedural model of democracy cannot make good on its promise of a fair process that treats all as equals, because it requires citizens to view their deepest commitments as mere "interests" or "preferences" that can be entered into a system of *quid pro quo* political bargaining. However, many citizens *cannot* adopt such an understanding of their deepest commitments; they hold that to do so would be to violate, abandon, cheapen, defile, or denigrate that which they take to be of ultimate value. And why should they consent to a political system that requires *this*? For, according to the religious believer, political legitimacy is itself contingent upon a society instantiating the truth or God's will.[13] Insofar as proceduralism precludes this, democracy as understood on the procedural model is illegitimate.

---

[12] It should be added that, for some religious believers, obedience to God, even at the expense of – or perhaps *especially* at the expense of – this-worldly well-being, is *necessary* for true, that is, other-worldly, self-preservation.

[13] This is the force of much of the religious political rhetoric in currency in the United States, such as the claim that the United States was founded on "Christian principles" or is a "Christian nation." See, for example, P. Buchanan 2001: 180ff. Note also Newt Gingrich, "We must reestablish that our rights come from our Creator, and than an America that has driven God out of the public arena is an America on the way to decay and defeat" (2005: xxi).

Thus, the procedural account has not supplied the needed justification of democracy; it has at best merely relocated the question of justification. Of course, this leaves entirely open the question of what the religiously committed citizen may do in *response* to the failure of justification. That the state has failed to meet its justificatory burden does not alone entail that rebellion is justified; the failure of justification merely raises the question of what should be done. This is a matter I shall take up in the final section of this chapter.

I have deliberately cast the preceding argument in the form of a dialectical exchange between a proceduralist and a certain strip of ardent religious believer. Before moving on, it should be emphasized that this was strictly a simplifying device. The presuppositions of proceduralism are easily highlighted when brought into contrast with the commitments of a certain kind of religious belief. Although certain types of religious believer perhaps provide the most obvious foil for the procedural view, similar exchanges between proceduralists and differently committed interlocutors – including proponents of various secular moral doctrines – are easy to imagine.

For example, return to one of the four glosses above. Consider the controversy over teaching evolution in public schools. Imagine how a biologist is likely to react to a recent decision by the Kansas Board of Education to eliminate the requirement that evolution be taught in biology courses in the public schools. Of course, that the decision was reached by a fair and democratic process will not convince the biologist that the decision is *correct*. But, more importantly, the biologist is likely to regard the decision as *illegitimate* and intolerable. It bears repeating that the judgment that the democratic result is illegitimate leaves open the question of what should be done in response. The point that concerns us here is that the biologist is likely to insist that *something* must be done to correct the intolerable result; that is, from the biologist's point of view, teaching evolution in a biology curriculum is *non-negotiable*, and hence the Kansas result simply *cannot stand*, despite the fact that it was produced by a properly democratic procedure.

A proceduralist might attempt to reconcile the biologist to the decision by pointing out that since the Board's decision does not *outlaw* the teaching of evolution, but only abolishes the *requirement* that evolution be taught, the result coerces no one and furthermore implies no evaluative judgment whatsoever concerning what the biologist takes to be most valuable with respect to science education. The proceduralist may continue that, as it merely gives individual school districts the freedom to choose what material is covered in biology classes, it does not require anyone to *endorse* an anti-evolution view, or any particular view on the matter. The biologist will almost certainly see this proceduralist reply as entirely beside the point. According to the biologist, what counts as biology, and thus what counts as a proper biology curriculum, is not a matter of choice, and it surely is not a matter that can be properly decided by means of a popular vote. That is, according to the biologist, the content of a biology curriculum is not the kind of thing that should be subjected to the democratic decision process; to decide the curriculum by popular vote is to treat science and myth, truth and nonsense, and knowledge and ignorance as equals. It is, therefore, to *misunderstand* profoundly the nature of the values and purposes of biology education. According to the biologist, there could be no proper biology education without an evolution *requirement*; in fact, the biologist may go further and argue that insofar as proper science education is a prerequisite for intelligent and effective democratic citizenship, the decision to eliminate the evolution requirement from public education is a blow against democratic legitimacy itself. So why should the biologist accept a democratically produced decision that renders instruction in the theory of evolution optional in the biology curriculum of the public schools?

Notice how this dialectic closely resembles the exchange considered earlier between the proceduralist and the religious believer. Similar interactions can be provided for the other cases glossed above. To repeat, there are important differences among the cases, but all share the following logical structure: each is a case in which the democratic process has produced a result that violates some value that one party to the dispute takes to be the *sine qua non* of democratic legitimacy. In such cases, the fact that the democratic process had been applied properly is not enough to settle the question of justification. And so proceduralism does not resolve the paradox of democratic justification.

What's the matter with Kansas?

I close this section of the chapter by raising a further critical point against the procedural view. The procedural view not only fails to resolve the paradox of democratic justification, it renders inexplicable the prevalence of the kind of disputes we have been discussing. The most obvious case in point is the issue of gay marriage. On the procedural view, public opposition to gay marriage should be more or less restricted to a few religious fundamentalists. However, it in fact strikes a large portion of the population of the United States as a crucial political issue. Why should this be? Recall that on the proceduralist analysis democratic votes are expressions of citizens' interests. It follows, then, that the proceduralist must conclude that large numbers of citizens take it to be in their interest to restrict marriage to heterosexual couples. Yet it is difficult to imagine how opposing gay marriage serves anybody's interests. To be sure, some claim that extending marriage to homosexuals will cheapen, trivialize, or make less secure heterosexual marriages. But as an empirical matter this seems highly implausible. Others claim that allowing homosexuals to marry will dissolve traditional family bonds. But, again, this seems highly implausible. Moreover, it should be noted that if people were so strongly motivated to oppose policies which could be seen to empirically cheapen heterosexual marriage or imperil family bonds, we should find strong opposition to no-fault divorce laws, and strong support for other policies that would prevent marriage among persons not sufficiently mature or serious; but we do not. The fact is that there is no plausible story to tell to the effect that gay marriage harms others, or harms society, or obstructs the interests of heterosexual couples. Why all the fuss, then? On the procedural view, it is a mystery why anyone should care about gay marriage, other than gay couples who are denied the privileges of marriage. And yet large numbers of people *do* care about gay marriage enough not only to oppose it, but to vote in favor of amendments to their state constitutions which define marriage in strictly heterosexual terms. Many believe that the US Constitution should be amended to include a definition of marriage.

The proceduralist must conclude from this that large numbers of people are deeply mistaken about their own interests. And this in turn calls the proceduralist to develop a theory to account for the pervasiveness of the mistake. In order to address existing and prevalent political phenomena, proceduralism requires a theory of the manipulation of popular opinion. That is, the only response the proceduralist has to the prevalence of issues that defy procedural analysis is to declare that mainstream America is profoundly deluded. Consequently, the procedural view violates its aspiration to be a non-normative theory of democracy. As our imagined religious believer suspected, the procedural view is committed to a series of claims regarding the bases on which citizens ought to cast their votes, the way in which citizens ought to understand their moral commitments, and how they ought to rank their moral and material concerns. In short, the procedural response to the paradox of democratic justification denies the moral pluralism that we earlier argued is the natural outcome of the liberties of conscience that democracy protects.

To see how this works, consider Thomas Frank's popular 2004 book, *What's The Matter With Kansas?* According to Frank, the fact that conservatives have succeeded in recent elections proves that people are "getting their fundamental interests wrong" (2004: 1) and, moreover, that individuals are suffering from an "illusion" (2004: 7), a "distortion" that leads good people "astray" (2004: 242). Frank's substantive position is that conservatives have succeeded because they have mastered the politics of false advertising. Although they continue to govern on the basis of what Frank sees as the old-fashioned Republican commitments to big business and the elimination of social welfare, the conservatives have managed to focus the attention of the working class on a set of cultural issues, such as abortion, gay marriage, "family values," blasphemous art, the arrogance of "Hollywood liberals," the radicalism of tenured university professors, and so on. Hence, according to Frank, the conservatives campaign on the basis of one platform, but govern on the basis of another. On Frank's analysis, "Values may 'matter most' to voters, but they always take a backseat to the needs of money once the elections are won" (2004: 6). And so Frank contends that average voters are duped into voting *against* what he insists are their most fundamental concerns, their true interests. He describes this phenomenon like this:

Vote to stop abortion; *receive* a rollback in capital gains taxes. *Vote* to make our country strong again; *receive* decentralization. *Vote* to screw those politically correct college professors; *receive* electricity deregulation. *Vote* to get government off our backs; *receive* conglomeration and monopoly everywhere from media to meat-packing. *Vote* to stand tall against terrorists; *receive* Social Security privatization. *Vote* to strike a blow against elitism; *receive* a social order in which wealth is more concentrated than ever before in our lifetimes, in which workers have been stripped of power and CEOs are rewarded in a manner beyond imagining. (2004: 7) (original emphasis)

The continuing success of this blatant bait and switch on the part of the Republicans perplexes Frank to the point of exasperation. Endorsing proceduralism, Frank writes that "most of us think of politics as a Machiavellian drama in which actors make alliances and take practical steps to advance their material interests"; however, in a revealing contrast, he acknowledges that contemporary politics rejects this framework, and is instead "a crusade in which one's material interests are suspended in favor of vague cultural grievances that are all-important and yet incapable of ever being assuaged" (2004, 121).[14] Elsewhere, he faults this "crusade" model for its "systematic erasure of the economic" (2004: 127).

---

[14] If it is true, as Frank claims, that "most of us" see politics in procedural – he says *Machiavellian* – terms, then it is difficult to explain why the crusade model he laments pervades our politics. One wonders who Frank takes himself to be addressing as "us."

All of this simply begs the question. Frank's analysis *presumes* that an individual's "fundamental interests" are his economic interests; moreover, Frank insists that the extent to which any individual holds that his own economic well-being may be trumped by other objectives is the extent to which that individual is deluded, or the victim of some conservative con job. But surely other explanations are available. Never once does Frank consider the possibility that an increasing number of individuals in the United States are politically moved by commitments that cannot be reduced to, or explained in terms of, "material interests," and that consequently these individuals feel called to act politically for the sake of respecting or realizing those commitments, even at the expense of their own economic well-being. More importantly, Frank never considers the possibility that the conservative voters in Kansas are *fully aware* of the bait and switch perpetrated by the Republican candidates they elect. It may be that the conservative voters in Kansas see *all* politics as a dishonest and corrupt con game, and so they vote for the candidates who at least give *lip service* to the correct value commitments, regardless of the actual material consequences of conservative victories. Or, alternatively, it may be the case that citizens who, for example, oppose abortion on religious grounds take themselves to be *morally obligated* to vote for pro-life candidates, regardless of the likely negative impact on their pocketbooks, their public schools, their small businesses, and their neighborhoods.

Frank repeatedly discusses Republican victories in terms of a "back-lash" (2004: *passim*), an irrational and unreasoned knee-jerk reaction. This reveals that he takes the conservative trend to indicate that conservative voters – remember, roughly half of the American electorate! – are either the selfish beneficiaries of the Republicans' big business economic agenda that destroys middle-class America, or the benighted and foolish victims of "conservatism's populist myth" (2004: 239). According to Frank, then, all conservative voters are either despicable or irrational, and no respectable case can be made for conservatism. *This* is to reject the kind of pluralism of minimally plausible moral positions that democracy entails.

It should be emphasized that it may be the case that the conservative agenda – whatever it may be – is deeply flawed and morally corrupt. Frank does not argue this; he merely asserts that it is. But this kind of assessment is very different from the one that Frank offers, which encourages us to view more than half of our fellow democratic citizens as knaves or fools. Yet Frank's claim that half of his fellow citizens – conveniently, the half with whom he disagrees – are either too corrupt or too stupid for democratic citizenship smacks of gross oversimplification. In any case, it is a strike against any proposed analysis of democratic politics that it requires us to characterize prevalent political phenomena in this way. A mode of political analysis that entails that millions of people who are otherwise reasonable, intelligent, and sincere are the victims of a silly and obvious deception that seriously undermines their well-being might, after all, be correct; however, given the extravagant implications of the procedural view, one should consider exploring alternate hypotheses.

III DEEP POLITICS

Let us pause for a moment to take stock. Thus far I have argued that contemporary democracy confronts a paradox in that the very freedoms secured by democratic politics tend to undermine the conditions under which it would be possible for democracy to meet its own conception of legitimacy. To be specific, the liberties of conscience secured by a democratic constitution lead to a pluralism of moral commitments among the democratic citizenry. Yet, where there is a pluralism of moral commitments, there will be a plurality of moral conflicts, and some of these conflicts will engage the values and commitments that citizens take to be *fundamental* and hence non-negotiable. I then argued that the standard proceduralist response to the paradox cannot succeed because it presumes a particular view about the *nature* of citizens' moral commitments; it presumes that citizens are willing and able to view their deepest commitments as bargaining chips to be entered into an aggregative decision mechanism.

But there is good reason to think that citizens cannot adopt such a self-understanding without transforming and thus violating the values they hold most dear; for, according to many citizens, their moral commitments – along with their particular understandings of justice, liberty, dignity, equality, and the right and the good – are *prior* to their democratic commitments in the sense that the legitimacy of democracy is thought to *follow* from their moral commitments. Hence, in cases where democratic politics conflicts with some value that is held to be more basic, one cannot justify democracy by simply appealing to the features of the democratic process itself, because, in such cases, the legitimacy of the democratic process is precisely what the conflict calls into question. But in such cases, some decision or other must be made; something must be done and this means that some values will prevail over others. What can be said to those whose fundamental values lose out in the democratic process? Accordingly, proceduralism merely relocates, and does not respond to, much less resolve, the paradox of democratic justification.

From paradox to crisis

It is, of course, possible to live with paradox. For many citizens, the procedural account of democracy serves as an adequate validation of democratic politics, and for other citizens, the question of democratic legitimacy never even occurs to them. Accordingly, the paradox of democratic justification need not result in any *practical* political crisis. However, as I have suggested above, many of our most pressing political controversies share a structure that indicates that citizens, and not just political theorists, are confronting the paradox of democratic justification. To cite the obvious example which we have already discussed, pro-life citizens see legal abortion as the state-sponsored murder of innocent citizens, and they hold that a government that does not protect the lives of its innocent citizens is *ipso facto* illegitimate; pro-choice citizens see legalized abortion as necessary for the liberty and equality of women, and they hold that a government that fails to secure these goods for all citizens thereby loses its claim to legitimacy. Obviously, there could be no political rapprochement of the sort envisioned by the procedural model between conflicting parties who each see their position as the *sine qua non* of political legitimacy. There could be no *principled* compromise between these two parties, for each sees the values at stake as identifying non-negotiable requirements for political legitimacy as such. The abortion controversy is not unique in this respect; the prevalence of similarly structured contemporary controversies indicates that citizens are increasingly turning to their deepest moral commitments for guidance and instruction in political affairs. As these commitments tend to identify sources of *ultimate* authority and *fundamental* value, they cannot be bargained with and so do not fit into the aggregative model offered by the procedural view.

What this means is that present political controversies of the sort we have been discussing suggest that the paradox of democratic legitimacy is generating a legitimacy crisis in modern democracies. Citizens are questioning why they should accept the democratic status quo at the expense of their fundamental values. Hence, democracy is losing its grip on citizens who feel increasingly that the current state of politics is morally intolerable. We confront a democratic citizenry that does not accept the morally thin market assumptions of the procedural model; we confront a citizenry that increasingly believes that democratic politics must conform to their deepest value commitments or else lose its claim to legitimacy. We confront what I shall call a *deep politics*.

Deep politics as a problem

The problem posed for democracy by deep politics should be clear enough. When citizens hold opposing moral and religious doctrines, but insist that democracy must instantiate their deepest commitments or else lose its claim to legitimacy, someone must lose out. Every democratic decision concerning a controversial issue will generate discontent in some sector of the citizenry. In certain cases, this discontent will rise to the level of a denial of legitimacy. As I mentioned above, the judgment that a given democratic outcome is illegitimate and, therefore, cannot stand leaves open the question of what democratic citizens are justified in doing in response. The options run the gamut from the obviously anti-democratic and violent to various acts of protest and petition that lie clearly within the framework of democratic politics. What reason can be given to those whose fundamental values lose in a democratic decision to pursue the democratic means of response and not the anti-democratic ones?

To help clarify matters, let us consider an admittedly overused example. For many citizens, the overturn of *Roe* v. *Wade* would represent a serious lapse in democracy's legitimacy, and would undoubtedly incite a variety of responses. Let us consider the main lines of response that are available:

(1) *Relocation*. Relocate to a country in which the desired rights and policies are in place.

(2) *Rebellion*. Engage in acts of uncivil disobedience, including violence, threats, riots, destruction of property, unlawful protest, terrorism, and so on, and resist legal punishment for crimes.

(3) *Civil disobedience*. Resist and engage in protest within circumscribed moral constraints, but publicly and openly disobey the law, and willingly accept legal punishment for crimes.

(4) *Petition*. Obey the law, but engage in all available legal measures to effect a change in the law, including voting, campaigning, lawful protest, lobbying, consciousness-raising, coalition-building, public criticism, debate, activism, and so on.

I begin with a few observations. I trust that it is clear that options (3) and (4) represent *democratic* responses, whereas (1) and (2) do not. Of the non-democratic options, (1) is typically morally superior to (2), though it should be noted that relocation is not open to all citizens, and under certain conditions may not be open to any. Furthermore, it should be noted that the relocation option raises additional moral difficulties concerning the conditions under which it would be immoral for a citizen of one country to relocate to another.[15] It also bears mention that there may be some cases in which the only morally permissible option other than relocation is petition; that is, there may be cases of legitimate complaint in which civil disobedience is not morally available. We need not dwell on these and related complications, because the moral rankings and subtleties of the options are not to the present point. The question, then, is why our imagined pro-choice citizen should pursue the options of civil disobedience and petition rather than relocation or rebellion. Put otherwise, why should a citizen who sincerely believes that a given democratic outcome violates a basic and necessary condition for political legitimacy nonetheless sustain his commitment to democratic means to social change? Under such conditions, why not pursue non-democratic means to one's political ends?

Many citizens will give the Hobbesian answer: one should sustain democratic commitments, even in cases of lapsed legitimacy, because the cost of open rebellion is too high. But the Hobbesian answer offers a reason of the wrong kind. We are not concerned with the question of why it would be *prudent* or instrumentally rational for citizens to not rebel, but with the question of why citizens *morally* ought to pursue democratic means to their political ends. For it is natural to think that the rebellion option is morally justified only when no democratic option is available, such as when the political order is democratic in name only, or not democratic at all. But what justifies this thought?

Exit, voice, and loyalty

At this point it will prove useful to introduce a framework developed by Albert Hirschman in his classic book, *Exit, Voice, and Loyalty* (1970). Roughly, Hirschman reasoned that when individuals are disappointed by the performance of an institution that is supposed to serve them, they have two options. First, they may *exit*, that is, they may withdraw from the institution and take their business elsewhere, so to speak. To return to our categories above, both relocation and rebellion are forms of exit. Second, they may exercise *voice*, that is, they may sustain their relationship with the institution in question, but voice their dissatisfactions with the expectation

---

[15] Presumably there are conditions under which it would be morally wrong to desert one's country. Though I cannot argue the case here, I contend that citizens in the United States who relocated to a foreign country because they did not endorse the results of the 2004 election acted immorally.

that service will consequently improve. Petition and civil disobedience are forms of democratic voice. Hirschman thought that voice is crucial to the maintenance and improvement of institutions; hence, he held that institutions need to discourage exit if possible. He further reasoned that exit is discouraged, and voice encouraged, if institutions can nurture a sense of *loyalty* among their members. Consequently, Hirschman argued that loyalty was crucial to the success of institutions of almost every kind, from firms, businesses, and clubs to governments and, indeed, entire societies.

A slightly modified version of Hirschman's framework can be applied in characterizing the problem posed to democracy by deep politics. It is surely the case that the health of a democracy depends on its citizens' willingness to exercise voice. This is done most typically through political participation in the form of votes and the other standard democratic channels represented by the petition option we described above, though we must add that civil disobedience is often a form of voice as well. Recall that the essence of voice is the pursuit of democratic means to redress political grievances.

In democratic politics, exit comes in many forms, though we can identify two broad categories of exit: *obstructive* and *non-obstructive*. Let us begin by identifying a few obvious forms of non-obstructive exit, remembering, of course, that these designations are neither exhaustive nor exclusive. One kind of non-obstructive exit is the kind of political *abstention* exemplified by certain insular religious sects in the United States. Abstention consists in full, or nearly full, withdrawal from democratic politics, including refraining from voting and other forms of political participation.[16] According to the abstentious citizen, politics under any regime is to be, insofar as possible, shunned as an unhealthy or morally inappropriate distraction. Closely related to the abstentious citizen is the *cynical* citizen. Like the abstentious citizen, the cynic non-obstructively declines to participate politically. However, the cynic's withdrawal from democracy is motivated by a general frustration with democratic politics. That is, the cynic does not exit for the purpose of more completely attending to a spiritual calling, but out of exasperation. Finally, we can add to our list of non-obstructive mode of exit the *indifferent* citizen, whose exit from democratic politics is not the result of some negative assessment of the political scene, but rather the result of a simple lack of interest.

The foregoing forms of exit are non-obstructive in that none seeks to dismantle or undermine the standing democratic regime. Those who

---

[16] Withdrawal may also involve seeking exemptions from certain democratic laws, as in the case of the Amish, who do not pay federal taxes.

engage in non-obstructive exit simply want to be left out of the political process.[17] Accordingly, non-obstructive exit carries with it no alternative or competing political program, and so does not involve any positive political action on the part of those who exit. We may characterize non-obstructive exit as exiting from not only *democratic* politics, but from politics as such.

Consider next two obstructive forms of exit: *revolution* and *conspiracy*. Revolution is exemplified most fully by domestic organizations that actively seek to overthrow the existing political order, typically by overt means of violence, terrorism, intimidation, and force. According to the revolutionary, the standing democratic order must be not only shunned and resisted, but abolished at almost any cost and as quickly as possible. Contrast the revolutionary with the conspirator. Whereas the revolutionary seeks to incite overt conflict in the present, the conspirator employs more covert and subtle means, taking a long-view approach to social upheaval and often working, at least initially, within the limits of established democratic law. That is, like revolutionaries, conspirators plot the overthrow of the existing democratic order, but, unlike revolutionaries, adopt a strategy according to which the successful upheaval of society must begin from *within* the bounds of democratic politics. Accordingly, conspirators, at least initially, exercise the voice option. They lobby, campaign, rally, demonstrate, canvass, pro-test, and petition; however, these activities are enacted with a view to building a coalition of sufficient strength to eventually overthrow or funda-mentally transform the democratic order. For this reason, conspiratorial activity is, in the short run, difficult to distinguish from legitimate demo-cratic participation, but the long-run aspirations of the conspirator are in essence no different from those of the revolutionary.

It may be said, then, that revolution and conspiracy represent a mere difference in means; they both aim to disrupt and eventually dismantle the standing democratic order and replace it with another order. To be sure, revolutionaries and conspirators frequently characterize their ambitions in democratic terms; they claim to seek democracy "in a higher sense" or a system in which people are "truly free." But they nonetheless aspire to create a politics that differs fundamentally from the existing democratic order. Hence, we may say that, unlike non-obstructive exit, obstructive forms of exit carry with them decidedly political aspirations. Consequently, obstruc-tive exit represents a withdrawal not from politics as such, but from *democratic* politics, at least as we know it.

---

[17] I leave aside the complication that some non-obstructively exiting groups exit for the purpose of maintaining a local form of governance in accordance with their own sectarian principles.

With this rough sketch of a modified Hirschmanian framework in place, the problem of deep politics can now be stated succinctly. As I noted above, Hirschman thought that loyalty was the key to encouraging voice and discouraging exit; however, in modern democracies, citizens are not required to share common moral or religious loyalties. In fact, as was mentioned earlier, it is thought by many that in modern democracies widespread consensus over moral and religious essentials can be maintained only by oppression, and thus should not be a *desideratum*, or even an *ideal*, of any properly democratic order.[18] In any case, the lack of agreement at the level of fundamental moral commitments – what I earlier called moral pluralism – seems to be a present and persistent feature of modern democracy. Therefore, citizens not only do not share common loyalties, but in fact maintain conflicting and opposed loyalties. And so the problem of deep politics consists, then, in preserving the voice option among citizens who are divided at the level of fundamental loyalties.

Our most pressing political controversies reveal that we are divided not only at the level of policy; we are also morally divided at the level of our fundamental commitments and deepest loyalties. Accordingly, there is much more at stake in contemporary politics than policy and law; for many citizens, present policy and legal issues call into question the very legitimacy of democracy itself. Unless we can formulate a compelling reason why citizens ought to pursue democratic means to their political ends in cases in which democracy threatens to fail to reflect their deepest commitments, we should expect increasing instances of exit. In many cases, exit will be of the non-obstructive kind, but in some exit will take more hostile, obstructive forms. And in certain cases, non-obstructive exit will lead to obstructive exit. In any case, both forms of exit are hazardous for democracy. Can anything be done?

---

[18] I am, of course, thinking again of Rawls, who writes, "a continuing, shared understanding on one comprehensive religious, philosophical, or moral doctrine can be maintained only by the oppressive use of state power" (2005: 37). But this thought is shared by theorists otherwise opposed to Rawls, see, for example, Phillips (1991: 131), Sanders (1997), and Young (2000: 49).

CHAPTER 2

Against the politics of omission

In Chapter 1, I presented the problem of deep politics. To repeat, the problem emerges out of the fact that citizens of contemporary democracies increasingly turn to their respective moral commitments – religious and secular – for guidance in political action. Yet citizens are deeply divided at the level of these commitments. Accordingly, contemporary democratic citizens do not regard themselves as engaged in a process by which their individual preferences are aggregated to make public policy that is fair and hence justifiable to all; instead, citizens increasingly see themselves as embroiled in a zero-sum contest among conflicting and incompatible religious and moral visions: a civil war by other means. As these visions represent deep commitments about *fundamental* matters of the good, it is difficult to see how democratic processes can be justified to those whose values lose out. Those who lose have a strong incentive to exercise what Albert Hirschman (1970) fittingly characterized as "exit." But since many citizens take the project of instantiating their deepest value commitments in the political order to be morally imperative, and perhaps overriding, their "exit" is not likely to take the form of a total (and peaceful) withdrawal from politics; rather, it is likely to manifest in a rejection of the idea that their political ends should be pursued by democratic means. That is, they will exit from *democratic* politics, not politics as such.

Hence, contemporary democracy confronts a potential legitimacy crisis: how can we justify democratic politics to persons divided at the level of fundamental commitments who fully understand that democracy means that *someone's* values must lose out? The traditional answer, according to which each of us has reason to retain our loyalty to democracy because democracy allows for politics without bloodshed, is increasingly fragile in a world in which individuals hold that their respective moral visions must be pursued at any cost. That is, the traditional, quasi-Hobbesian view that democratic norms are dictated by the motive to seek peace fails when people reject the idea that peaceful co-existence among diverse individuals trumps their individual conceptions of justice, salvation, purity, or the good.

In this chapter, I shall examine the most influential attempt to date to resolve the problem of deep politics, namely, the *political liberalism* of John Rawls. Finding the Rawlsian response inadequate, I shall then turn to a critical examination of the alternate response more recently proposed by Jeffrey Stout. With these criticisms in place, we will be well-positioned to undertake in Chapter 3 the development of what I contend is a more viable response to the problem of deep politics.

Before embarking, a word of caution is in order. The political philosophy of John Rawls, in all its various and fascinating elements, is the focus of an already vast secondary literature that has been steadily expanding for more than thirty years. This is a good indication of the enduring importance of his work and the depth of his philosophical vision. However, it is perhaps another consequence of Rawls's many virtues that there is at present no single account of his political philosophy that commands the assent of all Rawls scholars, much less all political philosophers. There is an especially high degree of disagreement among the experts concerning the elements of Rawls's thought that I am about to discuss, namely Rawls's political liberalism and the doctrine of public reason that lies at its core. In what follows, I do not take myself to be engaged in Rawls scholarship. The aim is rather to discuss Rawls and some prominent Rawlsians as proponents of an especially intuitive strategy for addressing the problems we are concerned to examine. I will present a version of Rawls's view that follows a common line of interpretation, leaving the thorny issues of Rawls scholarship to the side.[1] Although in the present chapter we will be critical of the Rawlsian approach, we will have occasion in Chapter 4 to identify and adopt what I take to be crucial insights of Rawls's view.

I THE RAWLSIAN RESPONSE

Background to political liberalism

Rawls's response to the problem of deep politics is a view he called *political liberalism*. Before proceeding, the concept of political liberalism must be clarified. First, to avoid confusion, note that the term *liberalism* will here be used in its *philosophical* sense. Although the term is used in contemporary parlance to denote a political platform devoted to welfarist distributive

---

[1] Those wishing to pursue the interpretative issues can do no better than Freeman 2007.

policies, it is employed in political philosophy to denote the theoretical framework within which contemporary politics functions. Roughly, this framework is constituted by a commitment to individual rights and corresponding restraints on state action. Liberals and conservatives, in the senses of those terms employed in popular political discourse in the United States and elsewhere, disagree about the extent of individual rights and the proper scope of state action; liberals tend to hold that among the individual rights are rights to a certain level of economic and social support that must be provided by the state, whereas conservatives see state action always as a threat to liberty, and hence they emphasize individual responsibility and initiative. In this way, liberals and conservatives in the popular sense are both committed to liberalism in the philosophical sense; they both hold that political justice is fundamentally a question of how to protect individuals and recognize their rights. We may go as far as to say that liberalism in its philosophical sense forms the intellectual backdrop of any modern constitutional democracy. A political order which does not countenance individual rights and constraints on state authority roughly of the sort with which we are familiar is by our lights insufficiently democratic. The term *democracy* as it is used today most often means *liberal democracy*.[2]

But what justifies this general approach to political theory? Why should politics *begin* from the recognition of the individual and her rights? And what is the source of her rights? The modern tradition of political philosophy – a tradition that begins roughly in the sixteenth century with Machiavelli, continues through Locke, Montesquieu, Rousseau, Hume, Smith, Jefferson, Kant, and Mill, and persists today – is united in thinking that there is some abiding *moral* justification for liberalism. Typically, philosophical defenses of liberalism claim that liberal political arrangements are entailed by some moral fact about human beings as such. In John Locke and Thomas Jefferson it is the fact of divinely conferred natural rights that entails a liberal political order. For Immanuel Kant, it is the unique value of the human capacity for rational agency, what Kant called "dignity." In the thought of John Stuart Mill, the intrinsic value of pleasure, and the corresponding moral requirement of maximizing it, entails a politics based in individual liberty. In all cases, the claim is that only a liberal regime can recognize, secure, realize, respect, or manifest this basic moral fact about humanity; the conclusion, then, is that only a liberal political order is just.

Since liberalism has it that the state exists for the sake of protecting individuals and their rights, liberals must confront the question of

---

[2] For further discussion of these issues, see Talisse 2005: ch. 2.

anarchism: why should there be a state at all? Robert Nozick has framed this thought especially well. He writes:

> Individuals have rights, and there are things no person or group may do to them (without violating their rights). So strong and far-reaching are these rights that they raise the question of what, if anything, the state and its officials may do. How much room do individual rights leave for the state? (1974: ix)

Hence Nozick (1974: 4) claims that the fundamental question for political philosophers is "Why not have anarchy?"

I cannot here survey liberal attempts to respond to this question; the point is that liberals are committed to the idea that, since states are fundamentally *coercive* institutions, the legitimacy of any state is something that must be *proven* or *demonstrated* to the individuals that are its citizens (and possibly others). Even though they reject anarchism as a positive political proposal, liberals must see something like anarchy, or the absence of political authority, as the philosophical *default position*; consequently, the very idea of a political order stands in need of justification. Hence, liberalism countenances a strict conception of political justification. As Jeremy Waldron puts it:

> The liberal insists that intelligible justifications in social and political life must be available in principle for everyone, for society is to be understood by the individual mind, not by the tradition or sense of community. Its legitimacy and the basis of social obligation must be made out to each individual … (1993: 44)

According to the liberal, then, the legitimacy of the state requires that the state be justifiable, at least in principle, to "every last individual" (Waldron 1993: 37).

Consequently, the traditional task of the liberal political philosopher was not simply to devise a moral justification for liberalism; the task was to provide a justification that could convince all citizens. That is, in order to meet its own conception of political legitimacy, the liberal political order must be able to justify itself in terms that can command the assent of all who are expected to live under its authority. Failing this, the state is not legitimate.

Traditional liberal theory thus proceeds on the assumption that it is possible to formulate a moral case for the liberal state that could not be reasonably rejected. The thought driving Rawls's *political* liberalism is that this traditional liberal assumption is false. Rawls formulates the point as follows: "The question the dominant tradition has tried to answer has no answer" (2005: 135). By this he means that there is no deep moral, philosophical, or religious theory – what Rawls calls a "comprehensive doctrine" – that can justify liberal politics, because all comprehensive doctrines can be rejected by reasonable persons.

Hence, the contrast between Rawls's *political* liberalism and what he calls *comprehensive* liberalism (2005: 199ff.). Whereas comprehensive liberalism looks to some comprehensive doctrine to provide the justification for the liberal regime, Rawls's political liberalism "starts from within" the political tradition of constitutional democracy (2005: 14), and attempts to collect and organize the "basic ideas and principles" implicit in this tradition into a "coherent political conception of justice" (2005: 8). In this way, Rawls attempts to provide the required justification of liberal politics without getting embroiled in philosophical controversy; he aspires to arrive at a justification of liberalism that is, as he says, "freestanding" (2005: 10).

Freestanding political theory

With this sketch of the background motivations for Rawls's political liberalism in place, we may now proceed to examine the details of Rawls's views that are most relevant to the problem of deep politics.

Rawls begins his analysis by identifying what he calls the "fact of reasonable pluralism," which is obviously closely allied with what I had called *moral pluralism* in Chapter 1:

Under political and social conditions secured by the basic rights and liberties of free institutions, a diversity of conflicting and irreconcilable – and what's more, reasonable – comprehensive doctrines will come about and persist if such diversity does not already obtain. (2005: 36)

Recognizing that a "reasonable pluralism" of comprehensive doctrines is the "inevitable outcome" of human reason working under free institutions (2005: 37), Rawls casts the central problem of political philosophy in the contemporary world as follows:

[H]ow is it possible for there to exist over time a just and stable society of free and equal citizens, who remain profoundly divided by reasonable religious, philosophical, and moral doctrines? (2005: 4)

One way to answer this question is taken up by neo-Hobbesians such as Stuart Hampshire (1999), Chantal Mouffe (2000), and John Gray (2000). These theorists contend that under conditions of pluralism there could be no political justification in the usual sense, but only the attempt to "domesticate hostility" (Mouffe 2000: 27) by forging a truce among proponents of contending doctrines. Although it offers a kind of non-comprehensive justification for liberalism, Rawls is correct to reject this kind of response; according to Rawls, a truce is "political in the wrong way" (2005: 142). Where democratic politics is adopted as a truce – what Rawls calls a "mere *modus vivendi*" (2005: 145) – there will be no stability, because a truce is insufficient to motivate ongoing allegiance to the democratic process. Where the political order is endorsed by citizens as the terms of a truce, the only motivation for upholding the agreement is the desire to avoid all-out conflict. But one seeks to avoid conflict only for as long as one judges conflict to be too risky or otherwise too costly. However, should the balance of power appear to shift far enough in a favorable direction, at least one party to the truce will have no motivation to keep the agreement; consequently, they will "exit" the bargain, and conflict will resume.

Rawls's own answer to the above question has it that the theoretical core of democratic politics must be formulated at such a level of generality so as to imply or implicate no specific doctrine in particular, but nonetheless be *compatible* with all reasonable comprehensive doctrines. In this way, individuals holding any one of the various reasonable philosophical, moral, and religious comprehensive views could tell *their own* justificatory story about democracy. Hence, citizens otherwise deeply divided could all agree about the legitimacy of the political order, and each will be motivated by moral reasons to uphold the political values associated with that order, regardless of fluctuations in the distribution of power. More importantly, since each citizen will see the democratic order as the proper expression of his comprehensive doctrine in the political sphere, each will be sufficiently motivated to uphold the democratic principles in cases in which his own political views lose out. In this way, all citizens will have a compelling moral reason to endorse democratic politics, but they will not all have the *same* reason. Rawls called this kind of agreement *overlapping consensus* (2005: 15). Overlapping consensus presents a middle way between the kind of unanimity that is impossible under conditions of pluralism and a Hobbesian truce amongst adversaries.

An account of democratic politics that aims to win an overlapping consensus among proponents of diverse and conflicting comprehensive doctrines must not itself employ or implicate any particular comprehensive doctrine; it must be freestanding. How can a freestanding account of democracy be constructed? Rawls contends that political justification must begin by looking to the "public culture" of contemporary liberal societies as a "shared fund of implicitly recognized basic ideas and principles"; the task of the political theorist is to "organize" these into a "coherent political conception of justice" (2005: 8) without invoking philosophical controversy. Rawls contends that the act of organizing the ideas and principles implicit in contemporary democratic societies is "the most we can expect" from political theory; he adds, "nor do we need more" (Rawls 1985: 410).

Hence Rawls recommends a strategy of "avoidance," according to which political theory must deliberately eschew deep commitments and "avoid philosophy's longstanding problems"; that is, according to Rawls, we must "stay on the surface, philosophically speaking" (Rawls 1985: 395). This view of the practice of political theory in turn entails a view of the practice of democratic citizenship. To explain: politics is not exhausted by the activities of political theorists. Citizens working within a democratic framework must choose policies, cast votes, decide cases, and wage campaigns. In these activities, citizens confront the same difficulty facing the democratic theorist; that is, they must attempt to reason with and persuade each other despite the fact that they are deeply divided at the most fundamental levels, and this requires citizens to "consider what kinds of reasons they may reasonably give one another when fundamental political questions are at stake" (2005: 441). Rawls hence proposed a model of public political discourse on which citizens "conduct their fundamental discussions within the framework of what each regards as a political conception of justice based on values that the others can reasonably be expected to endorse" (2005: 226).

In public political discussion, then, citizens "should be ready to explain the basis of their actions to one another in terms each could reasonably expect that others might endorse as consistent with their freedom and equality" (2005: 218). This means that, as in political justification generally, citizens "are not to appeal to comprehensive religious and philosophical doctrines" in properly public discussion (2005: 224). That is to say, that properly public political discourse is based in a principle of "nonentanglement" (Holmes 1995: 206), which requires that citizens advance only those premises derived from the "shared fund" of implicitly recognized principles and ideals; citizens cannot "proceed directly from [their] comprehensive doctrine" (2005: 455). Questions that cannot be discussed within these bounds, and issues that lie beyond the shared fund of basic principles, are removed from the political agenda (2005: 157).[3] Rawls called this attenuated

---

[3] *Cf.* Nagel, "Where no common standpoint is available at any level to authorize the collective determination by democratic procedures of policies about which individuals find themselves in radical disagreement because of incompatible values, it is best, if possible, to remove those subjects from the reach of political action" (1991: 164).

mode of public discourse "public reason," and identified the supreme court as its "exemplar" (2005: 216). In fact, Rawls proposed the following intuitive test to see whether a given line of reasoning is properly public:

> To check whether we are following public reason we might ask: how would our argument strike us presented in the form of a supreme court opinion? Reasonable? Outrageous? (2005: 254)

The strictures of public reason do not apply only to reasons offered in public discussion or debate. Public reason places constraints upon political reasoning *per se*. Hence, public reason prohibits citizens from consulting their moral, philosophical, and religious convictions when deliberating about how to vote (2005: 243). That is, citizens who vote for a candidate or proposal solely on the basis of reasons drawn from their deep convictions are failing at democratic citizenship. Consequently, citizens of faith who hold on the basis of religious reasons that abortion is a grave moral evil and who for this reason vote for pro-life candidates are being, as Rawls says, *uncivil* (2005: 217), because, by deriving political policy from premises that their fellow citizens could reasonably reject, they are attempting to employ the coercive power of the state in the service of a moral percept that democratic citizens need not endorse, and in fact might oppose. Moreover, citizens who insist upon appealing to non-public reasons in public discourse are *ipso facto* unreasonable (2005: 59), and consequently may be dealt with coercively.[4] Rawls writes:

> [A] given society may also contain unreasonable, irrational, and even mad, comprehensive doctrines. In their case the problem is to contain them so that they do not undermine the unity and justice of society. (2005: xvi)

In this way, the Rawlsian response to the problem of deep politics is to propose a *politics of omission*. As we have seen, the politics of omission works on at least two distinct but clearly related levels. The first omission occurs at the level of the *political agenda*, where especially divisive issues are placed beyond the reach of political action. The second omission occurs at the level of *political deliberation*, where citizens and representatives are required to conduct public discussion and deliberation in terms that do not draw from or presuppose their deepest moral commitments.

There is a further feature of the politics of omission that is worth highlighting. Consider a citizen who not only believes that abortion is a grave

---

[4] "It is unreasonable for us to use political power ... to repress comprehensive doctrines that are not unreasonable" (2005: 61). Hence, it may be fully reasonable in some cases to use political power to repress *unreasonable* comprehensive doctrines.

moral evil, but actually has compelling *arguments* in support of that judgment. Let us suppose, for example, that a citizen has a knock-down argument in favor of the Thomistic ensoulment doctrine, and so is justified in holding that her judgment that abortion is murder is *true*.[5] On the Rawlsian view, not even the *truth* of a moral doctrine is sufficient to gain admissibility into properly public political deliberation; the fact that a doctrine is *controversial* among reasonable persons renders it inadmissible. According to Rawls, "politics in a democratic society can never be guided by what we see as the whole truth" (2005: 243). But here we are not imagining a citizen who *merely believes* the Thomistic ensoulment doctrine, or merely *sees it* as true, but actually has a decisive argument in its favor. So we must ask: why isn't the *demonstrable truth* of some particular religious view sufficient for its admission into democratic politics? Why doesn't the demonstrable truth of a doctrine render all controversy with regard to it as *unreasonable*?

Here one may be tempted to deny that it is possible to develop a decisive argument in favor of any specific moral doctrine. Brian Barry pursues this line, claiming that "there is no conception of the good that nobody could reasonably reject" (1995: 169). But this temptation must be resisted by those who, like Rawls, are pursuing a freestanding response to the problem of deep politics, for to deny that decisive arguments in favor of specific moral doctrines are possible is to commit to some variety of moral skepticism. Moral skepticism is a moral doctrine in its own right, one that is as controversial and contestable as any other moral doctrine. Consequently, an account of democratic politics that is premised upon moral skepticism fails to be freestanding; it is thus *not* a solution to the problem of deep politics, it is just another instantiation of the problem.

A more promising path is suggested by Bruce Ackerman and Charles Larmore, who offer what may be thought of as a *conversational* justification of the omissions required by Rawls's model. Ackerman writes:

When you and I learn that we disagree about one or another dimension of the moral truth, we should not search for some common value that will trump this disagreement ... We should simply say nothing at all about this disagreement and try to solve our problem by invoking premises that we do agree upon. In restraining ourselves in this way, we need not lose the chance to talk to one another about our deepest moral disagreements in countless other, more private contexts. (1989: 16–17)

---

[5] I shall return to this example throughout. It is important, however, to emphasize that nothing crucial turns on the example being that of a committed *religious* believer who opposes abortion on Thomistic grounds. As I shall note below, roughly the same arguments can be run using the commitments of *any* moral doctrine that lies beyond the constraints of public reason, such as certain radical democratic, feminist, and even rival liberal views.

Larmore makes the point more succinctly: "In the face of disagreement, those who wish to continue the conversation should retreat to *neutral ground*, with the hope of either resolving the dispute or bypassing it" (1987: 53).

The "restraint" and "retreat" mentioned by Ackerman and Larmore do *not* entail the skepticism advocated by Barry. Restraint instead entails no grand philosophical pronouncement at all; it simply makes a *pragmatic* recommendation for what Nagel has described as "a kind of epistemological division between the private and the public domains" such that "in certain contexts, I am constrained to consider my beliefs merely as beliefs rather than as truths, however convinced I may be that they are true, and that I know it" (Nagel 1987: 230). One accepts this epistemological division for "purposes of conversation" (Larmore 1987: 53) only; therefore, no deeper epistemic ramifications are implicated.

Hence, we see that the politics of omission involves restrictions on not only the *agenda* and *vocabulary* of democratic politics; it also prescribes a general "norm of rational dialogue" (Larmore 1987: 53) for politics which presumes that citizens "are indeed interested in devising principles of political association" (Larmore 1996: 142), and as such recognize the need to "keep the conversation going" (Larmore 1987: 53) in order to do so. Thus, the norm of rational dialogue requires a general subordination of the epistemic to the political, or, in other words, a subordination of truth to acceptability. As Rawls says, political justification is a "practical" and not an "epistemological" problem (2005: 44). That is, the politics of omission requires us to think of political justification in decidedly *non-epistemic* terms; political justification is more a matter of the *sociology* of liberal democracy, or a matter of what liberal democrats tend to accept as true.

To explain: when operating within public reason, citizens do not aim for outcomes based on the epistemically best reasons, but rather for the outcome that best concurs with the basic judgments and intuitive principles implicit in the public culture of the kind of constitutional democracy with which we contemporary citizens are familiar.[6] Public reason takes these basic commitments of constitutional democracy as "fixed points" (2005: 124) and requires that citizens' contributions to public discourse recognize them. In other words, on the Rawlsian view, the admissibility of a reason, argument, or principle into public deliberation is strictly a matter of its *content* rather than its *ground*; correspondingly, the reasonableness of a

---

[6] There is a fascinating literature examining whether public reason is "complete," that is, *capable* of producing determinate outcomes on questions of basic justice; see especially Reidy 2000.

person is a matter of *which views he holds* rather than of *the extent to which he supports his views by reasons*. In this sense, public reason is an *epistemically closed system*; no position that lies beyond the "shared fund" of common and implicitly endorsed principles, no matter how tightly argued or well-supported, could be politically justified in a Rawlsian order. The *truth* of one's comprehensive doctrine, and hence the truth of the moral and political prescriptions that follow from that doctrine are, on the Rawlsian account, *irrelevant* to justice in a liberal democracy. A further implication is that there could be no properly public discussion about the merits of the politics of omission itself, and no public discussion about the appropriateness of public reason as a model of political discourse.

In this way, the Rawlsian model is epistemically closed in two senses. First, the public admissibility of a doctrine or premise is independent of its epistemic value; second, the parameters of public reason itself are, once established, beyond properly public debate. According to Rawls, public reason must be epistemically closed in order to meet "the urgent political requirement to fix, once and for all, the content of certain political basic rights and liberties, and to assign them special priority"; he continues, "Doing this takes those guarantees off the political agenda" (2005: 161).

The exclusion objection

A common line of criticism attacks public reason for being inherently exclusionary. In an ironic instance of overlapping consensus, the *exclusion objection*, as we shall call it, is found in the work of theorists who otherwise agree on very little. Radical democrats, such as Seyla Benhabib (1992; 1996), Nancy Frazer (1992), and Iris Young (2000: 36ff.; 2003) argue that since public reason proceeds from a strict delineation of a "proper" political vocabulary, it implicitly privileges the status quo, which, even in contemporary liberal democracies, is hardly the image of justice. Further, they argue that since public reason seeks to constrain the political agenda so as to remove the most controversial issues, it comes to nothing more than an *apologia* for existing power structures, structures which typically crowd out the voices of the weak and vulnerable. As Benhabib observes:

All struggles against oppression in the modern world begin by redefining what had previously been considered private, nonpublic, and nonpolitical issues as matters of public concern, issues of justice, and sites of power that need discursive legitimation. (1992: 82)

Natural Law theorists Robert George and Christopher Wolfe apparently agree with the radical democrats:

> Public reason … almost always has the effect of making the liberal position the winner in morally charged political controversies. It does this in effect by ruling out of bounds substantive moral argument on behalf of nonliberal positions. (2000: 2)

The principal target of this particular version of the exclusion objection is a fateful footnote in Rawls's *Political Liberalism*, where he claims that "any reasonable balance" of the values typical of a constitutional democracy "will give a woman a duly qualified right to decide whether or not to end her pregnancy during the first trimester," and "may allow her such a right beyond this, at least in certain circumstances" (2005: 243, n. 32). In the same footnote, Rawls further contends that any comprehensive doctrine that denies a duly qualified right to abortion is "to that extent unreasonable"; from this, he concludes that "we would go against the ideal of public reason if we voted from a comprehensive doctrine that denied this right" (2005: 244, n. 32). According to George and Wolfe, these points reveal that the Rawlsian "method of avoidance" (Rawls 1985: 395) is itself a morally committed, and hence contestable, principle that privileges Rawls's own moral convictions and places out of bounds, by an act of mere stipulation, all opposing views.[7]

The civic republican Michael Sandel generalizes the kind of criticism raised by George and Wolfe. Sandel laments the "political costs" of Rawls's method of avoidance, arguing that Rawlsian public reason "is too sparse to contain the moral energies of a vital democratic life" (1998a: 217). He worries that where public discourse is attenuated in the ways Rawls envisions, citizens will express and engage their moral commitments in undesirable, volatile, non-democratic ways. The liberal theorist William Galston shares Sandel's concern and writes:

> It is difficult to imagine that any liberal democracy can sustain conscientious support if it tells millions of its citizens that they cannot rightly say what they believe as part of democratic public dialogue. (1999: 43)

Ronald Dworkin concurs:

> Liberals will not succeed if they ask people of faith to set aside their religious convictions when they take up the role of citizen. That role demands sincerity and authenticity, which is impossible for such people unless they keep their religion very much in mind. The schism over religion in America shows the limitations of

---

[7] But see Rawls 2005: 479 n. 80.

Rawls's project of political liberalism, his strategy of insulating political convictions from deeper moral, ethical, and religious conviction. (2006: 65)

The exclusion objection has been met with both a clarification and a qualification. As for the clarification, Larmore explains:

Rightly conceived, [public reason] does not thwart the uninhibited political discussions which are the mark of vigorous democracy. We can argue with one another about political issues in the name of our different visions of the human good while also recognizing that, when the moment comes for a legally binding decision, we must take our bearings from a common point of view. (2003: 383)

Larmore reminds us that the restrictions of public reason apply only to decision-making contexts, not to political discussion generally, hence he claims that the requirement that "the most divisive issues" be removed from the public political agenda (2005: 157) does not quell discussion among citizens in non-public domains. In fact, like Larmore, Rawls affirms that lively debate about controversial issues, conducted by means of non-public reasons, is a vital activity within the "background culture" of a liberal democracy (2005: 220).

Now for the qualification. Rawls's original statement of the idea of public reason in the 1993 hardcover edition of his *Political Liberalism* prompted the criticism that the speeches delivered by Martin Luther King, Jr. against segregation and Lincoln's Second Inaugural Address fail to satisfy Rawls's criteria for properly public reasoning. In work following the original publication of *Political Liberalism*, which has since been incorporated into the 2005 "expanded edition" of the work, Rawls introduced "the proviso" (2005: 462) as a revision of public reason's vocabulary restrictions. According to the proviso, citizens in properly public discussion may invoke reasons drawn from their comprehensive doctrines provided that they are prepared "in due course" to offer public reasons to supplement the non-public ones (2005: 462).[8] Hence, Rawls's considered view is that non-public reasons are admissible in public discourse, but as promissory notes only.

This twofold Rawlsian rejoinder is unsatisfying. Although the exclusion objection is often formulated so as to suggest that it is aimed at public reason's agenda and vocabulary restrictions, it should be understood instead to be aimed at its non-epistemic character. What public reason excludes is not the radical democratic, Thomist, and civic republican *positions*, but rather the *reasons* associated with those doctrines. More precisely, public reason cannot recognize a Thomist's reasons *as* reasons. Accordingly, even

---

[8] Apparently, Larmore rejects the proviso (2003: 386).

an irrefutable proof of the Thomistic doctrine of ensoulment is insufficient to render reasonable a Catholic's public opposition to abortion.[9] Presumably, this is due to the fact of reasonable pluralism, which has it that a sound demonstration of x is insufficient for a proof of the falsity of all views inconsistent with x.

But why should our Thomist, or anyone else for that matter, endorse such a pluralism? Here, the Rawlsian must be careful. He cannot offer a philosophical *argument* for his pluralism – to do so would be to violate the very idea of a freestanding political theory.[10] The question of the truth of reasonable pluralism, or even of why one should accept reasonable plural-ism, is a question to which a freestanding theory "does not speak" (2005: 128).[11] This will strike the Thomist as dishonest and hypocritical; however, to object to the silence is to be unreasonable, and thus someone the state must endeavor to "contain" (2005: xvi).

In this way, public reason is *epistemically* exclusionary. Regardless of how widely it is construed, public reason cannot acknowledge the *epistemic force* of the arguments advanced in favor of positions that do not accept its constraints, and cannot give *reasons why* such arguments should be disre-garded. It can only assert that "the zeal to embody the whole truth in politics is incompatible with an idea of public reason that belongs with democratic citizenship" (Rawls 2005: 442). Yet this is simply to beg the question, and the association of truth with zealotry implicitly denies that the positions in question have any epistemic merit. Rawls's proviso confirms this: that persons who advance non-public reasons in political contexts are obliged to supply public reasons "in due course" indicates that non-public argu-ments ultimately *can do no justificatory work* no matter how epistemically sound they may be. But this raises a serious question about the proviso. Insofar as a citizen may introduce non-public reasons only if he is confident that there is a compelling *public* reason for his view, then why should anyone bother with the non-public reason in the first place (Gaus 2003a: 199–200)? The proviso, it seems, is thus merely symbolic. However, those who would raise reasons drawn from their deepest moral convictions must

---

[9] See Joshua Cohen's discussion of the Papal encyclical *Evangelium Vitae*, in which an anti-abortion argument is presented that claims to be independent of any specifically religious claims. Cohen asserts, without argument, that the Pope appeals to a "conception of reason" that is "itself sectarian" (1998: 196).

[10] Contrast the philosophically robust pluralisms of Gray (2000) and Galston (2002); both theorists criticize Rawls on this point. Rawls is defended against Gray's criticism in Talisse 2002, and Galston is criticized in Talisse 2004.

[11] That is, the freestanding theorist must take a vow of "epistemic abstinence" even about the value of his own commitments. On this, see Raz 1990 and Estlund 1998.

reject the idea that those reasons are lacking in justificatory force, and they similarly must reject the idea that raising them in public discourse is merely a symbolic gesture. Although public reason may allow everyone a *voice*, it grants a *hearing* to only a few (*Cf.* Goodin 2003: 178).

The advocate of the politics of omission will concede this point but question its critical force. He may argue as follows: citizens who insist on presenting arguments that presume the truth of their own comprehensive doctrines are failing at proper democratic citizenship because they implicitly reject the fact of reasonable pluralism, recognition of which is necessary for the stability of a modern democratic regime (Rawls 2005: 441). Thus, the insistent Thomist, civic republican, and radical democrat are all destabilizing forces, and surely a democracy, like any regime, should be expected to endeavor to secure its own stability. So whereas it may be the case that public reason cannot duly recognize the epistemic merits of all views, there is no reason why it should be required to do so. To be sure, the reply continues, the aim of securing the stability of a democratic society under conditions of reasonable pluralism commits one to a kind of moral position, namely one that at the very least holds that a democratic society is *worth* preserving and that we should try to "find some way of living together that avoids the rule of force" (Larmore 1996: 151). But this is surely only a *minimal* moral commitment, and those who reject it are rightly dismissed.

This is a cogent reply, but it confronts a difficulty. Recall that the politics of omission was introduced as a way to maintain democratic stability among a population divided at the level of deep commitments. But there is good reason to expect that the politics of omission will generate *instability*. The argument for this claim draws from some recent work in the epistemology of groups bound by common beliefs.

Group polarization and crippled epistemology

In several recent works, Cass Sunstein has called attention to the statistical regularity known as *group polarization*. Group polarization means that "members of a deliberating group predictably move toward a more extreme point in the direction indicated by the members' predeliberation tendencies" (Sunstein 2003a: 81). Importantly, the term *extreme* does not in this context refer to points on a political spectrum of opinion, such as "radical" and "conservative" or "Left" and "Right"; rather, it is defined internally, that is, only by reference to persons' doxastic tendencies prior to discussion. Simply put, "like-minded people, after discussions with their peers, tend to end up thinking a more extreme version of what they thought before they started to talk" (2003b: 112). Let us consider a few of Sunstein's own examples:

(1) A group of moderately pro-feminist women will become more strongly pro-feminist after discussion.
(2) After discussion, citizens of France become more critical of the United States and its intentions with regard to economic aid.
(3) After discussion, whites predisposed to show racial prejudice offer more negative responses to the question of whether white racism is responsible for conditions faced by African Americans in American cities.
(4) After discussion, whites predisposed not to show racial prejudice offer more positive responses to the same question. (2001a: 23)

Group polarization "has been found all over the world and in many diverse tasks" and does not discriminate along educational, class, ethnic, gender, or political lines (2003a: 82). It has been shown to be operative in judicial panels, legislatures, political parties, religious organizations, and civic groups (2003b: 111). Moreover, the polarization effect is amplified in cases of what Sunstein calls "enclave deliberation," which is "that form of deliberation that occurs within more or less insulated groups, in which like-minded people speak mostly to each other" over extended periods of time (2001b: 75–76).

Group polarization shows that deliberative bodies of like-minded persons are *epistemically unstable*. The concern here is not the instability as such – change or shift of belief is not necessarily bad, and, indeed, tenacity can often be a vice in itself. Rather, the danger is that the shifts in belief due to group polarization occur only in the direction of the more extreme and without regard for reasons. That is, when a group polarizes, the members come to adopt increasingly more extreme versions of their former positions, and this movement is not occasioned or driven by the introduction of new or better arguments. When groups polarize it is because of the social-dynamic features of insular deliberative groups, not reasons or evidence (Sunstein 2003a: 82).

The danger of group polarization is not limited to the hazards associated with the perpetual shift towards extreme views. There is a danger also in that extreme views require extreme cognitive means for their preservation, what Russell Hardin has fittingly called "crippled epistemology" (2002). That is, those with extreme views attempt to "protect" their beliefs by "keeping [themselves] in the company only of others who share [their] beliefs"; in this way, the extreme beliefs "get reinforced constantly" despite the fact that "those beliefs might be shared by at most a tiny fraction of the world's population" (Hardin 2002: 10). The result is the emergence of a "norm of exclusion" (Hardin 2002: 9), which dismisses anyone who does not accept the preferred view. Hardin explains:

Isolation of people in a group with relatively limited contact with the larger society generates paranoid cognition, in which individuals begin to suppose the worst from those they do not know or even from those with whom they are not immediately in communication. (2002: 11)

The point is that, in order to maintain an extreme view, individuals must embed themselves in a social context that encourages them to lose the capacity to engage rationally with those with whom they disagree. Accordingly, as groups polarize, their members increasingly come to see all opposing views as not simply mistaken, but as nonsensical or incoherent. Hence, they increasingly come to see those who hold opposing views as wicked, benighted, ignorant, and stupid. To be sure, these attitudes are difficult to sustain; ordinary and everyday interactions tend to disconfirm the thesis that nearly everyone outside of one's own circle of like-minded colleagues is foolish or evil. This is why groups that hold extreme views often devise and employ complex epistemic mechanisms to control or limit individuals' interactions with persons outside the group. For example, extremist groups typically promote elaborate conspiracy theories that dismiss or explain away any countervailing considerations; further, they typically incorporate intricate pseudo-histories – usually involving a persecution mythology – that at once valorize the group and demonize those outside the group, thereby discouraging interaction between members and non-members. Frequently the language of chosen-ness is employed to explain how it could be that so many live in ignorance of the vital truths around which the group is organized.

To bring the Sunstein and Hardin insights together: doxastically homogenous groups polarize towards more extreme beliefs in the direction of their pre-deliberative commitments. When groups polarize in this way, their views grow increasingly out of step with the dominant views of those in the mainstream of society. Hence, ordinary social interaction with those outside the group becomes awkward and potentially threatening. A "crippled epistemology" develops which sustains, or even augments, the group members' confidence in their views by explaining away the fact that so many others disagree. Hence, the group grows to see those outside as dupes, fools, or even willful conspirators against the truth; accordingly, the group grows increasingly unable and uninterested in engaging with the outsiders and increasingly incapable of seeing them as fellow epistemic agents.

Omission and instability

For these reasons, the phenomenon of group polarization poses a distinct threat to democratic politics under conditions of moral pluralism. I shall next argue that the politics of omission can plausibly be expected to foster conditions under which group polarization is likely. It follows from this that the politics of omission is likely to generate *instability*. The politics of omission – "the strategy of avoidance" – is, therefore, a non-viable response to the problem of deep politics.

That the constraints imposed by public reason are likely to generate deliberative enclaves should be clear. Citizens are very deeply committed to comprehensive doctrines that conflict with the politics of omission on several levels. Citizens of faith present a conspicuous, though not the only, example. Many religious believers hold not only that abortion is a grave moral evil, but also that their opposition to abortion must not be relegated to what Rawls calls the "background culture" (2005: xx) of society. That is, they will resist the politics of omission because, for them, opposition to abortion is a fully *public* moral obligation; on their view, to acquiesce in a politics that places the issue of abortion off the political agenda is to commit a serious moral wrong. As Nicholas Wolterstorff has argued:

It belongs to the *religious convictions* of a good many religious people in our society that *they ought to base* their decisions concerning fundamental issues of justice *on* their religious convictions. They do not view as an option whether or not to do so … Their religion is not, for them, about *something other* than their social and political existence; it is *also* about their social and political existence … (1997: 91) (original emphasis)[12]

Agreeing with Wolterstorff, Christopher Eberle has argued that many religious believers take their religious obligations to be "totalizing"; Eberle explains:

They will take their obligation to obey God to extend to whatever they do, wherever they are, and in whatever institutional setting they find themselves. *A fortiori*, they'll take their obligation to obey God to extend to the political realm. (2002: 145)

Such citizens will accordingly reject the Rawlsian distinction between public and non-public. Interestingly, the situation is not altogether different for the kind of radical democrat we mentioned earlier who disagrees with

---

[12] Compare Dworkin's claim that for many Americans "their religious convictions *are* political principles" (2006: 64).

the Rawlsian not only on substantive issues of justice and equality, but also on the question of the *very nature of the political*. That is, the radical democrat maintains that part of what is at stake in our most central controversies is the "character of public life itself, as well as the meaning and scope of accepted political values" (Bohman 1996: 86). Again, since public reason begins from a strict delineation between the public and the non-public realms, it *cannot* countenance a public deliberative space in which these fundamental issues can be reasonably engaged; it must "put the 'values' of public reason beyond political contestation" (Bohman 1996: 86). In this sense, then, there is literally *no way* for persons who hold such views to raise their concerns and press their arguments in properly public contexts. Accordingly, the politics of omission must generate *epistemically excluded groups*.

Consider now the predicament of those persons that the politics of omission epistemically excludes: believing, correctly, that there is no point in raising their arguments in public, they will likely form small groups devoted to the advancement of their position; these groups will meet regularly to discuss the group's views and devise strategies for disseminating their message. Conditions will be ripe for polarization. To repeat: as the groups polarize, individuals will not only come to hold more extreme versions of their initial position, but will become epistemically crippled. They will come to see themselves as excluded, victimized, and oppressed; naturally, they will also grow increasingly dismissive of opposing views, and will regard those that affirm them as either evil or benighted. Fanaticism will set in, the overlapping consensus will give way to a *modus vivendi*, and hence precisely the kind of instability Rawls sought to avoid will result.[13] More importantly, a different kind of instability is likely to emerge, namely, the kind associated with fanaticism, hatred, and violence (Sunstein 2003b: 12).

In this way, the politics of omission engenders a politics of epistemic exclusion, and thus of non-engagement. But the salient lesson of the group polarization phenomenon is that non-engagement is democratically hazardous. It exacerbates rather than resolves the problem of deep politics. Therefore, the politics of omission fails.

---

[13] Hence, Hardin, "Winston Churchill reputedly quipped that fanatics are people who cannot change their minds and will not change the subject. He got their epistemology just right in his first point. But perhaps he got them wrong in his second point. It is not so much that they will not change the subject. Rather, they cannot change it, because they have no other subject. That is the nature of their crippled epistemology, without which they would not be fanatics" (2002: 21).

Some examples

It may be objected that I have been merely speculating or exaggerating. However, if it can be granted that certain regions of our public political discourse omit certain positions in the way described above, it can be shown that my speculations about epistemic exclusion are not implausible.

Carol Swain (2002) has recently published an alarming study of what she calls the "new" white nationalist movement in contemporary America. Swain's analyses are based on interviews conducted with ten prominent white nationalists; the transcripts of these interviews are available in a book edited by Swain and Russ Nieli (2003). An examination of the strikingly similar narratives offered by the white nationalists reveals the pattern of group polarization and crippled epistemology described above. For example, both William Pierce, the recently deceased founder of the neo-Nazi National Alliance and author of the infamous *Turner Diaries* (the book which inspired Timothy McVeigh to commit his act of terrorism) and Lisa Turner, the Women's Information Coordinator of the white supremacist World Church of the Creator, claim to have been motivated to political action by what they perceived to be a systematic refusal on the part of mainstream society to engage their ideas and arguments. It is important to note that their complaint is not that people were not *convinced* of their positions, but rather that the public space of political reason-giving was closed to them; hence, they characterize mainstream white America not as simply *mistaken* about matters of race and equality, but as "brainwashed," "conditioned" and "propagandized" (Swain and Nieli 2003: 258, 264). Pierce and Turner claim to have been "forced" to "build" their own "infrastructure" (Swain and Nieli 2003: 261) for disseminating their arguments. They both point to the Internet as their most effective recruitment tool (Swain and Nieli 2003: 266, 250). Perhaps not surprisingly, Sunstein (2001b) has shown that, insofar as it enables individuals to pre-select and filter the information to which they will be exposed, the Internet is a powerful source of polarization in contemporary society.

Swain explicitly draws the connection I have suggested between epistemic exclusion and group polarization when she writes:

Sunstein's analysis [of group polarization] seems to describe something clearly at work among many of the white nationalist leaders interviewed ... I believe that one reason why many of the members and potential members of their organizations have such little exposure to alternative viewpoints is because of the overall feebleness and lack of honesty that currently dominates discussion about controversial racial issues in America. (2002: 10)

Believing that America is "increasingly at risk of a large-scale racial conflict" (2002: 423), Swain makes a recommendation similar to Sunstein's: "What is most needed now … is for white nationalists to be heard and debated in mainstream forums where their data and ideas can be openly evaluated and subjected to critical assessment" (2002: 35). Despite the maneuvers designed to loosen the agenda and vocabulary restrictions of public reason, its *non-epistemic* character means that the kind of debate called for by Swain is not possible within a framework of "freestanding" politics. Recall that Rawls's political liberalism *begins* from the presumption of characteristically liberal democratic values, such as equality regardless of race, gender, or ethnicity; it regards these matters as settled and fixed, thus not open to public debate. Political liberalism hence cannot countenance the kind of debate Swain is calling for. Nor can it countenance such public debate concerning a wide array of other controversial moral issues.

A critic may respond that I have exaggerated the point. He may say that the fact that I have turned to fringe groups for my examples shows that my analysis is lacking in force. After all, the critic may continue, we should expect that in any society there will be some small number of persons on the fanatical fringe. Yet those on the fringe are *properly* excluded, along with their views and purported arguments. Hence, the critic concludes, the dangers I have described are not particularly pressing, at least not for mainstream society; thus, the politics of omission is stable after all.

But note that the problem is not that the politics of omission excludes those on the fanatical fringe of society; rather, the point is the more Millian one that, by excluding the arguments and reasons advanced in support of fringe positions, the politics of omission helps to create social conditions under which extremist groups can flourish, grow, and become more extreme. That is, by creating conditions under which fringe views are inadmissible in proper political discussion and so are dismissible as simply uncivil, unreasonable, and inappropriate, the politics of omission encourages those who espouse such views to take their message underground, so to speak, and to attempt to propagate their views in controlled, non-public forums where they can insulate themselves from critics. It is precisely in such forums where the tendency toward group polarization is especially high. Thus, the issue is not the exclusion of extremist views, but rather the inability of the politics of omission to combat the *spread* of extremism.

On this count, the data concerning the accelerated growth of racist and hate groups in recent years are disconcerting. According to Swain, "Over the decade of the 1990s there was a substantial increase in the activities of racist 'hate groups' in America" (2002: 75), and a recent report by the Southern

Poverty Law Center finds an increase between 2003 and 2004 in the number of active hate groups in the United States.[14] The surge in the popularity of these organizations is, of course, due to an array of factors, and no simple analysis can claim to provide the final explanation. However, part of the story surely involves the success of various groups in "mainstreaming" their image and message. According to Swain's description, the "new" white nationalist movement is characterized by "new tactics, new symbols, and new language designed to allay the fears of citizens repelled by more extremist approaches characteristic of the older racist right" (2002: 25). She continues:

Unlike the older racist right epitomized by the 1950s- and 1960s-era Ku Klux Klan, the new white nationalist movement that has emerged in America over the past two decades is preeminently a movement of discourse and ideas. It seeks to expand its audience largely through argument and persuasion ... In this regard, it is more akin to Leftist and Green parties around the world than to the older style white supremacy groups. (2002: 25)

A central tactic in the effort to mainstream racism is essentially semantic: the strategy is to redescribe the characteristic aims and objectives of the group in terms familiar to mainstream white citizens. Accordingly, many groups adopt names that employ familiar terms from the popular political culture, such as "Euro-American Student Union" and "The National Organization for European American Rights" (Swain 2002: 28). But the strategy is not restricted to the names of the organizations; it extends also to the terms that are used to formulate the *content* of the racism. This is confirmed by Swain and Nieli's interviews with white nationalist leaders. In these interviews, racism is cast as "pride" (Swain and Nieli 2003: 126), hate as "awareness" (Swain and Nieli 2003: 258), and white supremacy as a "civil rights" (Swain and Nieli 2003: 167) "activist" (Swain and Nieli 2003: 244) movement concerned primarily with the "education" (Swain and Nieli 2003: 262) of whites in America who are ignorant.

This is exactly what one should expect. Where politics is organized around a general principle of non-entanglement designed to avoid confrontations between competing deep commitments, the very content of the concepts that shape and direct our political institutions is left underdetermined; they are left up for grabs. The task then falls to citizens to fill in the precise details of these concepts. Hence, we shall all agree to be "democrats"

---

[14] The SPLC counts 762 hate groups active in 2004; that is a slight increase from the 2003 number of 751. "Hate Group Numbers Up Slightly in 2004," www.splcenter.org/center/splcreport/article.jsp?aid=135 (accessed April 22, 2005).

who share great concern for "freedom," "justice," and "equality," and who believe in "open dialogue" and "critical discourse" as a means to their achievement, but we shall not agree about the meaning and scope of any of these terms. Accordingly, the "shared fund" of "implicitly recognized basic ideas and principles" (Rawls 2005: 8) upon which public reason is based is left underdetermined and thus available for easy co-optation. The accounts given by Swain and Sunstein strongly suggest that this is occurring.

Although I have been focusing on the tendency of the politics of omission to create conditions favorable to groups on the fringe, the point can be extended to matters of mainstream politics. The narrative of a society deeply divided, with each camp incapable of speaking the other's language, is by now common. At present, this division narrative features many of the signals of polarization and crippled epistemology, for one of the main features of this narrative is the claim that it is either *useless* or *impossible* for the divided parties to rationally engage their differences; each side casts the other as either wicked or mindless and in any case unresponsive to reason or unwilling to participate in honest and open debate.

For example, consider Patrick Buchanan's words at the 1992 Republican National Convention:

There is a religious war going on in this country, a cultural war as critical to the kind of nation we shall be as the Cold War itself, for this war is for the soul of America.[15]

In an earlier piece titled "This is the Battle for America's Soul," Buchanan clearly identifies the moral dimension of the "cultural war":

The arts crowd is after more than our money, more than an end to the congressional ban on funding obscene and blasphemous art. It is engaged in a cultural struggle to root out the old America of family, faith, and flag, and re-create society in a pagan image. (1990)

According to Buchanan, then, the battle lines in the war for America's soul are clear: all that is good, wholesome, sacred, and "ours" is under attack by an "arts crowd" – notice: a *crowd*, an impersonal "it" – that aims to destroy "old America." Nowhere is it suggested that the so-called "arts crowd" presents *arguments* for its positions; instead, the "arts crowd" is presented as a mob, struggling to gain the power to defile American society. Surely, this kind of "crowd" cannot be reasoned with; hence, moral divisions produce not disagreement or debate, but a *cultural war*.

---

[15] Patrick Buchanan, "1992 Republican National Convention Speech," www.buchanan.org/pa-92-0817-rnc.html (accessed May 29, 2007).

Less overt examples are easy to find. Much of the popular literature emerging out of the 2000 and 2004 elections in the United States employs the "two Americas" narrative, positing an impassable divide between red and blue states. Similarly, popular political commentary, on both the Left and the Right, promotes the view that all opponents are intellectually defective and thus unworthy of engagement. Hence, the conservative commentator Ann Coulter (2004) advises her readers to talk to liberals only "if you must." Fortunately for them, she has undertaken the chore of developing for her followers a script of "how to talk to liberals." Apparently, according to Coulter, one need not actually *listen* to what one's opponents say in order to talk to them; talking to them (of course, only when one must) amounts to dismissing them *regardless* of what they might say.[16] Picking up on this general line, the conservative Michael Savage contends that his liberal opponents – possibly more than half of all adult Americans who vote, mind you – suffer from a "mental disorder" (2005), whereas Mike Gallagher (2005) contends that they are lunatics. A similar state of affairs prevails in the world of liberal commentary. For instance, in his "fair and balanced" examination of those with whom he disagrees, the liberal Al Franken (2003) casts those on the Right as "lying liars," and Michael Moore (2002) characterizes Republicans as "stupid white men." Of course, since reasoned dialogue requires that a norm of truthfulness be in place among intelligent participants, there is literally no point in talking with stupid liars. The message on both the Left and the Right is clear: anyone who disagrees with us is not worth talking to.

The rhetoric of insularity and crippled epistemology that pervades popular political commentary has been elevated to the level of a theory in the work of cognitive-scientist turned political strategist George Lakoff (2002; 2004; 2006; 2008). Lakoff begins from the observation that:

> Contemporary American politics is about worldview. Conservatives simply see the world differently than do liberals, and both often have a difficult time understanding accurately what the other's worldview is. (2002: 3)

According to Lakoff, this difficulty derives from the fact that our worldviews, and thus the language we use to formulate our political opinions, are couched in conceptually thick systems of meaning and metaphor. Accordingly, although liberals and conservatives may employ the same

---

[16] The charge of intellectual ineptitude is present even in Coulter's more recent book: *Godless: The Church of Liberalism* (2006). The message here is that liberals are irrational hypocrites who reject God but nonetheless belong to a church. Her more recent *If Democrats Had Any Brains, They'd Be Republicans* (2007) simply continues the trope.

terms to articulate their views, the *meanings* of those terms differ so greatly that liberals and conservatives are in essence speaking different languages.[17]

One might presume that the difficulty each side has in understanding the other's worldview is the *problem* to be overcome by a cognitive-scientific analysis of political discourse. But this is not the case according to Lakoff's analysis. The trouble, as Lakoff understands it, is that the conservative worldview predominates contemporary American politics. This means that the conservative system of meanings and metaphors "frames" the policy debates in American society. To use one of Lakoff's more nifty examples, consider that policies that cut taxes are popularly characterized as "tax *relief*" (2004: 23). But the very notion of *relief* already presumes the conservatives' *moral* conclusion that taxes are a *burden* that should be lifted. The trouble is that once the public policy debate concerning taxes is framed in such terms, the liberal position is at a loss, for they are stuck with the ungainly task of arguing that *relief* is something to oppose. In this way, "progressives have ceded the political mind to radical conservatives" (2008: 2).

Lakoff's advice to liberals is to invent and promulgate their *own* frame, one that embeds decidedly *liberal* values and policies (2006: 245ff.). That is, according to Lakoff, the lesson to be learned is that the liberal and conservative positions are "impossible to compare because they presuppose opposite moral systems" (2002: 385).[18] He continues:

There are no neutral concepts and no neutral language for expressing political positions within a moral context. Conservatives have developed their own partisan moral-political concepts and moral-political language. Liberals have not. (2002: 385)

Lakoff suggests that "the best thing that can be done for the sake of a balanced discourse is to develop a meta-language – a language about the concepts and language used in morality and politics" (2002: 385). Elsewhere, he emphasizes the need to reach a "higher rationality" that is able "to step outside of our own political beliefs and to see how moral and political reasoning works for both ourselves and others" (2006: 15).

The problem with these suggestions is that it is not clear why Lakoff should presume that such a meta-language would be itself "neutral"; a second-order language *about* the language of moral and politics should be subject to the

---

[17] In what follows, I will not bother to criticize the simple-mindedness of Lakoff's political taxonomy, according to which there are but two worldviews operative in contemporary democratic politics in the United States.

[18] I leave aside the objection – obvious and compelling, in my view – that to say that A and B are "opposite" is to compare them. If they were indeed impossible to compare, it would not be possible to discern that they are based in "opposite moral systems."

same ideological influences as any first-order worldview. Similarly, a "higher" rationality would be subject to all the framing effects and meta-phorical influences of the *lower* rationality we typically employ and hence could not "step outside" of it. That is, any attempted meta-language (or "higher rationality") will be subject to the same analysis that Lakoff has developed of our first-order moral and political language.

Indeed, one can easily develop such a critique of Lakoff's proposed meta-language. Lakoff characterizes the conservative–liberal divide in terms of two moral systems; according to Lakoff, conservatives subscribe to a "strict father morality," and liberals hold a "nurturant parent morality" (2002: 33f.; 2006: chs. 5 and 6). Surely a critic would be right to point out that these characterizations are not value-neutral and are therefore objectionable. A conservative critic will object to the association of conservative politics with a moral vision that is based in a decidedly *male* role. According to the conservative, this image is objectionable because it embeds into a purported description the normative judgment – a popular one among liberals – that conservatism is chauvinistic, misogynistic, or the politics of the "old boys' club."

To be clear, my point is not to dispute the aptness of Lakoff's character-ization of the moral tendencies driving the conservative program – I need to take no view on the matter – but rather to suggest that if we accept Lakoff's claim that "There are no neutral concepts and no neutral language for expressing political positions within a moral context" (2002: 385), there is no reason not to extend the analysis to the concepts in a meta-language used to describe first-order systems of concepts. To employ Lakoff's own language, he has simply proposed a new frame within which to describe two influen-tial ways of thinking about politics; however, since there is no "neutral language for expressing political positions within a moral context" (2002: 385), there are no descriptions that are not at the same time pre-scriptive. That is, on Lakoff's view, all purported descriptions embed normative judgments about the things described; hence, the entire frame-work of the "strict father" and the "nurturant parent" embeds the moral judgment that the conservative moral system is antiquated, paternalistic, male-oriented, anti-egalitarian, oppressive, and authoritarian, while the liberal morality is supportive, liberating, egalitarian, loving, encouraging, and caring. This is a description that no conservative would embrace.

Amazingly, this is precisely the point of Lakoff's analysis! The salient implication of Lakoff's view is that honest and sincere debate between liberals and conservatives is quite literally impossible (Lakoff 2002: 385). On Lakoff's view, since moral and political terms are themselves

semantically embedded in the more general liberal and conservative worldviews, there can be no rational give and take among the contending parties;
indeed, he claims that liberals and conservatives employ "two very different
forms of reason" (2006: 15). Hence, his advice to liberals is to create a "moral
discourse to counter conservatives"; in order to do this, liberals must "get
over their view" that "straightforward rational literal debate on an issue is
always possible" (2002: 387; *cf.* 2006: 255). The implication is, again, that
liberals and conservatives need not engage each other, because they frankly
cannot. Accordingly, his discussion about "how to take back public discourse" (2004: ch. 1) contains no examination of the respective merits of
liberal and conservative *arguments* or *positions*; it instead presents a *strategy*
for replacing the conservative frame for a liberal one. More importantly, the
moral question of the *worth* of characteristically liberal policy initiatives, as
compared with conservative alternatives, lies beyond the scope of possible
debate; similarly, the question of why one *should* be a liberal rather than a
conservative is rendered nonsensical. In the end, then, Lakoff is offering a
strategy by which progressive ideals can come to dominate American
politics, but the strategy requires relinquishing the belief that those very
ideals are worth striving for.

Democratic politics is, on Lakoff's view, simply a matter of two worldviews competing for dominance. The "higher rationality" he calls for is a
purely *instrumental* rationality designed to identify effective strategies for
persuading people to adopt your views, yet it proceeds from a theory of
moral commitment which precludes the task of giving an account of *why*
one's worldview is *morally better* than any other. Indeed, Lakoff's view
denies the possibility of moral reasoning and moral disagreement altogether. That is, on Lakoff's view, democracy can be nothing more than an
ongoing propaganda contest among incommensurate and hostile moral
standpoints.

The lessons from these examples should be clear. Given the recent
advances in communications and media technology that increasingly
make it easier for individuals to "filter what they see" (Sunstein 2001a: 8)
and thus to "live in echo chambers of their own devising" (Sunstein 2003b:
106) and inhabit "information cocoons" (Sunstein 2006: 9), the threat of
epistemic self-insulation is especially present even in mainstream politics. A
model of political discourse that omits reference to deeply held commitments and that denies that such commitments are legitimate bases for
political action creates an incentive for citizens to exit the public sphere
and pursue their political ends in non-public, insular, and non-democratic
arenas. As Michael Sandel observes:

Where political discourse lacks moral resonance, the yearning for a public life of larger meanings finds undesirable expressions. Groups like the "moral majority" and the Christian right seek to clothe the naked public square with narrow, intolerant moralisms. Fundamentalists rush in where liberals fear to tread. (1998a: 217)

However, the proper response to this state of affairs is not the communitarian one of saturating public discourse with the language of a supposedly shared substantive moral vision. The communitarian impulse simply to trade a variety of "narrow, intolerant moralisms" for a single, communal moralism is no solution to the problem of deep politics. Rather, the solution lies elsewhere.

Beyond omission

Let us pause to review the argument thus far. The freestanding response to the problem of deep politics calls for a politics of omission in which citizens avoid appealing to their moral and religious commitments in public political debate and deliberation. The thought is that, since we disagree about matters of deep moral commitment, politics should be conducted in terms that draw only from the "shared fund" of "implicitly recognized basic ideas and principles" operative in contemporary democratic societies. But the very idea of a politics of omission will strike many citizens as morally objectionable in itself: they will see certain of their moral commitments as demonstrably *true* and they will take the project of politically instantiating those commitments as a non-negotiable imperative of basic justice. Since the politics of omission is rooted in a non-epistemic view of political justification, the demonstrable truth of a contested moral proposition is insufficient to render it a proper basis for political policy. But this is itself a commitment that a freestanding political theory cannot justify, since to attempt to do so would be to abandon freestandingness. As a result, the politics of omission involves what persons of faith and others will see as a "gag rule" (Holmes 1995) which ultimately cannot be defended. In practice, this will encourage the formation of deliberative enclaves, which in turn produce group polarization and crippled epistemology. The result is a politics based in the kind of *modus vivendi* truce that Rawls is correct to regard as insufficiently stable. Hence, the politics of omission fails.

To be sure, the argument is focused on the likely consequences of overtly implementing the Rawlsian proposal rather than endorsing its more general theoretical contours. In fact, it is difficult to reject the thought that the politics of omission exhibits the right *aspirations*; indeed, Nagel is surely correct to propose that "we should not impose arrangements, institutions, or requirements on other people on grounds that they could reasonably reject" (1987: 229). Similarly, Larmore is right to say that, "When two people disagree about some specific point, but wish to continue talking about the more general problem they wish to solve, each should prescind from the beliefs that the other rejects" (1987: 53). But what reason do deeply divided citizens have to seek to continue the conversation with their moral opponents? Why should citizens see those with whom they disagree as persons *worth* talking to at all, rather than, say, as adversaries to be marginalized, silenced, or defeated?

Larmore is correct to emphasize that the politics of omission presupposes that citizens already "share a form of life that embodies a commitment to equal respect" (1996: 142).[19] But this raises two intertwined questions: (1) why should our justification of democracy be premised upon the presumption that citizens that are otherwise deeply divided nonetheless share a common commitment to equal respect?; and (2) why should the content of the commitment to equal respect be interpreted in the way that entails a politics of omission?

With regard to the first question, to presume a common commitment to equal respect seems no less controversial than to presume a common commitment to almost any other moral principle. The value of equal respect is no less contestable than the value of respect for authority or of faithfulness to a tradition, for example. The democrat will reply that equal respect is a fundamental *democratic* value, whereas respect for authority is *not*; thus, equal respect is a core value for *us*. But this reply simply begs the question of justification; it does not answer it.

As for the second question, the precise nature of the commitment to equal respect is subject to a variety of interpretations, not all of which are practically consistent with the others; hence, the view that respect requires omission is but one view among many. For example, one can imagine a view according to which the entire strategy of "non-entanglement" is constitutive of a policy of *disrespect*. On such a view, we respect our fellow citizens' deep moral commitments by "engaging, or attending to them – sometimes by challenging or contesting them, sometimes by listening and learning from them – especially when those convictions bear on important political questions" (Sandel 1998a: 217). Any attempt on the part of the advocate of

---

[19] Compare Nussbaum, "Rawls starts from the idea of equal respect and shows that only a political conception that separates certain key moral/political values from religious ideas will appropriately preserve that all-important value" (2008: 361).

the freestanding approach to democracy to respond to these questions will involve the introduction of a substantive moral doctrine and, therefore, will constitute a violation of freestandingness.

The general point is not that the aspiration for a politics based in common ground is misguided, but rather that the Rawlsian proposal begins from a common ground that is simply *stipulated*. But common ground is, almost by definition, the kind of thing that *cannot* be simply stipulated; common ground must be *achieved* and *worked for*. The task of forging common ground cannot proceed from *ex ante* stipulations about the content of "implicitly shared" democratic principles and what counts as properly public deliberation. Rather, the search for common ground must proceed from a politics "founded upon the legitimacy of a debate as to what is legitimate and what is illegitimate" (Lefort 1988: 39). Such a politics requires an *epistemically open* procedure that can sustain a real debate between contending positions. The aim of such debate is not the implausible one of reasoned consensus; the aim is rather to reach outcomes that are sufficiently based in processes of collective reasoning to motivate even those who disagree with them to continue to participate (Bohman 1996: 33). In other words, if we want to "find some way of living together that avoids the rule of force" (Larmore 1996: 151), we must pursue a *politics of engagement*. This is precisely what the politics of omission precludes. We find the beginnings of a politics of engagement in the recent work of Jeffrey Stout, so it is to him that we now turn.

II STOUT AND IMMANENT CRITICISM

In his recent book, *Democracy and Tradition* (2004), Jeffrey Stout addresses the problem of deep politics by offering an analysis of the role of religious commitment in popular political discourse. His focus on religion does not mean that his view cannot be generalized to address the problem in its broader dimensions. So, although in examining Stout's view we shall fix on cases involving religious commitment, we can easily extend the discussion to include deep commitments of other kinds.

Stout is driven by what he sees as an emerging crisis in the relationship between democratic politics and citizens of faith. Stout writes:

We are about to reap the social consequences of a traditionalist backlash against contractarian liberalism. One message being preached nowadays in any of the institutions where future preachers are being trained is that liberal democracy is essentially hypocritical when it purports to value free religious expression … Over the next several decades this message will be preached in countless sermons throughout the heartland of the nation. (2004: 76)

Insisting that "All democratic citizens should feel free to express whatever premises actually serve as reasons for their claims" (2004: 10), Stout launches his own version of the kind of objection to the politics of omission I developed above. His aim, in part, is to devise an "alternative under-standing of public reasoning" (2004: 10). Like Rawls, Stout thinks it is important that such a view be one that contemporary citizens can endorse as something other than a Hobbesian truce; that is, whereas Rawls seeks an overlapping consensus, Stout seeks an account of democratic public reason-ing that citizens can accept without "resentment" (2004: 92ff.).

It is important to emphasize that citizens of faith come to resent the politics of omission because they consider it hypocritical. From their perspective, omission is introduced for the sake of acknowledging and respecting the deep commitments of all citizens; however, in practice, the politics of omission does not place an equal burden on all citizens. For example, the strictures of public reason require more from religious citizens than from citizens who hold secular commitments, because the latter commitments are more easily translated into properly public reasons. In this way, the politics of omission seems "rigged" against the commitments of citizens of faith. Recall the claim made by George and Wolfe, cited earlier:

Public reason … almost always has the effect of making the liberal position the winner in morally charged political controversies. It does this in effect by ruling out of bounds substantive moral argument on behalf of nonliberal positions. (2000: 2)

Echoing Galston (1999: 43), it could be said that when a large proportion of citizens view standing democratic processes as hypocritically rigged against their fundamental commitments regarding justice, it is difficult to imagine how anything other than a *modus vivendi* politics can result. And a *modus vivendi* is insufficiently stable for democratic politics.

The source of secularization

Stout correctly thinks that if resentment is to be avoided, a case for secularized public discourse must be made to citizens of faith *from within* their own religious perspectives. Accordingly, central to Stout's view of the proper role of religious reasons in democratic political deliberation is his account of the secularization of public discourse. According to Stout, it is a mistake to suppose that secularized public discourse is, as some critics suppose, the result of anti-religious impositions by the liberal state. Stout contends that "Secularization was not primarily brought about by the triumph of secularist ideology" (2004: 102); rather, the politics of omission developed *among* religious thinkers who saw that they were "not in a position to take for granted that their interlocutors are making the same religious assumptions they are" (2004: 97). Hence, the impetus for secularization was not the desire to do away with religion, but instead "the increasing need to cope with religious plurality discursively on a daily basis under circumstances where improved transportation and communication were changing the political and economic landscape" (2004: 102).

Stout contends, then, that the extent to which our current modes of political exchange feature elements of omission is not something that citizens of faith must resent, for the prevalence of a secularized mode of public discourse is *not* indicative of a secularist mode of politics (2004: 93), and does *not* "reflect a commitment to secularism, secular liberalism, or any other ideology" (2004: 97). Hence, Stout's position is opposed to the views of other religious thinkers, including John Milbank, Alasdair MacIntyre, and Stanley Hauerwas. According to Stout, these theorists manifest an unwholesome resentment toward modern democracy. Rejecting this resentment, Stout asks, "if theological premises … receive little discursive attention for this perfectly understandable reason [i.e. religious plurality], why would anyone have just cause for resentment of the resulting type of secularized discourse?" (2004: 99). According to Stout, to resent secularized public deliberation is effectively to resent religious diversity itself (2004: 99).

Let us grant Stout's genealogical account of secularization. But it is still not clear how Stout's genealogy is supposed to motivate contemporary citizens of faith to accept secularized discourse without resentment. According to one possible reading, Stout's argument runs as follows: secularization has its origin in religious traditions and not in a secularist ideology; therefore, contemporary citizens of faith should *now* embrace secular discourse. But this reading of the argument should be resisted; for on this reading, Stout is unabashedly committing the genetic fallacy. Charity demands that we look deeper for a cogent reading of the argument.

We can begin to see the deeper argument by noting that, like Rawls, Stout appeals to pluralism. According to Stout:

> Our society is religiously plural, and has remained so for several centuries despite constant efforts on the part of its religious members to appeal to their fellow citizens with reasons for converting to a single theology. (2004: 100)

The argument thus seems to be pragmatic; according to Stout, "there is no point in trying to wish the social reality of religious diversity away, or in resenting this diversity as long as it lasts" (2004: 100). But this is puzzling. Let us grant that religious plurality is a near-permanent condition of contemporary democratic societies; nonetheless, it does not follow from this that we must not (or simply should not bother to) *resent* this fact. The point is that the observation that pluralism is here to stay is not sufficient to motivate a wholehearted acceptance of religious diversity. However, such acceptance *must* be motivated, since adopting it is, in many cases, tantamount to revising one's religious doctrine. But Stout cannot produce the required motivation without committing to a specific philosophical view that will inevitably be as contestable as the religious doctrines it is supposed to harmonize. So Stout seems to be caught in the same dilemma that haunts the Rawlsian proposal.

Stout's pragmatism

Stout here takes a pragmatic tack. Rejecting an overt politics of omission, he allows that "All democratic citizens should feel free to express whatever premises actually serve as reasons for their claims" (2004: 10), but contends that the fact of religious diversity means that sectarian reasons will be *impotent* in political discourse, and the arguments that employ them will be *unsuccessful*. Stout writes:

> And this consequence of theological plurality has an enormous impact on what our ethical discourse is like. It means, for example, that in most contexts it will simply be imprudent, rhetorically speaking, to introduce explicitly theological premises into an argument intended to persuade a religiously diverse public audience. If one cannot expect such premises to be accepted or interpreted in a uniform way, it will not necessarily advance one's rhetorical purposes to assert them. (2004: 98–99)

Stout's thought seems to be that the *practice* of public discourse will lead citizens of faith to adopt willingly a secularized mode of discourse and accordingly embrace religious pluralism non-resentfully. Citizens who persist in practicing sectarian discourse will find themselves frustrated and their objectives obstructed.

In this respect, Stout seems to differ from Rawls. Recall that, on Rawls's view, public reason involves *ex ante* constraints on the kinds of reasons and arguments that could be admitted into public discourse. Stout's view, by contrast, involves no *ex ante* constraints; rather, Stout sees secularization as an *ex post* or pragmatic strategy. Again, what generates this turn to secularized discourse is the realization that *sectarian arguments are ineffectual.* Hence Stout's case for secularized discourse runs like this: if you want to persuade your fellow citizens to adopt your view, it is better to not employ religious reasons, because raising such reasons "does not work" (2004: 94).

Immanent criticism

Stout's proposal seems a good fit with the kind of politics of engagement that I sketchily described at the end of the previous section. In fact, Stout proposes a mode of engagement by means of which common ground may be won; he calls this "immanent criticism" (2004: 90). When engaged in this mode of discourse, the immanent critic adopts the premises of the person he aims to criticize, and then attempts to demonstrate either that the conjunction of the adopted premises is a contradiction or that the premises support his own preferred conclusion. In this way, the immanent critic *adopts the position* of his interlocutor and attempts to show that the interlocutor has a reason *from within his own view* to revise his position.

But note that immanent criticism, if it is to be democratically efficacious, is a two-way street in the sense that it presupposes that the party to be criticized is *willing* to allow his most central commitments to be critically engaged by someone who does not already share them, but has merely *adopted* them *ad arguendo*. Of course, it may be the case that, for certain modes of religious commitment, the very project of merely *adopting* the religious perspective in question – rather than, say, *embracing* it – is futile. One could easily imagine a religious believer claiming that an immanent critic *cannot* simply *adopt* his religious premises; in order to truly *occupy* the position of the religious believer, it could be argued, one must *really commit* to the truth of the religious doctrine. Anything less than full commitment is a mere *pretending*, and no criticism derived from a *pretended* religious perspective is worth taking seriously. According to this kind of religious believer, immanent criticism is a *conceptual impossibility*.

But it is likely that this mode of religiosity is relatively rare. Let us suppose then that most versions of religious commitment prevalent in contemporary democracies allow for the conceptual possibility of immanent criticism. Nonetheless, Stout's model faces a difficulty. The very practice of immanent criticism requires the participants to see each other roughly as discursive equals, each qualified to engage in moral reasoning, each with the authority to interpret and assess moral claims, each a cognitive creature that is morally autonomous, neither subordinate to the other, and so on. In other words, in order to engage in immanent criticism, each must see the other as a fellow democratic citizen. Stout confirms this, stating:

Implicit in our way of treating one another is a conception of ourselves as citizens who (a) ought to enjoy *equal standing* in political discourse; (b) deserve respect *as individuals* keeping track of the discussion from their own distinctive points of view; and (c) have a personal and perhaps religious stake in the exercise of *expressive freedom*. (2004: 82)

But now things seem to have gone awry. Recall that we were looking to the model of immanent criticism as a way to *motivate* democratic commitments among deeply divided citizens. Now we see that the model of immanent criticism *presupposes* those very commitments.

Non-entanglement redux

Thus, the model of immanent criticism faces the same difficulty confronting the "conversational" justification of the politics of omission offered by Larmore and Ackerman discussed above. Recall that the conversational justification for the politics of omission has it that "In the face of disagreement, those who wish to continue the conversation should retreat to *neutral ground*" (Larmore 1987: 53). Accordingly, the conversational justification is purely *conditional*; it says that if one *wants* to continue the conversation, one should omit reference to controversial premises. The immanent criticism model is similarly conditional; that is, it says that *if* one wants to forge common ground with others, or *if* one wants to engage others in the way that democrats typically do, then, when engaging deep moral differences, one should try to argue from one's interlocutor's premises. But it is not clear that Stout's model can motivate citizens to seek common ground in the first place.

To be sure, Stout claims that his book "addresses readers in their capacity as citizens" (2004: 5). This means that he asks his readers to adopt a certain "point of view," namely that of "someone who accepts some measure of responsibility for the condition of society and, in particular, for the political arrangements it makes for itself" (2004: 5). He continues that "To adopt this point of view is to participate in the living moral tradition of one's people, understood as a civic nation" (2004: 5). In this way, Stout's argument is addressed to those who already accept the moral tradition that obtains at present in the United States. This moral tradition prescribes a mode of politics in which citizens owe to each other equal respect and the kinds of political reasons that can be accepted by all. In this way, the model of immanent criticism follows from the democratic moral tradition that Stout presupposed. Therefore, it does not *justify* that tradition to those who do not already embrace it.

Consequently, Stout's position is subject to the same kind of objection that I launched against the Rawlsian proposal. Stout's account of the democratic moral tradition is but one such account among many, and hence is itself contestable. This is especially obvious today, where the "moral tradition" of the United States is appealed to on all sides of pressing social issues, including gay marriage, social security reform, foreign policy, the appointment of Supreme Court justices, and so on. Just as advocates of the politics of omission stipulate the content of the "shared principles" that shape the constraints on public reason, Stout stipulates a particular interpretation of the democratic moral tradition, one that emphasizes Whitman, Ellison, and Dewey and not Jesus, Locke, or Madison. Insofar as the model of immanent criticism is rooted in Stout's interpretation of that tradition, he cannot give to those who reject that interpretation any reason to undergo immanent criticism, or to engage in a process of forging common ground. And so it seems that Stout's immanent criticism model is but another non-entanglement strategy: those who do not begin from Stout's own interpretation of the democratic moral tradition are simply not engaged.

III CONCLUSION

In this chapter, I examined two well-developed responses to the problem of deep politics. Both proposals begin from the recognition of the plurality of deep commitments among democratic citizens, and both attempt to develop a strategy for democratic politics to proceed in spite of deep conflicts. I have argued that both proposals share a common flaw: they presuppose that despite the depth of moral disagreement, there is nonetheless an identifiable moral commitment that all reasonable persons share which can be appealed to as a basis for democratic politics. In the Rawlsian case, this common commitment is to the "duty of civility" (2005: 217), or the principle of "equal respect" (Larmore 1996: 142), according to which citizens must seek to justify their political actions in terms that others can be reasonably expected to accept. But, as we have seen, and as Thomas Christiano (2001) has argued in a different context, the freestanding nature of the Rawlsian enterprise prohibits the attempt to *justify* this supposed duty. In Stout's case, we are asked to countenance a "living moral tradition" (2004: 5) in which all democratic citizens participate that recommends immanent criticism as a model of public engagement across moral and religious divides. But, again, Stout offers no *justification* for the idea that citizens of faith should expose their most fundamental beliefs to the scrutiny of outsiders. On both views, a politics of omission is recommended as a

prerequisite for "keeping the conversation going" among divided democratic citizens; but nothing is said about why citizens should bother having
such conversations, rather than simply hiving off with like-minded fellows
in order to strategize and plot.

There is an additional similarity between the two proposals, one that
points to a quite different way of responding to the problem of deep politics.
The similarity consists in the shared premise that the ground for democratic
politics, the story we tell about why one should adopt the democratic
standpoint, must be an essentially *moral* ground. Again, both Rawls and
Stout have sought after a moral commitment that is minimal enough to be
acceptable across otherwise deeply divided citizens, but nevertheless substantial enough to support democratic commitments. The problem is that
there are no such moral commitments. Any moral principle substantial
enough to generate a democratic politics will be controversial across divided
comprehensive doctrines, and any moral principle minimal enough to win
consensus across deep moral divides will be too thin to support democratic
commitments.

Does this render the problem of deep politics irresolvable? I think not.
The two proposals discussed in this chapter share a common mistake in
presuming that the justification for democratic politics must lie in a *moral*
principle. But not all commitments are *moral* in character, and not all
normativity is essentially moral. There are other kinds of commitments
that may prove both sufficiently non-controversial and substantial to provide a justification for democracy. I contend that there is a core of sound
epistemic commitments that satisfy this description; that is, I hold that there
is a set of basic and non-controversial epistemic principles whose substance
entails a commitment to democratic politics. As it is crucial that these
epistemic principles be widely shared by persons who deeply disagree
about moral essentials, I shall argue that there is a "folk epistemology"
already implicit in the everyday workings of common discourse. In
Chapter 3, I shall make this folk epistemology explicit and argue that it is
sufficient for a justification of democracy.

Folk epistemology

Thus far the discussion has been devoted primarily to stage-setting. I have argued that the most popular responses to the problem of deep politics share the presumption that if we are to avoid a *modus vivendi* politics based in a Hobbesian truce, we must identify a "minimal moral conception" that could both support democratic politics and sustain the loyalty of citizens otherwise deeply divided over fundamental moral commitments. In this way, the dominant responses hold that democratic theory must be "freestanding," that is, free from deep moral entanglements but, nonetheless, sturdy enough to function as a moral foundation for democratic politics. In Chapter 2, I argued that this strategy is for several reasons non-viable. In general, the problem confronting the freestanding strategy is that even a minimal moral conception is contestable both in terms of its standing *qua* moral conception and as an interpretation of the "shared fund" of commonly accepted principles. This is especially so when the minimal conception places controversial constraints on citizens' political deliberation, advocacy, and action. In order to fill in the details of the freestanding account, one must tell a philosophical story about the normative appropriateness of the "shared fund;" but to tell such a story is to provide specific philosophical and moral *content* to that which was supposed to be freestanding, thereby inviting the kind of moral controversy that was supposed to be circumvented.

The alternate route to be pursued in the present chapter and Chapter 4 rejects the presumption that our justification of democratic politics must begin from decidedly *moral* premises; instead, it looks to what we shall call *folk epistemology* for a justification of democracy. The strategy is to identify a collection of core epistemic commitments that can be plausibly expected to be shared among persons deeply divided over moral and religious fundamentals. Accordingly, our approach splits the difference between Rawlsian political liberalism and the more traditional comprehensive approaches. It retains the justificatory structure of traditional views; like them, it maintains that democracy is the political manifestation of some basic commitment that we all share. However, whereas the traditional views held that certain *moral* percepts – for example, natural rights, dignity, autonomy, liberty, self-ownership, and the like – were fundamental, our approach enlists a collection of folk epistemic principles to serve as the foundation of democratic politics.

The task at hand, then, can be divided into two parts. First, I must identify the epistemic principles and show that they are indeed shared across moral and religious divides. Second, I must show that the epistemic commitments that we share entail a commitment to democratic politics. In the current chapter, I shall undertake the first part of the task, leaving the second part to Chapter 4.

I THE IDEA OF A FOLK EPISTEMOLOGY

As should be evident, the argument of the book turns on the concept of a *folk epistemology*. *Folk epistemology* is a relatively new concept in epistemology. Accordingly, some care must be taken in introducing the idea. So I begin with some considerations which may to some readers seem highly rudimentary.

Theory and practice

Philosophers today commonly lament the separation of theory from practice. The principle that theory and practice must not be sundered is most often employed critically. Philosophers tend to think that to show that some theory does not bear the right relation to practice is to raise a serious worry about the theory. Frequently, theories are criticized for being impossible to manifest in practice, or for relying on implausible assumptions about the world of practice, otherwise referred to as the "real world." Sometimes, a theory is criticized simply for having *no* practical implications at all. Obviously, the demand that theory and practice remain in close contact is especially present in moral and political philosophy, but it is a staple of many of the most influential philosophical movements of the past century, including logical positivism, pragmatism, and naturalism, among others.

It is less often noticed by philosophers that the claim that theory and practice must be continuous has implications not just for theory, but for practice as well. To engage in a practice is to manifest, or instantiate, or enact some theory. To be sure, our commonplace practices are more or less automatic. We don't think much about what we are doing when we go shopping for running shoes or place a phone call or obey a traffic signal – we just *do* it. But in reality we never *simply* act, we never really *just* do it. Our acts are most often the result of decisions, plans, and intentions, and these are, in turn, *projections* into the future. That is, when we act, we aim to do *something*; we act *for the sake of* bringing about some or other result. Yet our actions typically are not simply stabs in the dark; that they are typically the outcomes of plans and decisions means our acts are also the result of our assessments of *present* circumstances, evaluations of the potentialities inherent within the present. When we act, it is often because we judge that there is something that *needs doing*; we find the current state of the world dissatisfying, incomplete, or lacking, and we act so as to remedy, correct, or at least alter the present. The forward-looking nature of action presupposes a prior assessment of the present. But our assessments of the present involve a backward-looking element; when we deliberate about what to do in a given situation we bring to bear on the present a fund of past experience, and the expectation that the past will resemble the future in the relevant respects. Again, most of the time, our actions seem to us to be automatic. But that we act without *thinking about acting* does not entail that we act *without thinking*, and it does not entail that our actions are engaged without the help of theoretical presuppositions.

Yet those presuppositions are not restricted to claims and observations about simple states in the world. Our actions, in order to be the kind of acts they are, occur within a complex system of social relations and institutions. For example, shopping for running shoes is a practice that presupposes an entire theory of ownership and market exchange. Similarly, the practice of driving a car involves a complicated system of rules. Without *that* theory of exchange, or one that closely resembles it, there would be no act such as shopping; similarly, without some appropriate system of rules governing the road, it would be impossible to drive.

I take it that these are obvious points. However, shopping and driving are not unique cases. Whenever you ask another person, "What are you doing?," you seek to bring observed behavior under the description of a known or familiar practice; likewise, whenever it appears to you that it would make sense to ask such a question, you implicitly acknowledge that the behavior in question is so describable, that it can be made *intelligible* to you. To act in any way that is not haphazard or random is to enact a practice, and to engage in a practice is already to instantiate a theory, consciously or not.

I have been using the word *theory* in a rather loose sense. It indicates a collection of principles, observations, and hypotheses that together comprise the cognitive background against which we think, talk, act, and interact. When we talk about theories less casually, such as when we are discussing scientific theories, we mean something much more particular. Theories in the formal sense – again, such as good scientific theories – must answer to an array of standards; among these are testability, fecundity, consistency, and the like. Failure to satisfy these standards renders the proposed theory inadequate *as a theory*. We may contrast the idea of a formal theory with that of a folk theory. To characterize a theory as a *folk* theory is not to malign it. Folk theories are, to be sure, pre-scientific and relatively non-systematic, but they earn their keep by being *useable* in a rough and ready, practical way. A chef does not need to know formal chemistry in order to do his job, because there is a folk chemistry that is learned more or less in the kitchen. Although the chef's understanding of chemical interactions does not qualify as *scientific* in the strict sense, the chef does have *some* kind of knowledge in that he is able to reliably *produce* certain results; more importantly, his knowledge enables him to *make predictions, correct mistakes, invent,* and *improvise*.

Generalizing, we can say that folk theories are unabashedly *instrumentalist* in their orientation; they are *tools* first and foremost. Consequently, folk theories are not answerable to the same standards to which we hold proposed formal theories. What counts in the case of a folk theory is that it *works* "on the ground" as it were. Accordingly, folk theories are necessarily *incomplete* theories; they do not aspire to capture and systematize *all* the phenomena, but only the phenomena that are most centrally relevant to the tasks at hand. The chef's theory of chemistry makes no pronouncements on substances and reactions that are irrelevant to cooking. Moreover, as folk theories arise under normal and everyday circumstances, they are not designed to work under abnormal or irregular circumstances. Folk theories are in this way theories not simply *by* but *for* the folk.

Folk epistemology and folk psychology

As mentioned above, in the chapters that follow, I shall propose a solution to the problem of deep politics that derives from what I will call *folk epistemology*. By *folk epistemology*, I mean something analogous to what philosophers of mind call *folk psychology*. Whereas *formal* or *scientific* psychology studies the full range of mental phenomena and behavior – from memory, sleep, intelligence, and perception to aggression, compulsion, and love – *folk* psychology refers to the "prescientific, common-sense conceptual framework that all normally socialized humans deploy in order to comprehend, predict, explain, and manipulate the behavior of humans and the higher animals" (Churchland 1994: 308). Folk psychology is manifest in the "everyday psychological discourse we use to discuss the mental lives of our fellow human beings" (Dennett 1996: 27), and it employs a collection of familiar concepts such as *belief, intention, desire, mood, pain, fear, memory, rage*, and so on. In addition, folk psychology involves a potentially infinite series of rough and ready explanatory principles, such as the following:

People who undergo surgery unanesthetized will generally feel pain
People who desire that P generally attempt to bring it about that P
If Alfred is in a bad mood, he generally will be irritated by things that he would otherwise find unobjectionable
If Betty is afraid of cats and believes that Fido is a cat, Betty will generally avoid encountering Fido. (*Cf.* Churchland 1994: 309)

The obviousness of these principles, and the familiarity of the concepts they employ, speak to their folk status. Accordingly, the man on the street exhibits a remarkable facility in ascribing to himself and to others states such as *belief, intention, understanding, pain*, and *seeing red*; he will with marked confidence attribute to himself and to others such complex states as *believing that Orcutt is a spy, wanting a sloop, understanding Chinese*, and *intending to visit Spain*. Furthermore, such concepts play a seemingly ineliminable role in his explanations of behavior. He will characterize his own action as arising from his beliefs, desires, and intentions, and in general will explain the behavior of others in similar ways. It is important to note that folk psychology proffers explanations of a certain kind, namely, *reason-giving explanations* (Dennett 1987: 48). That is, folk psychology does not offer explanations of behavior in terms of bio-physical causal mechanisms such as stimulus and response; it rather presupposes the general *rationality* of the agent whose behavior is to be explained. Accordingly, when we offer a folk psychological explanation of another's behavior, we often cite the *reasons* for the behavior, thereby ascribing to the agent the tendency to act on the basis of reasons. As Dennett has observed, folk psychological explanations not only "describe the provenance of the actions," they "at the same time defend them as reasonable under the circumstances" (Dennett 1987: 48). Again, the purpose of folk psychology is to help us to see the behavior of ourselves and others as *intelligible*. Hence, folk psychology not only countenances a range of mental states and a set of principles regarding how those states are coordinated with stimulus and action, it also involves a general normative commitment to viewing not just ourselves but our fellows as more or less rational.

As with most folk creations, our everyday folk psychological ascriptions are subject to a number of difficulties. First of all, folk psychology is far from a *complete* theory of the mind. That is, if we want an explanation of the full range of normal mental phenomena – sleep, fantasy, attention, imagination, anxiety, horror, pleasure, and the like – we shall have to turn to formal theories of the mind. This is even more obvious once we consider the range of *abnormal* mental phenomena. Second, folk psychology occasions several philosophical puzzles. To wit: does the fact that Jones believes that *Orcutt is a spy* entail that Jones believes that *the man in the red hat is a spy* if, unbeknownst to Jones, the man in the red hat is Orcutt? How does the state of *intending to visit Madrid* differ from the state of *intending to visit Spain*? Does a computer program that reliably translates English sentences into Chinese sentences *understand* Chinese, or, for that matter, English? What, after all, is a belief, anyway? Are beliefs like mental sentences, or are they more like pictures? If they are like mental sentences, in what language are they formulated? Do creatures that lack language *ipso facto* lack beliefs? If, alternatively, beliefs are like mental pictures, do they arise out of antecedent visual perceptions? What does the mental picture corresponding to the belief that 7 + 5 = 12 look like? Obviously, further complications of this sort can be raised, all of which point to the limits of folk psychology and the need for a formal psychological theory.

What is striking about folk psychology, however, is that, despite all of its limitations and imprecision, it is highly *successful*. Not only is the man on the street typically very proficient at predicting behavior, but all manner of endeavors involving the manipulation of human belief and expectation are effective precisely because we have recourse to a successful folk theory of human psychology. To take one kind of obvious example, the effectiveness of popular movies, especially those in the suspense-thriller and horror genres, depends precisely on the ability of the filmmaker to predict and control the expectations of the audience. Without the ability to provoke anxiety, anticipation, trepidation, and horror in an audience, these productions would always fall flat. And when they do fall flat, it is often because the filmmaker has failed at his folk psychological task.

Partly due to this success, the categories and concepts of folk psychology are so deeply entrenched in our practice that they are taken as the *explananda* of the philosophy of mind. That is, philosophers of mind typically take their task to be, at least in part, that of developing a philosophical theory of the mind that systematizes our folk practices and accounts for their success. Accordingly, different formal theories of the mind can be understood as differing attempts to capture or accommodate our folk practices. Thus, formal accounts of the mind that implicitly or explicitly deny that there are states that closely resemble folk concepts such as beliefs, desires, and intentions are in the eyes of many, *ipso facto* unacceptable.[1] Folk psychology thus does not itself fix a particular philosophy of mind, it is that which different formal theories of mind are, in part, theories of; it is what the formal theories are trying to capture.

My aim at present is to identify a set of epistemic concepts and principles that play a role in epistemology analogous to the role that the folk psychological concepts and principles play in the philosophy of mind. In other words, I aim to describe our folk epistemology. Folk epistemology is comprised of those concepts and principles that inform our everyday practices of believing, asserting, deliberating, reasoning, arguing, doubting, questioning, and disagreeing, and of ascribing these acts to others. If my characterization is successful, much of what I have to say will seem obvious, perhaps even trivial. Again, this is to be expected; since the attempt is to identify those commitments that underlie our ordinary and everyday epistemic practices, we should hope to encounter no surprises. Moreover, as the task is to characterize those phenomena that formal theories of epistemology attempt to capture, my depiction of folk epistemology aspires to be neutral among, and consistent with, any viable formal epistemology. The aim is to provide characterizations of our core epistemic concepts that are catholic (in the non-religious sense, of course). To be sure, my description of folk epistemology cannot avoid employing certain philosophically thorny terms, such as *belief, reason, evidence,* and *truth* as if they had clear senses. The hope, however, is that these terms can be used in a way that accurately captures the folk concepts while leaving the details of their precise philosophical character undetermined. After all, something like a neutral description of the concept of, say, belief must be possible if we are to make sense of the fact that there are different and competing theories of belief. To employ a common philosophical distinction, the competing theories offer opposing *conceptions* of the *concept* of belief. In attempting to describe folk epistemology, I am trying to get a grip on the folk concepts without proposing any philosophically controversial conception of them in particular. In any case,

---

[1] Of course, some philosophers have promoted a view known as *eliminativism,* which holds that folk psychology is a false and deeply misleading theory of the mind, one that is destined to be displaced by a developed neuroscience, in much the same way that the scientific theory of epilepsy displaced the folk theory of witches. But even the eliminativists feel the need to *account* for folk psychology. That is, they see fit to propose a story about how it arose and why it is so pervasive; eliminativists simply argue that folk psychology is not a *successful* theory (Churchland 1984: 45f.). See Quine 1985, Rorty 1979: ch. 2, and Churchland 1981.

if my account is successful, nothing in the following chapter should strike an epistemologist as philosophical news.

Before proceeding, a caveat is in order. Just as folk psychology is not a *complete* theory of the mind, folk epistemology is similarly limited in scope. Accordingly, there are many types of case in which our folk epistemic theory breaks down. Self-deception, delusion, wishful thinking, rationalization, displacement, epistemic akrasia, and other forms of generally irrational or corrupt believing are obvious cases in point. There might also be cases of non-corrupt believing – certain forms of religious faith, for example – that do not conform to our folk epistemic theory. But, again, in appealing to our folk epistemology I do not attempt to address the full range of epistemic phenomena. More importantly, the appeal to folk epistemology is not meant to suggest that there is no need for a formal theory of knowledge, and there is no doubt that once we have a correct formal theory in hand, some of our folk theory may need to be revised or jettisoned. I shall here be satisfied if my characterization of our folk epistemology strikes you as accurate with regard to the range of common and everyday cases of belief and belief-attribution.

Of course, it can be conceded that many of the most interesting questions and problems of epistemology arise when one considers cases of belief under what seem to be atypical or otherwise special conditions. Imaginative scenarios involving malicious demons, mad scientists, clairvoyants, doppel-gangers, and zombies abound in professional epistemology. However, in the present chapter, I shall follow Jonathan Adler (2002: 2–3) in considering matters from a decidedly ordinary perspective, and I ask my reader to join me in this. That is, I shall attempt to identify the epistemic principles underlying our *ordinary* epistemic activity under *ordinary* conditions. And so I ask my reader to consider the principles we are about to introduce from the point of view of everyday beliefs, such as, *Today is Thursday*, *Ronald Reagan was president in 1984*, *James Joyce did not author* Hamlet, and *Athens is the capital of Greece*. What we shall find, I think, is that part of what makes the thought experiments of current epistemology so fascinating to us is that these scenarios are designed to upset or distort our everyday epistemic *modus operandi*; here, the concern is to get a grip on the ordinary, the everyday.

Furthermore, the point of the project is to show that the folk epistemic commitments we are about to identify are indeed *our* commitments; hence, I ask my reader to indulge in one further deviation from the norm among professional epistemologists. The field of epistemology is largely fixed on the analysis of knowledge; that is, professional epistemologists tend to see their main task as that of discerning the necessary and sufficient conditions for knowledge. They pursue this mostly by means of examining contexts of *third-personal* knowledge attribution – the conditions under which it would be proper to say that some person or *subject, S,* knows some proposition, *p*. To be sure, this is a perfectly reasonable way of proceeding. However, the task I am undertaking is different. My concern is not with the necessary and sufficient conditions for knowledge; I am instead interested in examining our folk epistemic concepts and their interrelations. Consequently, I ask you to consider the matters we are about to discuss from a *first-personal* perspective. When considering everyday beliefs, one should consider *one's own* everyday beliefs, or, more precisely, everyday beliefs in *one's own case*.

The first-personalism upon which I am insisting will not only help in the task of making explicit to ourselves our everyday epistemology, it will also help us to resist the temptation to raise certain objections that are, in the end, premature. To explain: there is no doubt that among the general population various forms of irrationality and epistemic corruption prevail. We all have great stores of experience in dealing with persons who are epistemically inept and delusional, or who hold beliefs which seem to us to be sustainable only if one is especially epistemically vicious. As I am describing our folk epistemology, it will be tempting to object that the prevalence of epistemic ineptitude and epistemic vice undermines the proposed analysis. But this is too hasty. To explain: the judgment that epistemic stubbornness and evidence-avoidance, for example, are epistemically *vicious* is to affirm, at least implicitly, that there are, indeed, epistemic norms which such practices violate. Again, the task is to get a grip on the epistemic commitments we intuitively endorse. And since we each assess ourselves as at least passable as epistemic agents, I will proceed by asking you to consider matters *from your own perspective*. Whether in practice we tend to make good on those commitments is a different (though not unimportant) issue.

II PRINCIPLES OF FOLK EPISTEMOLOGY

Five principles

I begin by cataloguing the following five principles which I contend collectively constitute folk epistemology. They are as follows:
(1) To believe some proposition, *p*, is to hold that *p* is true.
(2) To hold that *p* is true is generally to hold that the best reasons support *p*.

(3) To hold that *p* is supported by the best reasons is to hold that *p* is *assertable*.

(4) To assert that *p* is to enter into a social process of reason *exchange*.

(5) To engage in social processes of reason exchange is to at least implicitly adopt certain cognitive and dispositional norms related to one's epistemic character.

There is much to say about each of these principles. In this section I shall consider each in turn.

(1) To believe some proposition, p, *is to hold that* p *is true*

The first principle identifies the three terms of folk epistemology which together comprise its conceptual basis: *belief*, *proposition*, and *truth*. To repeat: since I am trying to characterize our *folk* epistemology, I must not put too fine a point on the constituent concepts, lest I invite the kind of philosophical controversy I am hoping to avoid. So I shall say a few ordinary, and I should expect uncontroversial, things. Although the term *proposition* often functions in a technical way among philosophers to identify the abstract objects that sentences in natural languages express or refer to, I shall use it here non-technically. Let us say that a proposition is a statement about the way the world is, where *world* is understood in the broadest possible sense. I shall use the terms *proposition* and *statement* synonymously, to refer to declarative sentences, sentences about which it seems natural to ascribe a truth value. I shall use *p* as a variable standing for any such sentence.[2]

As with *proposition*, the term *belief* is the site of much philosophical controversy. Some hold that beliefs are mental states that purport to represent the world; some contend that they are dispositions to act; still others say that they are functional states of the brain; and so on. I shall attempt to circumvent all of this by again sticking to a non-technical use of the term. However, *belief*, even in its non-technical usage, introduces a few complications that should be addressed from the start. First, it is worth noting that the word *belief* is double-barreled. The term is used to refer both

---

[2] Obvious complications arise rather quickly. For example, when I say "I am the author of this footnote," I say something that is true. When you utter the very same sentence ("I am the author of this footnote"), you say something that is false. So it seems that sentences cannot be the truth bearers; moreover, it seems that the same sentence can express different propositions. Hence, philosophers are quick to distinguish between propositions (linguistic entities expressed by sentences), sentences (grammatical entities), and statements (occasions on which sentences are uttered or asserted). Things get thorny from there. But these matters need not concern us because the account that follows can easily be formulated in a way that incorporates the requisite distinctions.

to *that which one believes* and to the *psychological state* of believing.[3] This dual aspect of the term owes to the fact that a belief (a psychological state) is always a belief that some or other proposition is true. To explain, consider a statement such as:

I believe, but I believe nothing in particular.

This should strike us as peculiar, almost nonsensical. This is because belief is a kind of psychological state that attaches to a proposition, what we will sometimes call a *content*. In other words, a belief is always a belief that something or other (as specified by a proposition) is the case – a belief is always a *belief that p*.[4] Hence, we sometimes use the term *belief* to refer directly to the content, and we sometimes use the term to refer to the psychological state. In the latter sense of *belief*, the term is used in contrast with other psychological states, such as *doubt* or *disbelief*. The former sense of the term is in play when we talk about beliefs being either true or false; in these cases, we refer to the *content* of the belief and assess the truth of the belief on the basis of the truth of the proposition that is its content. This ambiguity in the term is unavoidable. In what follows, however, context should be sufficient to keep them distinct.

And here is a further ambiguity. In certain contexts, the sentence "I believe that *p*" indicates that the speaker wishes to distance herself from *p*; that is, "I believe that *p*" can function as a kind of shorthand for something like, "My best guess is that *p*, but don't blame me if it turns out that *not-p*." In such cases, the "I believe that" form functions as a hedge. In other contexts, however, to claim "I believe that *p*" is to contend straightforwardly that *p*; "I believe that *p*" is in such cases longhand for the simple assertion "*p*." In addition to these two uses, there are many others, such as when "I believe that *p*" is used as a *declaration* of one's commitment to *p*, as in an oath or a pledge, or when we mean to simply *express* where we stand with regard to *p*. Further variants are easy to identify.

Again, here I shall use *belief* to indicate a rather specific attitude: a belief is the state of *affirming* that the proposition which is its content is true. In this way, I shall use *belief* to refer to what philosophers sometimes call "full"

---

[3] By referring to a belief as a *psychological state*, I am not proposing any philosophical conception about what beliefs are. On any theory of belief, it will be correct to say that beliefs are psychological states, since competing theories of belief employ their own conception of what it is for something to be *psychological*.

[4] Some insist on a distinction between *believing that* and *believing in*. For example, one may believe *that* today is Thursday, but one believes *in* the afterlife. It seems to me that believing *in* is just a fancy version of believing *that*. Believing *in* the afterlife is the belief *that* there is an afterlife. But, again, we need not get bogged down in this issue.

belief. But this is strictly a simplifying measure; it is not to deny that there are different degrees of belief, and relevant difference between them. It is, however, to say that our folk concept of belief corresponds closely to the philosopher's conception of full belief; that is, when we attribute to Sue the belief that *p*, we take it that according to Sue, *p* is the truth, plain and simple. The same holds *a fortiori* in our own case.

It may come as a surprise that my gloss on the concept *truth* is relatively simple. In his *Metaphysics*, Aristotle taught us that "To say of what is that it is not, or of what is not that it is, is false, while to say of what is that it is, and of what is not that it is not, is true" ([1952] 1011b, 26). Simplifying, it can be said that a proposition is true if and only if it says of what is the case that it is the case. Hence, as was mentioned above, a given proposition admits of exactly one of two possible *truth values*; that is to say, for any proposition it is either *true* or (if not true, then) *false*. And this seems intuitive: it is either true that today is Tuesday or it is false that today is Tuesday. Either it is true that Joyce wrote *Hamlet*, or it is false that Joyce wrote *Hamlet*. Although Aristotle's insight about truth verges on vacuity, it is difficult to imagine how it could fail to be correct.[5] A more substantive statement regarding truth will invite the kind of controversy I am attempting to avoid, so I shall make do with Aristotle. (There will be more to say about truth below, when I consider the second folk epistemic principle.)

Hence, we have the first principle of folk epistemology. Its obviousness may obscure its force. To get a fix on its meaning, consider a statement that violates the tight connection the principle countenances between the concepts of belief and truth. For example, imagine someone who says:

I believe that today is Friday, but I know that today is Tuesday

Insofar as taking oneself to *know* that today is Tuesday entails that one takes it to be *true* that today is Tuesday, the statement comes to this:

I believe that today is Friday, but I do not believe it is true that today is Friday.

How peculiar this is! What could such a statement mean? How would we interpret such a statement were it made by another? Surely a person who asserts this belief is not simply confused about what day it is; there is a deeper problem with this belief. Ask yourself: what would it be like to hold such a belief? What accounts to the oddness of a belief like this?

---

[5] Some hold that sentences involving vague predicates, such as *John is bald*, are not obviously true or false. Others hold that instantiations of what is known as the *liar paradox* ("Everything I say is false.") show that some propositions are neither true nor false. Again, given our project, we can leave these issues to the side.

The oddness of statements of the form:

I believe that p*, but I do not believe that* p *is true*

can be explained by the simple fact that when we believe, we take it that *what we believe* – again, the proposition which is the content or our belief – is true. This is not to say that we take ourselves to be infallible or omniscient. Although we take each of our beliefs, considered one by one, to be true, we also take it that in the full collection of our beliefs, *some* of them are false. We simply do not know which ones are false. That is, although each of us holds the belief:

I hold false beliefs

we take each individual belief we have, considered one by one, to be true. And this is all that our first principle states.

Who could reject this much? Surely to reject the principle is to assert that you do not *believe* it, but *reject* it, which is to say that you see no reason to think it true. That is, when you say of a proposition, "I reject that," you typically are not merely *reporting* the psychological fact about yourself that you are not in a state of belief with regard to the proposition in question. You are in addition advancing an *assessment* of the proposition. To be specific, you are asserting that you see no good reason to accept it as true. Put in other words, when you *reject* a proposition, you do not simply *decline* to believe it, you also express the contention that it *ought not to be believed*. And this tight connection between believing that *p* and taking *p* to be true is all the first principle asserts.

(2) To hold that p *is true is generally to hold that the best reasons support* p
Philosophers are fond of saying – in the spirit of the first folk epistemic principle – that beliefs aim at truth. It perhaps would be more precise to say that when we believe, we aim to have beliefs that are true. To aim to have true beliefs is to aim for beliefs that say of what is the case that it is the case. Although Aristotle's nearly empty insight about truth is sometimes taken to entail, or at least suggest, a correspondence theory of truth, it is better understood as stating something like an adequacy condition for any theory of truth. That is to say, that the intuition captured by Aristotle is so manifestly correct that nearly all formal theories of truth attempt to accommodate it, and those that reject it expend great effort in the attempt to show why and how it may be jettisoned. Indeed, it is difficult to imagine how a proposed theory of truth that *denied* Aristotle's intuition could be viable; any such theory would require a lot of philosophical back-up. Since I am

trying to avoid committing to any particular formal theory of truth and hoping to eschew deep philosophical controversy, I resign myself to saying something hopefully uncontroversial about the function of the folk concept of truth.

To say that a proposition is true is to say that it will square ultimately with the best reasons, evidence, and argument. When one believes that p, one typically takes oneself to have sufficient reasons or evidence for taking p to be true. Similarly, when one finds compelling arguments for two contrary propositions, or can find no compelling arguments for any view on a given matter, one is conflicted about what to believe, or, indeed, whether to believe anything at all. And when one discovers that one has no evidence for p, or when one discovers that one's reasons fail or are defeated by countervailing reasons, one's belief that p typically recedes.

A word about the term *recedes* is in order before proceeding. The term is deliberately loose. I do not mean to say that whenever we find ourselves short on good reasons for our belief that p, we automatically stop believing that p. Nor do I mean to suggest that whenever we are convinced that our reasons for p are defeated by countervailing reasons, we necessarily come to believe *not-p*. Many things can happen in light of the realization that one's reasons for p are insufficient. To be sure, there are contexts in which such a realization will, indeed, cause one to relinquish the belief altogether. In other cases, the realization will cause one to dampen the *degree* of one's belief that p. In other cases, the realization will render one wary of employing p as a premise in future inferences. And sometimes the realization will simply result in a reluctance to express one's belief that p in mixed company. And so on. I need not take a stand on which reaction is called for under which circumstances. Rather, my point is the more general one that whenever we discover that something is awry with our reasons for p, we take it that not all is well with our belief that p. Frequently, this self-assessment leads us to take some kind of epistemic action with regard to the belief, and these actions run the gamut from inquiring further into p to digging in one's heels with regard to p.

For the sake of simplicity, let us understand by *reasons* any of the non-controversial (or at least not typically controversial) truth-indicators, such as evidence, proof, argument, expert testimony, confirming observations, convergence of belief among competent inquirers, and the like. The second folk epistemic principle says that to believe that p is to take it that the best reasons speak in favor of p. Some may take this principle to be an implicit endorsement of the controversial "ideal inquirer" or "end of inquiry" conception of truth associated with, among others, Charles

Peirce (1878).[6] On this kind of view, truth is *defined* as that which would be believed by ideal inquirers. The most obvious trouble with this kind of view is that it seems to say that the truth of *p consists in* there being good reasons to believe that *p*. But surely this puts the cart before the horse; it seems much more intuitive to think that there being good reason for *p* derives from the fact that *p* is true. That is, we are intuitively committed to the idea that truth explains justification – that the fact that *p* is true explains why there is good reason to believe that *p* – not the other way around. So the end of inquiry view of the matter is at the very least counter-intuitive.

To be sure, counter-intuitiveness is not always a sufficient reason to reject a theory. However, apart from its counter-intuitive implications, there are several objections to the end of inquiry view of truth. Some have argued that it is incoherent. Consequently, the worry that the second principle is committed to it is cause for concern. On reflection, however, the worry is groundless. Despite appearances, there is no definition of truth implied by the second principle, and no philosophical theory of truth, controversial or otherwise, lurking in what has been said thus far. The second principle is consistent with any viable definition or theory, because, on any serious or well-developed view of the matter, reasons, evidence, and argument are *indicators* of truth.[7] To see this, consider how odd a theory of truth would be were it to propose that evidence for *p* did not indicate the truth of *p*; surely we would have a hard time understanding such a theory as a theory of *truth*. And this is all the second principle commits us to with regard to the concept of truth: to hold that *p* is true is to hold that the best reasons support *p*.

Yet the second principle does not simply state the tautology that truth-indicators are indicators of truth. It additionally provides an elaboration of what our aiming to have true beliefs consists in. Hence, further explication is required. When we inquire, or deliberate, or wonder, or doubt, or question, we are looking for *reasons* to believe one proposition rather than another.[8] To repeat, when we are firm in our belief that *p*, we take ourselves

---

[6] Contemporary Peirceans have done a nice job of showing that Peirce himself did not hold the "end of inquiry" view that is often attributed to him. See especially Misak 2004a and Hookway 2000: ch. 2.

[7] Some hold that with regard to certain matters, the truth is underdetermined by even the best and most full array of reasons and evidence. The thought is that, even in light of all the evidence there could possibly be, certain questions would remain open. But these views do not reject our claim that reasons, evidence, and argument are truth *indicators*.

[8] To be sure, in some cases, we may be looking for a reason to have a belief at all – a reason not to suspend judgment. But this complication need not detain us; the view can accommodate whatever one might want to say about this.

to have forceful reasons for *p*. If we discover that our reasons in favor of *p* come up short or fail, we are compelled to take epistemic action with regard to *p*. Again, we may hunt for new reasons and evidence, or look for ways to deny the force of the opposing reasons, or withdraw our belief that *p* altogether. In withdrawing the belief that *p*, we may adopt a new belief, *q*, that we take to be a better fit with the best reasons available to us; or, alternatively, we may suspend belief altogether, or find ourselves conflicted. All of this is to say that we take our beliefs to be responsive to our reasons.

It bears emphasizing that the reason-responsiveness of belief does not entail that no one in fact holds irrational beliefs, or that no one in fact believes on the basis of bad reasons or no reasons at all. Rather it entails that when we believe, we *take ourselves* to be responding to reasons. Hence the assertion:

I believe that p, *but have absolutely no reason for thinking that* p *is true*

is similar to the statement considered earlier:

I believe that p, *but do not believe that* p *is true.*

Like the latter, the former involves a kind of peculiarity in that it is difficult to imagine how one can self-consciously sustain such a belief. That is, we would generally expect that one's belief that *p* would recede in light of the realization – the self-assessment – that one has no reason for thinking *p* true. Under such conditions, there are, of course, other attitudes that may be appropriate. For instance, in light of the realization that one has no reason for taking *p* to be true, one may *hope* that *p*, or *wish* that *p*, *imagine* that *p*, *guess* that *p*, or perhaps even *opine* that *p*. But one may not, under such conditions, wholeheartedly *believe* that *p*.

In fact, someone who sincerely claims to believe that *p* for absolutely no reason is likely to be seen to be in the grip of some kind of cognitive crisis, perhaps suffering from a variety of dissociative disorder. For not only do we hold that beliefs should respond to reasons, we hold that *our* beliefs should respond to *our* reasons. That is, we hold that when we believe we ought not only to have reasons, but be able to see the reasons as the basis for our belief.

Let us pause again briefly to introduce an additional bit of terminology that should prove useful. I shall say that one's belief that *p* is *untenable* if honest reflection upon one's reasons for *p* should cause one's belief that *p* to recede. To be sure, we sometimes use the term *untenable* to refer to that which we take to be *unbelievable*. But I do not mean to use it in this strong sense. A building that is *untenable* is one which one *should not* inhabit. Of course, that honest reflection *should* cause one's belief to recede does not entail that it *will* have such an effect. There are a variety of intellectual strategems we employ to preserve wholehearted belief in light of such defeaters – we rationalize, hedge, fudge, equivocate, dissemble, confabulate, evade, gerrymander, and self-deceive more frequently than we care to acknowledge. That we are particularly reluctant to acknowledge our own tendencies to employ these methods of belief-preservation indicates the degree to which we take them to be epistemically vicious. After all, there simply would be no point in covertly engaging in such activities if it were not for the fact that when we believe, we take ourselves to be responding to reasons. The claim thus far has been simply that to recognize that one has no reason for *p* typically renders one's belief that *p* is untenable.

Hence, on the view I have been developing, George Orwell's famous claim that "We are all capable of believing things which we *know* to be untrue" is not quite right. To see why, let us consider the Orwell quotation in full:

We are all capable of believing things which we *know* to be untrue, and then, when we are finally proved wrong, impudently twisting the facts so as to show that we were right. Intellectually, it is possible to carry on this process for an indefinite time: the only check on it is that sooner or later a false belief bumps up against solid reality, usually on a battlefield. (1968: 124)

That Orwell is mistaken is clear from the fact that he recognizes that in order to hold a belief which has been proven to be wrong, we must engage in a kind of epistemic self-deception; we must engage in the activity of "impudently twisting the facts" to serve the purpose of belief-preservation. Yet if we were really "capable of believing things which we know to be untrue," we should have no need to engage in the effort of fact-twisting. That instances of egregiously false but persistent believing are typically also instances of Herculean self-deception proves that we are *not* "capable of believing things which we know to be untrue," at least not in any literal sense. Again, the frequent employment of the many and varied mechanisms of epistemic self-deception speaks in favor of and not against our folk epistemic commitment to being responsive to reasons.

To be clear, let me repeat once again that the view I have been developing is not committed to the claim that no one *in fact* holds beliefs for which he has no compelling reasons. There are, to be sure, certainly all manner of irrational, ill-considered, and groundless beliefs in currency. Moreover, there are beliefs that arise from *causes* rather than reasons, as is most obvious in cases involving various forms of psychological disorder or manipulation. Again, the point is that, barring perhaps the most extreme cases of brainwashing, no one *takes oneself* to believe that *p* in the absence of reasons for *p*. Even the fool, who we might imagine believes that *p* for no reason at all, does not take himself to be a fool, at least not in this way. Similarly, the deeply deluded man who believes that aliens are monitoring his phone conversations *claims* to have based that belief on reasons. His purported reasons may derive from an elaborate conspiracy theory involving government cover-ups and other types of intrigue, and so his supposed reasons may not be reasons at all. But that is no matter, since the point is simply that when we believe, we take ourselves to be responding to reasons.

Roughly the same kind of reply can be made to considerations which draw from the findings of the various "debriefing" (Ross, Lepper, and Hubbard 1975: 881) and "belief perseverance" studies (Goldman 1986: 214; Adler 2002: 288). In these cases, volunteers are subjected to experimental conditions which bring them to believe that they are particularly competent at some task, such as distinguishing authentic suicide notes from fakes (Ross, Lepper, and Hubbard 1975: 882). After the belief has been formed, subjects are then told that the evidence upon which they came to believe in their competence at the task was, in fact, rigged, and that, consequently, they have no reason to believe themselves to be especially skilled at suicide-note detection. Even in light of this new information, subjects *continue* to believe themselves to be especially skilled at the task (Ross, Lepper, and Hubbard 1975: 888). Does this show that we can believe on the basis of what we regard as bad (or no) reason? Not at all; in fact, the cases support the folk epistemic principle. When subjects are confronted with the fact that their belief is baseless, they confabulate, rationalize, or cast about for *other* evidence that supports the belief; that is, subjects either dismiss the report that the initial evidence was rigged or they look for (or *invent*) reasons to support their belief (Adler 2002: 289).[9] Were it not for the need to regard one's belief that *p* as supported by one's best reasons, the effort required to preserve the belief would not be necessary.

It may seem that the widespread belief in the nonsense of professed psychics, astrologers, fortune-tellers, so-called UFO-logists, new-age healers, and the like constitutes a counter-example to the second principle. On the contrary, when we consider the matter, we see that the principle holds firm. One of the things that all nonsense peddlers have in common – other than the patent falsity of the views they propose – is the tendency to couch their claims in the language of evidence, reason, and even science. All

---

[9] Interestingly, Goldman suggests that the subjects might have good reason to reject the *debriefing* report as untrustworthy (1986: 216); subjects then may take their initial evidence as undefeated.

insist that they have hard evidence and decisive proof for their claims. Often, the claims to hard evidence and good reasons are accompanied by an additional story involving government cover-ups, suppression of the facts, official persecution, and other intrigue. Indeed, the prevalence among those who hold fantastical beliefs of intricate and complicated conspiracy theories simply proves our point. The fact that we take our beliefs to be reason-responsive explains the necessity of such machinations; if we simply did not care about believing on the basis of reasons, conspiracy theories would be wholly irrelevant.[10]

To further explicate the second principle, examine the matter from the first-personal point of view. One way to do this is to consider Bernard Williams's (1973) analysis of "deciding to believe." Imagine a case in which you learn that a beloved friend has been involved in a potentially fatal car accident. Imagine further that the precise details of the accident are not available, and so the condition of your friend is uncertain. Now, there is, of course, great comfort in believing that your friend is alive and well, and nearly no good is realized by agonizing over the possibility that he may be dead or very seriously injured. So, why not simply decide to believe that your friend is, indeed, alive and well? After all, it seems the rational thing to do.

The fact is that you *cannot* simply *choose* what to believe, your beliefs are not under your volitional control. At best, you may choose to undertake some program of action – brainwashing, for example – which can be expected to result in your *coming to believe* that your friend is alive and well. But note that brainwashing does not enable you to believe at will; rather, it helps to create the delusion that you have *reason* to believe that your friend is alive and well. Again, you cannot *simply* decide to believe that which you acknowledge you have no reason to think is true.

Importantly, this inability to choose your beliefs is not due to lack of effort or some kind of weakness. The inability derives rather from the *conceptual* requirement that, since beliefs aim at truth, they must be reason-responsive. That is to say, precisely *what it is* to have a belief is to be truth-aiming and thus reason-responsive. Consequently, any state regarding a proposition that is consciously recognized as not reason-responsive is *ipso facto not* a belief. As Williams explains:

If I could acquire a belief at will, I could acquire it whether it was true or not; moreover, I would know that I could acquire it whether it was true or not. If in full consciousness I could will to acquire a "belief" irrespective of its truth, it is unclear

---

[10] See Clancy 2005 for a sustained attempt to treat UFO abduction stories as rational, though, of course, deeply flawed and mistaken, attempts to explain unusual experiences, such as sleep paralysis.

that before the event [of choosing to believe it] I could seriously think of it as a belief … At the very least, there must be a restriction on what is the case after the event; since I could not then, in full consciousness, regard this as a belief of mine, i.e., something that I take to be true, and also know that I acquired it at will. (1973: 148)

That beliefs are reason-responsive does not entail only that we cannot form beliefs out of thin air or purely on a whim. It also requires that we take the basis of our beliefs *to be reasons*, that is, truth-indicative. So, to return to our example, just as you cannot simply decide to believe that your friend is alive and well, you cannot believe that it will rain next Tuesday on the basis of a coin flip, unless of course for some reason you take the coin to have prognostic – that is, truth-indicative – powers. Hence the statement:

On the basis of the flip of this here entirely ordinary coin, I believe that it will rain on Tuesday

comes to the same thing as:

I believe that p*, but have absolutely no reason for thinking that* p *is true.*

And we have already argued that this latter statement is untenable.

Similarly, the reason-responsiveness of belief entails that, when we believe that *p*, we generally take ourselves to *have access* to the reasons for taking *p* to be true. As I said above, we take *our* beliefs to be responsive to *our* reasons. Hence, it is typically not enough to sustain the belief that *p* to hold that there are compelling reasons for *p*; we must also take ourselves to *know what those reasons are*. To employ a bit of philosophical jargon, we can say that, for this reason, folk epistemology is *internalist*.

The internalist component of our principle will provoke at least two kinds of criticism. Some critics, known as *epistemic externalists*, hold that access to the reasons that justify *p* is wholly irrelevant to one's justification in believing that *p*. According to the externalist, when one believes that *p*, one generally takes it that there are reasons for *p*, but one need not take oneself to know what those reasons are. Others, we shall call them *fideists*, will contend that certain beliefs are of such a nature that if they are to be held, they must be held *despite* one's lack of access to the reasons that justify them.

Both kinds of criticism can be met by emphasizing the folk epistemic nature of the enterprise. To the epistemic externalist, I issue the reminder that the second principle offers only a description of how the reason-responsiveness of belief is generally understood; the principle does not attempt to establish anything philosophically nuanced about what is in fact required for justified belief. So, it can be conceded that the externalist might be correct to think that access to the reasons that justify *p* is not *necessary* for being justified in believing that *p*; however, the point still stands that we generally take ourselves to be bound by the internalist demand for access to the justifying reasons. The externalist may be correct to think that this demand is superfluous strictly from the point of view of epistemic justification, but it would be hard to imagine an argument to the effect that the internalist demand is wholly without epistemic purpose. That is, the folk epistemologist can allow the possibility that the externalist is correct in thinking that access to the reasons that justify *p* is not necessary for justified belief. Recall that the aim is to avoid having to commit to any particular theory of epistemic justification. The possibility of the truth of externalism can be admitted; however, it can be said to the externalist that having access to the justifying reasons may yet be necessary for satisfying some epistemic *desideratum other than* justification, such as *rationality* or epistemic *self-control*. So that folk epistemology recognizes the legitimacy of the internalist demand does not render it inconsistent with externalist theories of justification; in recognizing the internalist demand, folk epistemology makes no pronouncement about the philosophical nature of epistemic justification at all.

A similar reply can be made to the fideist. The folk epistemologist can grant the possibility that there are certain kinds of propositions such that, if they are to be believed at all, the believer must take herself to be not bound by the internalist demand. But, again, the second folk epistemic principle does not claim to establish anything particularly fancy or sophisticated about beliefs and their reasons; consequently, folk epistemology can allow for special cases of belief in which the internalist demand is out of place or in some way inappropriate. The expectation is that even the fideist will allow that within the general range of beliefs, when we believe that *p*, we typically take it that we have access to, and can provide, the reasons that support *p*. Perhaps there is a special class of beliefs that do not fit this mold, but that is not a problem for folk epistemology.

Before proceeding, let us consider a further and closely related kind of concern. Someone may object that our second folk epistemic principle introduces a commitment to an extreme version of the controversial view known as *evidentialism*. Evidentialism is the view according to which the degree of one's belief should be proportioned precisely to the strength of one's evidence. One immediate implication of evidentialism is that one should not believe against one's evidence or in the absence of evidence; as W. K. Clifford famously put the evidentialist view, "it is wrong always, everywhere, and for anyone, to believe anything upon insufficient evidence"

(1999: 77). The thought is that it is *irrational* or *epistemically irresponsible* to believe except on the basis of (and in proportion to) one's evidence.

The view I have been developing seems to go beyond Clifford in that it claims not simply that it is *wrong* to believe against one's evidence, but that it is *not possible* to self-consciously do so. I again follow Adler in drawing a distinction between "extrinsic" and "intrinsic" varieties of evidentialism (2002: 2). The version of evidentialism endorsed by Clifford is an "extrinsic" evidentialism, since it claims that the reason-responsiveness of belief is a requirement of *rationality*. By contrast, the stronger view that we have been developing is an "intrinsic" evidentialism, as it claims that reason-responsiveness is a requirement that is *internal* to belief itself rather than imposed from outside. So, whereas the extrinsic evidentialist holds that we *ought not* to believe except on the basis of our evidence, the intrinsic evidentialist holds that we literally *cannot* believe except on the basis of what we take to be our evidence.

Controversy arises, even in the case of evidentialism in its weaker, extrinsic form, when we consider religious belief, which, it is generally acknowledged, fails to satisfy the evidentialist ethic of belief as prescribed by Clifford among others. Opponents of evidentialism claim that, for a certain range of beliefs, it is not only psychologically *possible* to believe that for which one recognizes one has insufficient evidence, but one *may* hold such beliefs rationally. The question of whether it is possible to recognize that one lacks evidence for God's existence but nonetheless sustain wholehearted belief that God exists is deeply interesting, as is the question of whether it could be *rational* to sustain one's belief that God exists in light of one's admission that the evidence for God's existence is insufficient. Indeed, there is at present great controversy about these matters; again, since we are involved in developing a *folk* epistemology, we are trying to avoid such controversies.

However, even though it can be conceded that the second principle is evidentialist, its character does not require the folk epistemologist to pronounce on the issue of the rationality of religious belief, because most anti-evidentialists readily admit that evidentialism is correct with regard to the vast majority of our beliefs. Even William James, perhaps the most famous anti-evidentialist, held that evidentialism is correct except for a very narrow range of cases. More importantly, James also seems to have held that the *intrinsic* view of evidentialism is correct over the range of cases in which evidentialism holds. James asks:

Does it not seem preposterous on the very face of it to talk of our opinions being modifiable at will? Can our will either help or hinder our intellect in its perceptions of truth? Can we, by just willing it, believe that Abraham Lincoln's existence is a myth … ? Can we, by an effort of our will, or by any strength of wish that it were true, believe ourselves well and about when we are roaring with rheumatism in bed, or feel certain that the sum of the two one-dollar bills in our pocket must be a hundred dollars?

James's response is:

We can *say* any of these things, but we are *absolutely impotent to believe them*; and of such things is the whole fabric of the truths that we do believe in made up … (1977: 719, my emphasis).

We need not get bogged down in the exegesis of James's notoriously complicated arguments. Given the folk nature of the enterprise, it will suffice if the account I have offered captures the bulk of our ordinary, garden-variety cases of belief. Furthermore, I need not claim that there are *no exceptions* to the second principle, nor need I admit that religious beliefs are counter-examples to evidentialism. No matter how the questions regarding the rationality or rational permissibility of religious belief get resolved, any viable epistemological theory must acknowledge that *for the most part* when we believe, we take ourselves to be responding to reasons. In other words, most varieties of anti-evidentialism are a case of *special pleading* for beliefs of a very particular kind. So the worry about evidentialism is a red herring, as far as the folk epistemic project is concerned.

(3) To hold that p *is supported by the best reasons is to hold that* p *is* assertable

As many of the examples thus far employed have suggested, folk epistemology countenances a fairly strict symmetry between belief and assertion. According to the view being developed, to *assert* that *p* is to indicate, state, or express your belief that *p*; consequently, both assertion and belief are ways of *committing* to the truth of the proposition which is asserted or believed.[11] Of course, the symmetry does not go all the way down. The act of asserting *p* is necessarily public – it implies an *audience* to which the assertion is addressed – and so is subject to a wide range of qualifications that normally do not apply in the case of belief. For example, there are obviously contexts in which the act of asserting *p* would be inappropriate, rude, awkward, or immoral, *even though* p *is true*. Proclaiming that you love your mother in the midst of a casual conversation with a stranger in an elevator is a good

---

[11] *Cf.* Pascal Engel's discussion of the "belief–assertion–truth triangle" (Rorty and Engel 2007: 13ff.); see also Misak 2007.

example. By contrast, it is difficult to imagine how one could be wrong to
believe that *p* when *p* is true. Of course, there are clear cases of the efficacy of
"positive thinking"; for example, lost climbers who believe the truth concerning the direness of their circumstances tend to fare less well than those
who believe, falsely, that they are not in a desperate situation. But, again,
these are atypical, special cases, not the norm.

In any case, now that these asymmetries between assertion and belief
have been noted, they may be set aside because the task at present is not to
provide an analysis of the conditions under which it would be *proper* –
morally, or as a matter of conversational etiquette – to assert that *p*, but
rather to elaborate the role of assertion in our folk epistemic commitment to
reason-responsiveness.

Consider the function of the act of asserting *p* under the appropriate
circumstances, whatever they may be. As I have said, when you assert that *p*,
you express your belief that *p*, thereby indicating your commitment to the
claim that *p* is true, and thus supported by the best reasons. In this way,
assertion is different from *pronouncement* and *command* in that to assert is to
recommend – in certain cases, to recommend very strongly – the proposition which is asserted to one's audience in a way that is meant to stimulate
or engage their own reason-evaluating capacities. To be sure, a pronouncement or command may also be meant to recommend the proposition which
is pronounced or commanded, but it is to recommend irrespective of – or,
in the case of many familiar types of command, *in spite of* – the rational
faculties of the audience to whom it is addressed or, in the case of a
command, issued. In this way, it may be said that to assert that *p* is to
take responsibility for *p*, to recognize the burden of justification with regard
to *p*, and implicitly to offer to put one's reasons for *p* up for scrutiny if called
upon to do so. Indeed, to assert that *p* is to hold that one's reasons can
withstand the scrutiny of one's audience. Thus, it can be said that to believe
that *p* is to take *p* to be *assertable*.

Accordingly, the statement:

I believe that p, *but I have resolutely avoided subjecting* p *to the scrutiny of intelligent*
critics

involves a kind of infelicity. Although it may not be strictly untenable, it
nonetheless indicates a kind of epistemic failure, especially if we imagine a
case in which *p* is a statement concerning some non-mundane matter. As I
have said, to believe that *p* is to hold that the best reasons support that *p*. Yet
the claim that *p* is supported by the best reasons involves a complex
comparative judgment to the effect that (1) the strongest criticisms of *p* do

not succeed, and (2) the reasons that support alternatives to p are not decisive. This can be assessed only by actually examining the matter, and examining the matter requires that p actually be asserted and put up for scrutiny.

A critic may object that the third folk epistemic principle sets a requirement for belief that is entirely too demanding. Such a criticism could run that, on the third principle, every believer is implicitly committed to a particularly rigorous mode of inquiry with regard to his beliefs; more specifically, the critic might charge that, on the third principle, every believer is obliged to engage the arguments and reasons that can be marshaled against each of his beliefs. The critic may continue that this can hardly be a *folk* epistemic principle, since it is very rare to find a man on the street who in fact engages in this kind of self-scrutiny; it is much more common to find among persons who believe that p that they have almost no idea about the main criticisms of p or the reasons one might give against p.

The critic can be granted his description of the typical man on the street. Ordinarily, people have a feeble grasp of the reasons that can be given against their beliefs, and may be wholly unaware of the reasons that are given to support beliefs that compete with their own. Yet this concession is consistent with the third principle, since although the man on the street who believes that p may in fact have almost no idea of the arguments against p or for some competitor, q, he surely *takes himself* to have reasons sufficient to meet objections to p. That is, although he may *in fact* not grasp the arguments against p, he *believes* that he does. Similarly, he may in fact have no idea about the reasons that can be marshaled in support of beliefs that run contrary to his own, but he often *takes himself* to know that those with whom he disagrees on such matters are mistaken, irrational, or benighted. This is why, as was discussed in Chapter 2, much of our moral and political discourse – that is, our discourse about the things we tend to take most seriously – concerning issues of pressing concern is organized around the idea that one's opponents are epistemically defective, capable neither of launching a fair criticism of one's own views nor of formulating an intelligent positive position of their own. Hence, liberals portray conservatives as "lying liars" (Franken 2003), while conservatives claim that all liberals suffer from a "mental disorder" (Savage 2005), and generally should not be spoken to (Coulter 2004). As these examples (there are dozens of others) suggest, the aim of much of our popular political rhetoric is to encourage the impression that there *is* no rational opposition to one's own views, and hence no opposing arguments to address.

This kind of rhetoric is necessary only when it is recognized that reason-responsiveness generally obliges us to be responsive to the reasons of those with whom we disagree. Were the norm of considering the weight of our critics' positions not in place, it would not be necessary to erect straw-men of our opponents. However, straw-men abound. Accordingly, the third principle stands.

(4) To assert that p *is to enter into a social process of reason* exchange
The third principle of folk epistemology states that to believe that *p* is to take *p* to be assertable. To take *p* to be assertable is to take it to be able to withstand the scrutiny of critics; hence, to take *p* to be assertable is to be prepared to actually assert *p* under the appropriate circumstances. When one asserts that *p*, one incurs the *prima facie* epistemic obligation to provide reasons for *p* if called upon to do so. That is, to make an assertion is to enter into what Wilfrid Sellars called the "logical space of reasons" (1997: 76); it is to undertake the project of justification or at the very least present oneself as prepared to undertake it.

However, in supplying the *justification* of one's beliefs one simultaneously opens oneself to challenge and criticism. After all, one's reasons can fail under scrutiny; that is precisely what *scrutiny* is. That is, the logical space of giving reasons is a *dialectical* space in which one could find that one's justification comes up short. Again, when one discovers that one's justification for one's belief that *p* fails, one must take epistemic action: one must adopt a new belief, suspend belief and hunt for a better justification, or suspend belief altogether. In this way, to believe that *p* is to be *open* to challenge and criticism. But to be open in this way is also to be open to the possibility that one's belief is false or stands in need of revision. Again, it is important to stress that this is not to say that folk epistemology requires us to be skeptical about our own beliefs. One can take critics' objections seriously and recognize that one must confront hard questions without diminishing one's belief that *p*. Moreover, one can accept that *p* is true, but admit that one's particular understanding of *p* could be flawed or that one's formulation of *p* stands in need of refinement. Lastly, one can remain steadfast in one's belief that *p* while admitting, *ad arguendo*, that one could be persuaded that *p* is false. Our commitment to the truth of *p* entails only a *prima facie* openness to challenge and refutation.

Proper believing calls us to attempt to bring our beliefs under the scope of the broadest set of considerations and reasons we can find. Accordingly, folk epistemology involves a commitment to a norm of *including* dissenting and contesting voices. It must be inclusive in this way if it is to satisfy its own conception of belief as truth-aiming. For, like the statement that was considered above:

I believe that p, *but I have resolutely avoided subjecting* p *to the scrutiny of intelligent critics*

a statement of the form:

I believe that p, *but I have insulated* p *from criticism by insulating myself from potential critics*

indicates a kind of epistemic failure. Like the former, the latter is not strictly untenable, but it does obstruct the aspiration for truth, and so represents what we might call epistemic *bad faith*. If we aim to have true beliefs, and if this aiming requires that we attempt to square our beliefs with the best reasons, then we need to keep open the avenues by which we can encounter the strongest criticisms of our beliefs.

Thus, folk epistemic inclusion is not merely formal or procedural. When we believe that *p*, we must be not merely *willing* to hear criticism of *p*, we must *be open to* criticism and be prepared to take criticism seriously; put otherwise, we must be prepared to do more than simply *tolerate* our critics, we must be prepared to *engage* with them. Those whose lives and experiences are unlike our own tend to be the most adept at raising the kind of criticisms and counter-considerations that we have overlooked. Hence reason-responsiveness requires an *exchange* of reasons, and this requires a socially diverse pool of discursive partners.

(5) To engage in social processes of reason exchange is to at least implicitly adopt certain cognitive and dispositional norms related to one's epistemic character
As the account thus far has suggested, folk epistemology is *actional* rather than *contemplative*. It understands the fundamental cognitive categories in terms of the activities associated with truth-seeking; it contends that epistemology is something that we – *all* of us – *do*. Accordingly, we may add to the earlier discussion an additional important respect in which folk epistemology differs from many forms of professional epistemology. Professional epistemologies are often focused exclusively on the evaluation of *beliefs*; again, the leading question of professional epistemology is: *under what conditions does S's belief that* p *count as knowledge?* By contrast, folk epistemology involves the evaluation of *believers*. Folk epistemology sees that believing is the exercise of a certain kind of *agency*; it recognizes that epistemic evaluation in part concerns one's *epistemic character*.

Very roughly, epistemic character can be conceived of in terms of three distinct components: (1) cognitive skills; (2) belief-managing habits; and (3) epistemic dispositions. By *cognitive skills*, I mean the various cognitive abilities requisite to acquiring knowledge. These include the ability to concentrate or focus attention, to observe, to remember, to reason effectively, and much else. One's belief-managing habits include one's ability to evaluate and weigh evidence, anticipate and appreciate the force of countervailing considerations, separate out relevant from non-relevant factors, etc. Finally, one's epistemic dispositions include the attitudes one brings to bear on the epistemic enterprise itself, including how stubborn or tenacious one becomes in the face of counter-evidence, how one decides who are the relevant epistemic authorities in a given case, how quick one is to jump to unwarranted conclusions, and so on.

I cannot here undertake a full exploration of the concept of epistemic character; my remarks here must be limited to what is most central to the present aims. As we have seen, the process of justification is essentially a *social* process of reason exchange. As this process involves interactions between persons, it is subject to various norms. Although some have proposed that these norms be thought of in terms of formal rules (Habermas 1990; Cohen 1997), I contend it is better to conceive of them more loosely as providing a basic conception of epistemic or discursive etiquette. To be clear, the term *etiquette* should not be taken to indicate that the concern is with *politeness* or *courtesy*. Instead, the idea is roughly as follows: if we aim to have true beliefs, and if this aiming requires us to exchange our reasons with others, we must avoid adopting attitudes and habits that obstruct or frustrate the dialectical processes of examining and exchanging reasons. So, with regard to our interlocutors, we must be open-minded, attentive, honest, and charitable; we must try to avoid rushing to judgment, erecting straw-men, deploying *ad hominem* attacks and other dismissive tropes; in other words, we must play fair. With regard to our own position, we must be earnest, precise, and explicit; we must try to make our case in the clearest terms possible, avoiding obfuscation, equivocation, and sophism.

It bears emphasizing that this conception of discursive etiquette is emphatically *not* a moral conception; it is thoroughly *epistemic*. Someone who is cocksure and dismissive of counter-arguments is as epistemically blameworthy as someone who is especially prone to the fallacy of affirming the consequent. Similarly, someone who is unduly deferential to a supposed authority, or overly gullible, in forming his beliefs is as epistemically corrupt as someone who is especially careless in making observations. Despite the fact that being dismissive, or deferential, or careless, or especially prone to commit a fallacy could sometimes lead one to believe the truth, these facets of one's epistemic character will in the long run generate more false beliefs than true beliefs. All are ways of failing at the *epistemic* enterprise of aiming to have beliefs that are true.

It is also worth noting that the description of proper epistemic etiquette is *not* a call for what is sometimes called *civility* in the face of disagreement. Many theorists and commentators lament the adversarial and combative nature of contemporary society, especially with regard to moral and political discourse; they call for civility in such matters, equating civility with unity, cooperation, and consensus (Kingwell 1995; Carter 1998; Rodin and Steinberg 2003). The folk epistemic view rejects this. The kind of civility that is frequently called for tends to stifle discourse, inhibit criticism, discourage dissent, encourage pandering and patronizing modes of communication, and impose an artificial orderliness on public discourse. Consequently, this kind of civility also tends to privilege the status quo. Furthermore, the idea that public discourse should be governed by a norm of civility pushes disagreements and conflicts to the margins, where they usually develop into antagonisms.

Needless to say, on the view that I have been developing, proper discursive practice is not always, and perhaps not typically, civil in this way. As the folk epistemic view of proper discourse is driven by our common epistemic aspiration to have true beliefs, it must be acknowledged that public dialogue will often be agonistic and hence "uncivil" from the point of view of the conception of civility described above. Not all proper believers will agree about what proposition the best reasons support; nor are they likely to agree on what the best reasons are, or about how different kinds of reason are to be prioritized. However, insofar as they see themselves and each other as engaged in a common epistemic enterprise, their disagreements, though often intense and heated, can be *reasonable*, that is, driven by the shared aspiration to follow the best reasons. Hence, proper discourse does not have *consensus* as its immediate goal, and so does not see *dissensus* as a failure; in fact, it sees dissensus as a condition that could enable proper believing. In this way, proper discourse should be expected to be agonistic, not always and not necessarily calm, pleasant, and cooperative.

However, the discursive agonism that is advocated by the folk epistemic view is to be distinguished from the kind of *antagonism* that many proponents of civility rightly condemn. Antagonistic discourse is not driven by the mutual recognition of each party that the others are engaged in a sincere attempt to find and state the truth; rather, it is driven by a fundamental

distrust of the epistemic character of one's interlocutors. That is, antagonistic discourse is marked by a pervasive hermeneutic of suspicion with
regard to one's interlocutors; antagonists see each other as epistemic cons,
frauds, cheats, or imposters. Accordingly, the tactics and devices that civility
advocates tend to focus on and correctly decry – character assassination,
scandal-mongering, straw-manning, defamation, and so on – are properly
understood as responses to perceived epistemic foul-play or bad faith.
Consequently, the lack of civility in the sense these theorists adopt is *not* a
symptom of crumbling sociability and a lack of commonality; it is instead a
perhaps inadvertent *affirmation* of the value and need for the kind of
epistemic dispositions we have described. The proper response to widespread antagonism is not to overlay public discourse with a pall of con-
geniality, but to engage in more substantive and conflictual modes of
discourse.

III AN ELABORATION OF FOLK EPISTEMOLOGY

Thus far I have taken each folk epistemic principle individually and offered
an explanation of each. In this section, I shall offer an elaboration of a more
general sort by discussing the principles together, as an integrated epistemological framework. More specifically, I shall indicate and examine the
ways in which our folk epistemology is confirmed by common habits of
moral and political discourse.

Folk epistemology in practice

My primary contention thus far has been that the principles of folk
epistemology are well entrenched in our everyday epistemic practices.
Most generally, I have argued that when you make an assertion, those to
whom your assertion is addressed are typically entitled to ask for your
reasons. When the assertion in question is especially mundane, mundane
reasons typically will suffice, and the process of reason exchange will be
exhausted quickly. In other cases, the exchange may extend to several
rounds. Of course, the process of justification must end somewhere, and
there is indeed a point at which it would be inappropriate for an interlocutor
to press you further. But even in such cases, the inappropriateness does not
derive from there being a point at which your interlocutor *owes* you
epistemic deference or *must* acquiesce in your say-so, or simply *comply*
with what you have said; it rather is a matter of etiquette, courtesy,
politeness, or prudence. Similarly, to respond with hostility or indignation

to *any* request for reasons is not only rude, it betrays a failing of epistemic character. Someone who routinely refuses to enter his reasons into the dialectical space in which they may be evaluated betrays an insufficient concern for the truth of his beliefs.

From what has been said thus far, it might seem that folk epistemology applies only to uninteresting factual assertions about which there could be little by way of reasonable disagreement in the first place. Not so. The phenomenology of moral belief and assertion also squares with the tenets of folk epistemology. Persons who disagree about, say, the moral permissibility of abortion or the justice of a war typically do not take themselves to be merely expressing different preferences, or attempting to prescribe different attitudes and emotional dispositions, or even trying simply to persuade. Moral argument aims to win consensus *for the right reasons*; that is, moral argument aims to *convince* interlocutors by means of reasons and arguments that indicate the *truth* of our moral judgments. To be sure, when you and I discover that we disagree about some moral issue, we may, of course, elect to bracket the disagreement or change the subject, but, again, this is *not* an *epistemic* requirement. Quite the contrary; when we discover that we dis-agree, each of us infers that the other has made some kind of mistake, a mistake that reason, evidence, and argument could, at least in principle, address and correct. And if the setting is right and the issue pressing, we proceed to engage each other's reasons.

Indeed, the very fact that we countenance moral *disagreement* indicates that we are committed to the truth of our moral beliefs. Similarly, the fact that we engage in moral *debate* indicates that we take our moral judgments, and those of others, to be responsive to reasons. David Wiggins expresses the thought well:

Suppose I am convinced that something is so. Then it is disturbing to me if nobody else can be brought to agree with me. Why? Well, if something is so *either* it must be capable of impinging on others in the way impinged on me or I shall have in principle to account for its inaccessibility to all others. And if I could have accounted for that, then I should never have been disturbed in the first place by disagreement. (1987: 149)

To make the point in a slightly different way, we may say, following Cheryl Misak (2004b), that it is precisely our commitment to truth and reasons that makes disagreement *matter*. And this in turn means that the questions, objections, concerns, and contestations of those with whom we disagree matter. Unless we are prepared to take disagreement seriously, we are failing to aim at truth.

To be sure, this is not to deny the existence of demagogues and sophists. It is not to deny that moral discourse can be engaged for manipulative purposes. What *is* being claimed is that sheer moral rhetoric *cannot* present itself as such. The sophist who is interested only in persuasion cannot *confess* to his audience that he has no concern for the truth of his position. To say to an interlocutor or an audience:

I am trying by means of sheer rhetoric to persuade you of p, *and I have no reason to think* p *is true*

is to lose all chance of success. To persuade an interlocutor or an audience that *p* is to persuade that person or that audience that *p is true*. Consequently, the honest sophist is doomed; indeed, it should be noted that the very term *honest sophist* smacks of contradiction. This is because the honest sophist not only will fail to persuade, but also cause his audience to regard him as epistemically fraudulent and untrustworthy. And what kind of sophist is *that*? The honest sophist is arguably no sophist at all. But why should this be the case except for the fact that we take our moral beliefs, and our sources of moral instruction, to be answerable to the general folk epistemic tenets identified above?

Some may object at this point that my analysis is undermined by the fact that it explicitly embraces moral cognitivism (viz., the view according to which moral statements have truth values), whereas various versions of moral non-cognitivism are widespread. The critic might ask: what of the encroaching "dictatorship of relativism" the newly appointed Pope Benedict XVI (2005), and several politicians with him, has warned against?[12] What of the popular tendency to employ the emotive language of "feelings" when discussing moral issues?

The thing to note is that relativist and emotivist maneuvers that are most often employed in everyday moral discourse are *not* expressions of various non-cognitivist theories of moral statements; rather, they are introduced into discussion as moral conversation-stoppers. To explain: when someone engaged in a moral argument says something like, "It's all just a matter of opinion," you can be certain that he is not admitting that his *own* opinion is no better than yours, and he is *not* saying that it makes no difference to *him* that he believes one thing rather than another; instead, he is saying, "I want us not to discuss this matter further." That is, ostensibly relativist appeals in

---

[12] Hence, President Bush, "Pope Benedict XVI recently warned that when we forget these truths, we risk sliding into a dictatorship of relativism where we can no longer defend our values." May 20, 2005 address to a National Catholic Prayer Breakfast, at: www.whitehouse.gov/news/releases/2005/05/20050520.html (accessed May 24, 2005).

moral discussion do not usually indicate a commitment to relativism as a meta-ethic, but instead serve the strictly *pragmatic* function of changing the course of a discussion away from potentially divisive topics. In short, such maneuvers are attempts simply to change the subject.

But we should ask: why should an alleged moral relativist or emotivist be so eager to eschew discussion of his moral beliefs? Why should he be eager to change the subject? According to the relativist and the emotivist, remember, there is literally *nothing at stake* in moral discourse, so why be so adamant in avoiding it? The fact is, again, that the extent to which we are exercised in the least by the fact that others do not share our own moral beliefs indicates that we are committed to the view that there *is*, indeed, something at stake in moral discourse and that moral disagreement matters. If we find that some moral assertion of ours is without support, we will feel compelled to change our belief. But, given the nature of morality, we are *invested* in the truth of our moral judgments; they tend to serve as guides for how we behave, what we pursue, and what we treat as important. This investment explains the many mechanisms that we deploy in order to avoid discussion of these commitments in the presence of potential critics. Consequently, since the familiar relativist tropes, such as "it's all just a matter of opinion," serve to divert moral discussion, the frequency with which we encounter them is a good indication of the degree to which people *reject* relativism.

Hence, popular overtures raising the specter of relativism ring hollow. Moral relativism is a very sophisticated meta-ethical position advanced by only a few professional philosophers; it is decidedly *not* the reigning popular morality.[13] In fact, the frequency with which the threat of relativism is appealed to in popular discourse indicates relativism's abiding *unpopularity*. For if it were the case that relativism were so widespread as to threaten the "dictatorship" of which the Pope has warned, it could not serve as a popular bogey, and no politician could afford to speak out against it.

Finally, consider that current modes of political discourse confirm our folk epistemic principles. Note first that popular political commentary is couched in a self-image that is strikingly, and nearly exclusively, epistemic. Television news channels profess to offer "no spin zones" and "fair and balanced" reporting that is "accurate," "reliable," "honest," and "trusted." Popular books about contemporary politics and current affairs, the publication of which is now a multi-billion dollar industry, are also fixed on epistemic themes. Popular recent titles claim to expose "lying liars"

---

[13] See Boghossian 2006 for a sustained engagement with the most sophisticated forms of relativism in currency. See also Lynch 2004.

(Franken 2003), "idiots" (Gallagher 2005), "fanatics and fools" (Huffington 2004), and various other agents of "fraud," "illusion," "deception," "hypocrisy" (Schweizer 2005), "treachery" (Coulter 2003), and "downright stupidity" (Stossel 2006). In place of these, commentators promise "solutions" (Savage 2005), "common sense" (Schultz 2004), "reason" (Gore 2007), and "the truth (with jokes)" (Franken 2005). Similarly, critiques of the media target "bias" (Goldberg 2003), "spin" (Fritz, Keefer, and Nyhan 2004), "big lies" (Conason 2003), and "hoax" (Von Hoffman 2004). One author goes so far as to characterize the national news media as a "noise machine" that serves a right-wing agenda (Brock 2004), whereas another predicts a "meltdown" of the liberal media and its "weapons of mass distortion" (Bozell 2004), while Susan Jacoby has declared that we have entered an age of "unreason" (2008). Popular criticism of George W. Bush, both in the United States and abroad, has focused almost exclusively on his alleged lack of intelligence. Representatives are commonly criticized for being "partisan," that is, blindly loyal to a prefabricated party line and thus irresponsive to the arguments and reasons offered by their opposition. Campaigning politicians are fond of charging their opponents with "waffling," that is, basing their policy proposals and other agenda items on the results of popular opinion polls rather than on reasons and evidence.

These last two phenomena are telling. The charge of partisanship derives its critical force from a popular *rejection* of the idea that politicians should simply press their own party's agenda. Similarly, the waffling charge presupposes that politicians should *not* simply follow the popular opinion polls, but ought instead to follow the best reasons available to them. It should be noted that in both cases, the interest-based or proceduralist conception of democratic politics is implicitly rejected. For on a proceduralist view, partisanship and waffling are *exactly* what one should expect – indeed *want* – from politicians. Insofar as we tend to see partisanship and waffling as *defective* modes of political activity, we reject the proceduralist conception of democratic politics. The message of popular political commentary, then, is clear: truth matters for democracy and, therefore, reasons, arguments, honesty, and intelligence matter. Or, as Al Gore has put it, "The very idea of self-government depends on open and honest debate as the preferred method for pursuing truth – and a shared respect for the rule of reason as the best way to establish the truth" (2007: 58).

Consider next the new mode of political activism practiced by documentary filmmaker Michael Moore, among others. Moore's *modus operandi* is to confront the powerful with their own hypocrisy, to expose, as one of Moore's television series has it, the "awful truth." The thought that underlies all of his work is that the truth, which has been suppressed by the powerful, must be uncovered because truth, once uncovered, trumps power. That is, Moore has tapped into the deeply intuitive premise that power and authority derive their legitimacy from truth. From this it follows that "lying liars" and "useful idiots" (Charen 2003) are not legitimate holders of power. And so Moore presents himself as a Socratic hero, exposing contradictions and fallacious arguments, revealing hidden interests and allegiances, challenging popular nostrums, and shattering illusions; the force of these exercises is to demonstrate the illegitimacy of the authority of those he targets.

My point is neither to endorse nor condemn Michael Moore's methods or politics. The point is rather to emphasize that the deeply epistemic meta-narrative of the need to speak truth to power that is employed by Moore is a staple of our popular political culture. For example, during the 2004 presidential election in the United States, a group calling itself Swift Boat Veterans for *Truth* sought to demonstrate that Democratic candidate John Kerry's service in Vietnam rendered him "unfit for command" (O'Neill and Corsi 2004);[14] similarly, John Dean (2004) has sought to uncover "the secret presidency of George Bush," and Al Gore's most recent book casts the Bush administration as being devoted to an "assault on reason" (2007). Further examples are easy to find; in fact, our current political discourse is so focused on exposing cover-ups, lies, and distortions that it could be argued that our popular political culture is *obsessed* with truth. And so, again, the dynamics of our popular political culture confirms our folk epistemology.

I concede that for the most part these pervasive images of political truth-seeking and intellectual integrity are *merely* images. Claims to epistemic fairness, reasonableness, trustworthiness, and honesty function in today's popular political discourse mostly as strategies and slogans that serve marketing and public-relations objectives. However, in light of the market pressures operative in the modern media industry, we must conclude that such slogans are effective. And that these slogans are effective confirms that our description of folk epistemology is correct. Our popular political rhetoric employs such heavy doses of epistemic rhetoric because citizens tend to see themselves as rational epistemic agents who seek to base their political opinions on good reasons. They accordingly hold that reasons, evidence, argument, and truth *matter* for political discourse and decision. And they believe that these folk epistemic attitudes and practices should be reflected in their politics and respected by their politicians.

---

[14] An opposing group, "Texans for Truth," argued that Bush was an "unfit commander" (Smith 2004).

Is folk epistemology provincial?

Two final pieces of business must be addressed before moving on to argue that our folk epistemic commitments provide a justification for democratic politics and a solution to the problem of deep politics. In the present section, I address the concern that folk epistemology is provincial; in the next, I look at an objection according to which folk epistemology is unduly influenced by Enlightenment values which some deem obsolete.

To begin: a critic may accept the above description and elaboration, but contend that what I have been calling "folk epistemology" is merely a distillation of our relatively local epistemic folkways. This kind of criticism is likely to arise in light of certain claims, advanced in the name of post-modernism, pragmatism, feminism, and other trendy "isms," to the effect that all modes of reasoning, all epistemologies or "epistemes," are deeply cultural and historicized, and thus not generalizable across broad social and political divisions. The criticism will run that what I have been claiming is a more or less universal set of epistemic commitments that persons incur by virtue of the fact that they have beliefs at all is in fact merely a description of what Western people, or Western males, or Western males living in modern industrial democracies, or Western males living in the United States, or Western males living in the United States who teach philosophy in private Southern universities, happen to believe about themselves. If this kind of criticism goes through, the project of devising a justification for democratic politics is pre-empted. That is, if folk epistemology is provincial in the way in which the imagined critic alleges, then any justification for democracy based in folk epistemology will be circular, as it will simply state the epistemic prejudices of modern democratic citizens.

Fortunately, the criticism, despite its abiding popularity in certain academic circles, does not succeed. As it stands, the envisioned criticism simply confirms what it alleges to deny. The critic claims that practices of reasoning and arguing are historically and culturally specific, and so any account of epistemology that aspires to transcend a particular place and age must fail. But this is to say that our account of folk epistemology does not square with all the relevant evidence, and that there is good *reason* to be suspicious that our description is not *true*. Put another way, insofar as we are able to recognize the criticism *as* a criticism, we must take it to propose a *correction* of the account we have been developing. But to pose a *correction* is to commit to the idea that our assertions are truth-aiming and thus reason-responsive. That is, to issue a criticism is to already be committed to the folk epistemic principles I have identified.

The imagined critic may respond by saying that my rejoinder has conflated two distinct levels of discourse. He may say that it is *of course* true that his criticism, in order to be a criticism, must presume the very principles of reason that it ultimately seeks to attack. However, the criticism is aimed at the claim that these principles are *universalizable*; that is, the criticism is supposed to show that folk epistemology is provincial. Showing that the critic is employing the same epistemic norms identified in the folk epistemic account does not render folk epistemology non-provincial. Hence, the critic may conclude that the fact to which he initially appealed remains in place: persons situated within radically difference cultural, economic, historical, and social contexts do not reason, believe, justify, argue, and communicate in the ways prescribed by folk epistemology.

Here the critic has committed to an empirical claim, and, importantly, the data are not in his favor. In a fascinating article, William D. Harpine argues that "the evidence of modern ethnographic research is that the similarities in how people think, speak, and behave rationally are substantial" (2004: 350). His thorough review of the current data shows that:

Syllogism, deductive logic, inductive logic, the argument from authority, empirical observation, and hypothesis testing are widespread in diverse human societies. They are even found in cultures that share features common with Pleistocene hunter and gatherers. (2004: 355)

Harpine's conclusion should come as no surprise, for the opposing position is literally *unbelievable*. To see this, imagine a society that satisfies Richard Rorty's professed hope for a culture in which there is "no concern for truth" (1995: 290). That is, imagine a society in which your assertion that *p* is *not* generally taken to be an indication to others that you take it to be true that *p*. Or imagine a society in which truth and reasons simply do not matter. Now consider the consequences: under such conditions, there obviously could be no *disagreement* and no *criticism*, because there could be no differences in opinion, or at least no differences that could *make a difference* to opining parties. But then there could be no *agreement* and no *consensus* either, since these require a convergence of opinion and without truth and reasons there is nothing upon which opinion can converge. Moreover, there could be no *learning*, no *correction*, no *mistakes*, and no notion of epistemic *improvement*, since these require the concepts of truth and reason.

Could there be such a society? Even in a thoroughly hierarchical society in which every individual was inclined to unquestioningly fulfill her prescribed role, there would have to be some way to evaluate whether everyone was, in fact, fulfilling the correct role in the social order. Consequently, there would have to be a corresponding concept of what it would be to make a *mistake* or to *fail* to satisfy one's duties. And even in a completely authoritarian society, in which every last person was disposed to unquestioningly obey the commands of a ruler, there would have to be some way to evaluate whether the commands were *truly* obeyed and *correctly* interpreted.

In short, it seems *impossible* that there could be a society in which individuals did not subscribe roughly to the kind of folk epistemic principles we have outlined. Rorty's hope is incoherent because, as Huw Price has argued, "in practice we find it impossible to stop caring about truth" (2003: 187).[15] This impossibility is not a mere cultural inheritance or Western prejudice. As paradoxical as it may sound, the epistemic *friction* that exists between persons – the possibility of disagreements that *matter* (Misak 2004b) – is necessary if there is to be community of any lasting form (Price 2003: 181; *cf.* Price 1998). Accordingly, folk epistemology is not provincial.

Folk epistemology and the enlightenment

A related objection to folk epistemology derives from work in professional epistemology. In a well-known essay examining the place of religious reasoning in democratic politics, Nicholas Wolterstorff objects to what he calls the "Enlightenment understanding of how reason works" (1997: 98), which he contends underlies most – perhaps all – democratic theory, from John Locke to Rawls. According to Wolterstorff, this understanding bids us to "regulate our belief-forming faculties, and to regulate them with the aim of believing what is true and of not believing what is false" (1997: 84). Summarizing what he takes to be Locke's position, Wolterstorff describes this regulatory procedure as follows:

With some proposition in mind concerning the matter in question, one first collects evidence concerning the truth or falsehood of the proposition … Second, by the exercise of one's reason one determines the probability of the proposition on that evidence. And last, one adopts a level of confidence in the proposition corresponding to its probability on that evidence. (1997: 84–85).

---

[15] Engel pushes a similar line against Rorty (Rorty and Engel 2007: 16). *Cf.* Stout 2007.

On Wolterstorff's view, the Enlightenment understanding – roughly what we characterized earlier as *evidentialism* – is "untenable," and, more importantly, has been subjected to a "decisive" attack in recent epistemology (1997: 87).

Since folk epistemology involves the contention that when we believe that *p* we take ourselves to have sufficient evidence for *p*'s truth, and take ourselves to be well-positioned to articulate our reasons, it clearly fits into Wolterstorff's description of the Enlightenment understanding. Accordingly, something must be said about his objections to that understanding.

Roughly, Wolterstorff's objection to Enlightenment epistemology fixes on its evidentialist core; that is, Wolterstorff rejects the Enlightenment idea that one is entitled to hold a belief that *p* only when one has sufficient evidence for *p*. Summarizing his anti-evidentialist position, Wolterstorff contends:

Something about the belief, the person and the situation brings it about that the person is entitled to the belief. But that need not be another belief whose propositional content functions as reason for the [original] belief. (1997: 87)

To be sure, Wolterstorff's claim is not that one may believe willy-nilly. It is rather that the "Enlightenment understanding of how reason works" presupposes a false view of how epistemic agents are related to their beliefs and to the propositions proposed to them as candidates for belief. Recall that on the Enlightenment view, the epistemic agent is obligated (1997: 84) to gather and assess the evidence for some proposed proposition, *p*, *before* adopting it as a belief. According to Wolterstorff, this obligation presupposes a fundamental dualism between that which an agent believes and the cognitive mechanisms by which she evaluates evidence and forms her beliefs; that is, according to Wolterstorff, the Enlightenment view holds that the epistemic agent is *separable* from what she believes. In a passage that is worth quoting in full, Wolterstorff rejects this view:

The beliefs that we already have, however acquired, are not merely stored inertly in memory, waiting to be lifted out should the occasion arise. They become components in our programming. What determines whether I will believe [for example] the doctrine of transubstantiation, upon grasping it, is the beliefs that I bring with me to the enterprise. In forming beliefs in response to experience, I do not and cannot operate as a generic human being. I operate as a person with such-and-such a contour of habits and skills of attention – and so forth. What I come to believe is a function of my experience plus what I already believe. It is not just a function of my experience. The traditions into which we have been inducted cannot just be set on the shelf, cannot be circumvented. They have become components of ourselves as belief-forming agents: components of our programming. We live *inside* our traditions, not *alongside*.[16] (1997: 89)

It might seem that one could respond to Wolterstorff along the lines by which I dispensed above with the philosophical controversies concerning moral relativism and evidentialism: since the concern is to make explicit our *folk* epistemology, I need not embroil myself in deep philosophical quandaries. However, in the present case, this kind of response seems insufficient, for Wolterstorff claims that the fundamental orientation of folk epistemology has been decisively attacked and defeated (1997: 87). I cannot here engage all of the relevant twists and turns of the current debate in epistemology between "reformed epistemologists" like Wolterstorff and their critics. But surely something must be said.

First, let us note that if by *decisive* Wolterstorff means something like *definitively* or *conclusively*, then his claim that the Enlightenment view has been subject to a "decisive" attack is clearly overstated. Many, perhaps most, epistemologists reject Wolterstorff's reformed epistemology and endorse some version of the Enlightenment view. In fact, debates between evidentialists and anti-evidentialists are ongoing and constitute a large portion of the current literature in epistemology.[17]

But more importantly, let us note some of the philosophical features of Wolterstorff's position. Recall that, according to Wolterstorff, "We live *inside* our traditions, not *alongside*" them (1997: 89). What this means is that our beliefs "become components of ourselves as belief-forming agents" (1997: 89), and that we are, therefore, *unable* to step outside of our body of belief to evaluate it; any epistemic evaluation of a given belief one holds must proceed from the commitment to the general aptness of one's belief system as a whole, for every evaluation draws upon conceptions of evidence, rationality, probability, and correctness that are *internal* to one's "programming" (1987: 89). Hence, Wolterstorff claims that "In forming beliefs in response to experience, I do not and cannot operate as a generic human being" (1997: 89). The result, then, is that there is nothing that can be claimed about epistemic agents *as such*; standards of evidence and the rationality of any given instance of belief-formation must be understood to be relative to each particular agent's epistemic programming. According to Wolterstorff, "what we come to believe," and, indeed, what we are *justified* in believing, "is a function, in

---

[16] It should be made clear here that in the quotation just cited Wolterstorff takes himself to be explicating an anti-evidentialist position that he contends makes an appearance in the penultimate chapter of Locke's otherwise thoroughly evidentialist *Essay Concerning Human Understanding*. However, the view he here imputes to Locke is a fair representation of the non-Enlightenment epistemology of which he approves.

[17] See Axtell 2006 for a helpful review of the issues.

part, of what we already believe" (1997: 98); and since we undeniably believe different things, we operate with different programming. Wolterstorff concludes, then, that there is no common human faculty of reason and no common store of experience from which to derive the evidentialist epistemic standard which lies at the core of the Enlightenment view.

But one must ask: what is the status of Wolterstorff's own epistemological claims? How are we to understand Wolterstorff's view about "how reason works"? Is the very account Wolterstorff gives of how epistemic entitlement is partly a matter of what experiences and background beliefs one brings to the epistemic task *itself* simply a product of Wolterstorff's programming? Or does he take this account to state a truth about human reason as such? If the former, it is not clear how Wolterstorff can claim that his reformed view constitutes an "attack" on the Enlightenment view, nor can he hold that his own position is superior to Locke's; for on Wolterstorff's view, Locke's position is simply the result of *different* – he cannot say *mistaken* – programming. But if, on the other hand, Wolterstorff intends his account to state a *truth* about human reason as such, then it is not clear how it can avoid being an Enlightenment view after all. For if it purports to state a truth about human reason as such, then surely it purports that this truth is supportable by reasons, arguments, and evidence; moreover, it purports that the reasons, arguments, and evidence that support its view of human reason as such are *better* or *stronger* than the reasons, arguments, and evidence that support rival views of the matter.

Of course, there is much more to say with regard to theses issues. The result of this discussion, however, is this: folk epistemology is, indeed, an instantiation of the Enlightenment view that Wolterstorff seeks to discredit. However, it is not clear that his objections cut any ice, since unless they presuppose a roughly Enlightenment view of their own content, they undermine the very idea of criticizing another's epistemic framework (even Locke's). At the very least, then, the reformed epistemologists' attack on the Enlightenment view is not as decisive as Wolterstorff seems to think. Consequently, my original reply to Wolterstorff seems to stand: the long-standing debates of professional epistemology are not relevant at this stage of this project; here, the concern is only to capture our folk epistemic commitments, and these are decidedly in line with the Enlightenment understanding of how reason works.

IV CONCLUSION

In this chapter I proposed that there is an epistemic analogue to folk psychology, which I called folk epistemology. I then identified five principles of folk epistemology and argued that collectively these principles are implicit in our everyday moral and political discourse. Rejecting the idea that folk epistemology is merely a distillation of the epistemic folkways of citizens of contemporary democracies, I tried to make a case for thinking that folk epistemology captures something universal about the way rational creatures must regard their own beliefs. I then accepted the claim that folk epistemology is an instantiation of a more general Enlightenment view, but argued that this is not objectionable. In Chapter 4, I shall argue that the folk epistemology to which we are all implicitly committed entails a further set of commitments to democratic political norms and institutions.

Justifying democracy

It may seem that we have journeyed a great distance from our topic, which, you may remember, is democracy. However, if you will grant the arguments from Chapter 3 to the effect that the characterization I have offered of folk epistemology is accurate and not simply a distillation of our provincial epistemic folkways, then we are well on our way to justifying democracy. The argument of the present chapter is intuitive and can be stated succinctly: only in a democracy can an individual practice proper epistemic agency; put in other words, only in a democracy can one be a proper believer. Since we are already committed to proper believing, we are implicitly committed to democratic politics. Folk epistemology accordingly justifies democracy: democracy is the political entailment – indeed, the political *manifestation* – of the folk epistemic commitments each of us already endorses.

To be sure, there are many details to be filled in. This is what I shall undertake in the present chapter. It is worth emphasizing that, if my arguments prove to be successful, I will have devised a solution to the problem of deep politics. If folk epistemology justifies democracy, then citizens have a reason to sustain their commitment to democratic political arrangements despite the fact that they are deeply divided at the level of their moral and religious commitments.

I FOLK EPISTEMOLOGY AND THE JUSTIFICATION OF DEMOCRACY

The basic argument

I argued in Chapter 3 that believing commits us to certain activities. For example, I argued that the fact that we hold beliefs at all commits us to the norms associated with assertion, and chief among these is the norm of articulating, exchanging, and responding to reasons. Yet these activities can be engaged only within a certain kind of social context. That is, in order to engage in activities of reason-exchange and argument, not only must individuals be afforded the protections and liberties associated with freedom of thought and expression, they must also have access to a variety of reliable sources of information. Accordingly, a political order under which information is strictly controlled and the exchange of arguments and reasons is suppressed is incompatible with proper believing.

To see this, consider that statements of the following sort are all untenable in the sense that was identified in Chapter 3:

I believe that p, *but my belief is the result of propaganda*
I believe that p, *but my evidence has been rigged*
I believe that p, *but my sources of information concerning* p *are epistemically unreliable*
On the basis of epistemically corrupt reasons, I believe that p.

These are untenable because, when one acknowledges that one's belief that *p* was generated in one of these ways, one's belief typically recedes. This is so because the belief that *p* comes with a commitment to the idea that the belief was formed under epistemically suitable – not necessarily ideal, but not inappropriate – conditions. These conditions include open access to reliable and relevant information and the absence of agents of systematic deception.

This is not to say that there are no highly-propagandized societies, no persons who hold beliefs on the basis of sham but "official" reasons, and no fanatical "true believers." To repeat, the point is rather that no one *takes* himself to believe on the basis of rigged reasons or a party line. Even in the case of someone who really believes the party line in full (rather than simply *reciting* it for prudential reasons), she believes because she holds that the party's pronouncements are true, and are supported by the best reasons. To be sure, someone who epistemically defers to a *de facto* political or moral authority resolves to base her beliefs on the say so of the alleged authority. But in such a case, the believer takes herself to defer to the *appropriate* or *true* authority; she takes it that the fact that the authority decrees that *p* is, indeed, *evidence* that *p*, or at least a *good enough reason* for *p*. Of course, she might have a corrupt view of what evidence or a good reason is, but this is no matter; all we are committed to saying is that when one believes, one takes oneself to be properly responsive to reasons.

It is precisely our commitment to the norm of reason-responsiveness that makes propaganda necessary in dictatorial regimes.[1] But note that propaganda consists not simply in the presentation of the official doctrine as unquestionable fact. In addition to this, propaganda always contains proclamations of its own *epistemic* authority. The most obvious example of this is that the official newspaper in Stalin's Soviet Union was called *Pravda* ("truth"). Consider also the analysis of personality cults – here translated as "cult of the individual" – offered by Mao to the congress in Chengdu in 1958:

> There are two kinds of cult of the individual. One is correct, such as that of Marx, Engels, Lenin, and the correct side of Stalin. These we ought to revere and continue to revere forever. It would not do not to revere them. As they held truth in their hands, why should we not revere them? We believe in truth; truth is the reflection of objective existence … then there is the incorrect kind of cult of the individual in which there is no analysis, simply blind obedience. This is not right.[2]

Other examples are easy to find. The point is that a regime that seeks to control the beliefs of its populace cannot simply circumvent or disregard individuals' commitment to reason-responsiveness. If a tyrant is to succeed in controlling the beliefs of his subjects, he must reinforce the official doctrine by means of institutions that *mimic* the processes of proper reasoning; he must create the *illusion* that the official doctrine is supported by the best reasons. Of course, this is not to downplay the extent to which dictatorial regimes employ and rely on violence, or the threat of violence, to secure compliance; rather, the point is that insofar as a dictator seeks to control the *beliefs* of his subjects, he must present the desired beliefs as supported by the best reasons, as true.

In short, proper believing requires a social context in which reasons can be freely exchanged, compared, criticized, and challenged; this in turn requires a political order in which individuals can be confident that they have access to reliable sources of information. Minimally this suggests that proper believing requires that familiar democratic institutions should be in place, such as those institutions associated with the First Amendment of the United States Constitution: freedom of speech, freedom of conscience, freedom of the press, freedom of assembly and association, and protections for critics, skeptics, dissidents, and whistle-blowers.[3]

[1] Propaganda exists in all regimes, including democratic ones. The point is that propaganda is *necessary* in authoritarian states.

[2] www.marxists.org/reference/archive/mao/selected-works/volume-8/mswv8_06.htm (accessed May 16, 2007).

[3] It may require more, such as certain levels of economic and other forms of material support. These issues cannot be discussed here.

Furthermore, the activities of believing and asserting require us to acknowledge each other as *equal participants* in the epistemic enterprise of justification. To be clear: the requirement that we acknowledge each other as equal participants in the enterprise of justification *does not* mean that we must view each other as equally informed, or as equally correct in our judgments. Rather, it requires that we treat each other as *epistemic peers*. Epistemic peers recognize that they owe to each other reasons, and acknowledge that cogent criticism may come from anyone. Accordingly, the following beliefs are untenable:

Having consulted only those who also believe that p, *and having considered only those reasons that confirm that* p, *I believe that* p
I believe that p, *and because of my privileged social status, I need not consider objections to* p
Having browbeaten my critics into silence, I believe that p
Having forcibly silenced all potential objections, I believe that p.

As I argued in Chapter 3, proper believing requires not only that we *tolerate* criticism and persons with whom we disagree, but that we open ourselves to new challenges to our beliefs and new discursive partners; proper epistemic practice is in this way inherently epistemically *inclusive*. Yet this inclusiveness is not based in a *moral* requirement to extend a respectful ear to all; its motivation is fully *epistemic*.[4] Unless we take seriously the reasons and arguments of our critics, we are not doing our best with respect to the aim of having true beliefs. Proper believing commits us also to the idea that there are no *a priori* experts that are beyond question and no fixed epistemic hierarchies that are beyond challenge. Accordingly, proper believing commits us to a politics in which channels of political contestation and institutions of political change are open and accessible to all citizens. Thus, if we are to exercise proper epistemic agency in our own case, our politics must be governed by familiar democratic norms of inclusion, equality, accountability, and participation.

Finally, the acknowledgement that we are epistemic peers – equal participants in the epistemic enterprise – commits us further to the idea that we are equal *citizens* in the political community. As such we are equally *entitled* to voice publicly our concerns, raise our objections, challenge standing assumptions, assert our beliefs, and devise arguments in favor of our commitments. We individually cannot expect to arrive at true beliefs under political conditions where other individuals feel too intimidated, dominated, insecure, alienated, or vulnerable to raise their concerns and share their reasons. In short, proper believing commits us to treating others

---

[4] To be clear: there might be such a moral requirement. The point is that the kind of inclusiveness we are talking about at present is demanded by epistemic considerations.

as fellow epistemic agents, persons with whom we can do "discursive business" (Pettit 2001: 72). And this in turn commits to a political order in which individuals can see themselves, and are seen by others, not as subjects or subordinates, but as full citizens, that is, agents in the proper sense, persons not subject to the arbitrary power of another. Persons in this sense have "a voice that has some claim to be given a hearing, and an ear that can give an effective hearing to the voices of others" (Pettit 2001: 74).

This in turn calls for a political order governed by norms of democratic *franchise* and *authenticity* (Dryzek 1996: 5). Just as individual proper believers must engage in *inclusive* practices of reason-exchanging, so too must a political community of proper believers seek to *enfranchise* fellow citizens by securing the conditions under which they can participate in democratic processes of self-government. This participation, however, must be *substantive* rather than merely *symbolic*; that is, democratic franchise must be *authentic*, reasons and arguments must have a political purchase, democratic participation must be able to *make a difference*. Moreover, as democratic franchise and authenticity entail that political institutions be *responsive* to the democratic participation of citizens, institutions must be *accountable* to the citizens they serve; just as public democratic participation must have a political purchase, so too must public democratic *criticism* of standing institutions and policies. A politics based in franchise, authenticity, and accountability requires that familiar procedural institutions of democracy, including regular elections and referenda, the rule of law, and other checks on political power, are in place.

This is not to say, however, that democracy must be *direct*. The idea of a representative democracy is fully consistent with our folk epistemology, as long as we think of representative arrangements along roughly Madisonian lines. That is, we are to see the distinction between representatives and their constituents as marking a division of *epistemic* labor. No single individual has the cognitive and material resources necessary to inquire into each and every matter that must be decided in a contemporary democratic polity. Representative bodies, then, are not to be merely institutions of collective poll-watching, but they are to be *deliberative* bodies, charged with the task of arguing and exchanging reasons on behalf of citizens. In this way, representative democracy emerges out of the acknowledgement of the necessity of a division of epistemic labor.

To summarize the argument thus far: our folk epistemic commitments compel us to endorse basic democratic arrangements and institutions. Thus, folk epistemology justifies democracy. The folk epistemic justification addresses each of us – one by one – and claims that insofar as we each regard ourselves as reason-responsive epistemic agents, we must endorse a democratic politics, since only within a democracy is it possible to exercise proper epistemic agency. In this way, the folk epistemic justification begins from a collection of epistemic commitments we each have by virtue of the fact that we hold beliefs at all and shows that these commitments call for a democratic political order.

To be sure, folk epistemology entails a *democratic* political order in only a very broad sense of that term. The argument does not profess to fix the finer details of democratic government. For example, the folk epistemic argument is consistent with parliamentary and non-parliamentary arrangements, it can countenance different mechanisms for checking and balancing power among different governmental agencies, it allows for different systems of taxation, and so on. In a way, then, the folk epistemic argument is philosophically modest – the details of the institutional design of democracy are left undetermined, to be settled in other ways. Some might take this to be a failing of the approach. I do not think that it is, since it seems obvious that democracy can take many institutional forms. In fact, one should be wary of a philosophical conception of democracy that seeks to accomplish too much by way of institutional design. The point is to specify a conception of democratic politics within which such matters can be debated and decided democratically, not to draft a blueprint for designing democratic institutions.[5]

However one might regard the modesty of the folk epistemic approach on this score, it should be noted that the view is ambitious in a way that is not common in contemporary political theory in that it claims that even *anti-democrats* are implicitly committed to democracy. Even a professed enemy of democracy, insofar as she holds beliefs at all, is committed to the truth of what she believes, and so is committed to the idea that her beliefs are in line with the best reasons and evidence. But this commits her to the view that her beliefs could withstand criticism and survive objections. This is something that can be demonstrated *only* by engaging in the processes of critical debate and deliberation that are possible only within a democratic context. Accordingly, even the most brutal dictator who claims to care only about power and seeks only to manipulate and propagandize the people that are his subjects must care about the *truth* concerning the best or most effective way to achieve these ends. To this extent, he must care about reasons, evidence, and argument. And caring about these things means

---

[5] I note again that I will have occasion to comment on a few policy proposals in Chapter 5. To repeat, the point here is not to show how the folk epistemic view *entails* such policies, but rather that the folk epistemologist *could* support them.

undertaking the project of justification, the project of trying to arrive at the best belief available. That is, no tyrant can be a *complete* tyrant or a tyrant *all the way down*; tyranny requires that, at *some* level, reasons, and hence the open exchange of reasons, matter.

A critic could object that the folk epistemic view I have outlined is naïve about the degree to which democracy is vulnerable to demagoguery. The criticism would contend that I have proposed a view of the epistemic commitments of ordinary citizens that is inconsistent with the plain fact that we are all highly susceptible to believing on the basis of sham evidence, poor reasoning, smooth talk, and wishful thinking. This susceptibility should undermine our confidence in the claim that there is a cogent and respectable folk epistemology.

This criticism is misguided. As I discussed above, and as I will discuss later in this book, contemporary democracy is indeed plagued with the flattery of rhetoric and sophistry. The point to keep in mind at present is that the practices of demagoguery *presuppose* that proper epistemic norms are in place; the sophistical tropes employed by demagogues are in fact *parasitic* on folk epistemic norms – they uphold in rhetoric what they undermine in fact. To explain: democratic citizens are indeed moved by claims to truthfulness, sincerity, integrity, rationality, accuracy, open debate, fairness, and balance. This is because citizens are *correct* to demand these qualities of their politicians and their news media. The image of the "no spin zone" is, after all, the *correct* image for epistemically responsible journalism and news reporting. Demagoguery succeeds *precisely because* there is a widely shared epistemic commitment to truth and reason-responsiveness. Since the folk epistemic justification I have proposed makes explicit the commitments that are exploited by demagogues, it therefore makes us more aware of the ways in which these commitments can be manipulated and imitated. Moreover, making explicit to ourselves the folk epistemic principles we endorse helps to guard against mimics and imposters. When citizens are engaged in the process of justification prescribed by their folk epistemic commitments, they are less susceptible to rhetorical tactics. Far from implicitly denying the pervasiveness of demagoguery, or underestimating its force, the folk epistemic view provides the basis for an *analysis* of contemporary popular rhetoric, and thus provides a means for its *critique*.

Deliberative versus dialogical democracy

I have noted that the folk epistemic justification of democracy is modest on matters of institutional design and public policy; however, as our discussion of representation and the division of epistemic labor above suggested, the folk epistemic justification does indeed suggest a particular *conception* of democracy. Specifically, folk epistemology entails a conception that is in line with certain versions of the view known as *deliberative democracy*. At the core of the deliberativist program is the rejection of the idea that democracy is strictly a formal procedure by which individual preferences are fairly aggregated by a voting process governed by a majoritarian decision rule. Deliberativists contend that the essence of democratic legitimacy lies in processes of public deliberation and debate. It should be clear that the folk epistemic view of democracy shares this much with deliberative theories of democracy.

However, although I have written under the banner of deliberative democracy in other contexts, I have grown reluctant to fully embrace the label of deliberative democracy. To explain: there are several competing versions of deliberative democracy in currency. In fact, the term *deliberative democracy* is so widely used these days by so many different kinds of theorists that it is at this point almost without definite content. It will be instructive, then, to contrast the folk epistemic conception with a few of the more influential deliberativist views.

The most prominent versions of deliberative democracy contend that public deliberation is necessary to satisfy some characteristically democratic moral requirement. According to the Rawlsian "public reason" model that was discussed in Chapter 2, deliberation is the expression of our "duty of civility" (2005: 217). Following Rawls, Larmore holds that public deliberation governed by his "norm of rational dialogue" is necessary for "equal respect" (Larmore 1996: 142), and Joshua Cohen claims that deliberation is required to satisfy the democratic idea of equality among citizens (Cohen 1997: 412f.). The closely related, but nevertheless distinct, view proposed by Amy Gutmann and Dennis Thompson has it that the "reason-giving process" associated with public deliberation satisfies the "moral basis" for democracy, which is that "Persons should be treated not merely as objects of legislation ... but as autonomous agents who take part in the governance of their own society" (2004: 3).

I argued in Chapter 2 that the Rawlsian model founders because it places constraints on public discourse that it cannot adequately motivate. As it aspires to be a "freestanding" theory that avoids philosophical entanglements and "stays on the surface, philosophically speaking," the Rawlsian account cannot *justify* the conversational restraints it imposes; all it can do is say that such restraints follow from the "shared fund of implicitly recognized basic ideas and principles" (2005: 8) commonly endorsed in a liberal democracy. However, as our most pressing social conflicts are focused precisely on the proper interpretation of those institutions and principles, any appeal to them will presuppose some particular interpretation of their content and hence will strike some citizens as question-begging and in need of philosophical justification. The Gutmann and Thompson model, by contrast, makes no explicit attempt to constrain public discourse, but confronts the same difficulty we raised earlier against Jeffrey Stout's position. Just as Stout presupposes that citizens already share a commitment to democracy as a "living moral tradition" (2004: 5) that transcends the respects in which they are otherwise morally divided, Gutmann and Thompson base their deliberativism on "three principles – reciprocity, publicity, and accountability – that regulate the process of politics, and three others – basic liberty, basic opportunity, and fair opportunity – that govern the content of policies" (1996: 12). The difficulty is that the moral principles that are presupposed by Gutmann and Thompson's deliberativism surely are at least as contestable as the principles that are the subject of the moral and political disputes over which the deliberative process is intended to preside.

The general problem confronting moral versions of deliberative democracy should be obvious by now. The moral ground from which such views begin is always controversial, so any such conception of the deliberative process will strike some citizens as inappropriate, unfair, or "rigged" to favor certain political outcomes.[6] Moral versions of deliberative democracy thus beg the question posed by the problem of deep politics; rather than providing a reason for deeply divided citizens to sustain their democratic commitments when confronted with fundamental disagreements, these theories address only those citizens already well-disposed to deliberative democracy. As was emphasized at the beginning of this chapter, the folk epistemic view differs from these moral versions of deliberative democracy in that it presupposes no controversial moral commitments. Instead, it derives characteristically democratic commitments from the epistemic commitments that individuals incur by virtue of the fact that they are committed to the truth of their beliefs.

It may seem, then, that the folk epistemic strategy bears a close resemblance to the discourse-theoretic conception of deliberative democracy advanced by Jürgen Habermas (1990; 1996) and others (Benhabib 1996; Apel 1980). Indeed, there are significant similarities. Just as the folk

---

[6] George and Wolfe (2000) bring this charge against the Rawlsian view; Stanley Fish (1999) raises a similar criticism of Gutmann and Thompson.

epistemic view has it that democratic commitments are entailed by the folk epistemic principles we already accept, Habermas claims that democracy is a necessary *presupposition* of all proper communication. According to Habermas, communication requires that "participants coordinate their plans of action consensually, with the agreement reached at any point being evaluated in terms of the intersubjective recognition of validity claims" (1990: 58). That is, Habermas holds that proper communication is itself democratic in that it is necessarily non-strategic and aimed at reasoned consensus among equal discursive participants. This entails that radically anti-democratic speech involves what Habermas calls a *performative contradiction* – the act of expressing a radically anti-democratic position is *inconsistent* with the conditions under which such speech acts are possible. On the Habermasian view, then, the "inescapable presuppositions" of discourse (1990: 89) entail a democratic political order; in short, the claim is that, insofar as we communicate, we are implicitly democrats.

The ways in which the folk epistemic view diverges from the Habermasian program can be seen by examining an objection to Habermas. Despite Habermas's appeals to "inescapable presuppositions," anti-democrats, racists, sexists, and tyrants do indeed communicate. Habermas's rejoinder is that anyone who does not adopt the norms of discourse he has identified "voluntarily terminates his membership in the community of beings who argue" (Habermas 1990: 100). However, we should wonder whether this rejoinder has any hope of moving, or even addressing, the anti-democrat. Surely it would be reasonable to expect that, from the anti-democrat's perspective, the very point of his speech is to terminate his membership of the democratic discourse community. How, then, could this count as a *criticism* of the anti-democrat?

Habermas explains further that the voluntary termination is an "empty gesture" unless our anti-democrat is "willing to take refuge in suicide or serious mental illness"; Habermas contends that "as long as [the anti-democrat] is alive at all" complete separation from the community of those who communicate democratically is "inconceivable, even as a thought experiment" (1990: 100). Habermas's point now seems grossly overstated; the claim is that radical anti-democratic politics is literally "inconceivable" by anyone who is not mentally ill or suicidal. If only this were true! The important point is that the discourse-theoretic justification for democracy is addressed in the first instance to those who are already well disposed to democratic politics. That is, Habermas's argument purports to show that, since the legitimacy of democratic norms is guaranteed by communicative practice, the radical anti-democrat – if, indeed, there could be one – is rightly excluded from the antecedently existing "community of beings who argue." But the legitimacy of precisely that community is what the anti-democrat seeks to challenge in the first place. The Habermasian argument seems circular: it justifies democracy only to those who have already accepted membership in a democratic discourse community.

From the folk epistemic perspective, Habermas's position begins in the wrong place. Whereas it might be true, as Habermas alleges, that internal processes of cognition – such as those associated with weighing evidence and drawing inferences – are derived from prior acquaintance with the intersubjective phenomena of social interaction (and I need take no view on this matter), the justification of democracy need not begin with the social phenomena of communication. Unlike the Habermasian argument, the folk epistemic view begins with our individual habits and attitudes regarding our own beliefs, whatever they may be and however they may have arisen, and attempts to show that each of us is motivated, *from our own point of view*, to uphold epistemic norms which in turn entail democratic political norms.

The contrast can be stated in a different way. Whereas the Habermasian view begins from the intersubjective conditions of communication and argues to the subjective commitment to democratic politics, the folk epistemic view begins from the subjective commitment to proper believing and argues to the intersubjective commitment to the kind of social epistemic activity that can be engaged only within a democracy. Habermas's recent discussion of the place of religious reasons in public dialogue helps to flesh this out. Although Habermas proposes a conception of public reason that is broader than Rawls's in that it allows for the admissibility of religious reasons in public debate, he, like Rawls, holds that public religious reasoning must be subjected to certain constraints. Specifically, Habermas holds that religious citizens must seek to "translate" (2006: 13) their religious reasons into secular ones. Accordingly, Habermas adopts a view that is in the end not far removed from Rawls's *proviso* (2005: 462), which was discussed in Chapter 2. In justifying the translation requirement, Habermas argues simply that the requirement *applies to all* citizens, religious and secular alike (2006: 15–16). So the argument again moves from an intersubjective requirement to a subjective commitment.

The folk epistemic approach is superior to the Habermasian model because the description of the intersubjective conditions for communication with which the latter must begin will inevitably be contestable; accordingly, the Habermasian model is subject to the kind of criticism I raised against moral versions of deliberative democracy, namely, that it is "rigged" from the start to favor certain outcomes and preclude others. The folk epistemic approach avoids inviting this kind of charge because it begins from the first-personal epistemic point of view and the self-conception of believers. It asks individuals first to reflect on the epistemic commitments *with regard to their own beliefs*, and then argues that these commitments can be satisfied only within a certain kind of social and political order.

But suppose that someone were to charge that the conception of belief employed by the folk epistemic view was "rigged" to favor democratic politics. There is a compelling reply to be made on behalf of the folk epistemic view. The charge that the view is "rigged" or question-begging can count as an *objection* only if one presupposes the epistemic norm according to which premises of arguments must not simply embed their conclusions. In other words, the very charge that the folk epistemic justification is question-begging or in some other way formally defective must *presuppose* certain norms governing justification. Yet these very norms – norms according to which justificatory reasons must be put forward, evaluated, criticized, and shown to not beg the question – are the norms to which the folk epistemic case primarily appeals. The charge that the folk epistemic justification of democracy begs the question hence *presupposes* a commitment to the folk epistemic norms that have been identified.

Now let us consider a related criticism that attempts to apply the kind of objection I raised against Habermas to the folk epistemic view. One may charge that an implication of the folk epistemic view is that no one holds anti-democratic beliefs, that insofar as one is an anti-democrat, one is not really a believer. So, just as I have criticized Habermas for employing a view according to which communication itself requires that one argue in the way Habermas advocates, a critic could charge me with employing a conception of belief according to which being a believer means inquiring in the way I advocate. Yet it seems obvious that anti-democrats *do* hold beliefs despite the fact that they reject folk epistemology.

In response, I need to flesh out a heretofore implicit distinction between belief *de facto* and *de jure*. That is, the precise view is that *genuine* or *proper* believers must be democratic truth-seekers and that anti-democrats are *specious* believers. The folk epistemic claim, then, is not that no one holds anti-democratic beliefs or that anti-democrats are not believers; rather, the view is that anti-democrats are not – and *cannot* be – *proper* believers. The challenge is to produce an argument in support of this distinction that preserves the implication from folk epistemology to democracy but avoids the circularity found in Habermas's account.

The charge of circularity is defused by noting that the distinction between proper and specious belief derives from epistemic norms that are *internal* to belief – that is, internal to our conception of our own beliefs – rather than imposed from without. To return to points that were emphasized earlier, it is impossible to sustain your wholehearted belief that *p* once you are convinced that you have no reasons or evidence for *p*. This is not to say that it is impossible to believe that *p* and *in fact* have no reasons for *p*; it is rather to say that for any particular belief you hold, *p*, you *assess yourself* as having reasons sufficient for *p*. Epistemic self-deception and failure is very common, but doxastic persistence in the face of recognized – self-assessed – epistemic failure is exceedingly difficult, and in some contexts impossible. Genuine beliefs are those that do not recede when the believer recognizes the way in which they were generated. Thus, the distinction between genuine and specious belief is a distinction between self-aware and deluded epistemic agents. Our claim is that self-aware epistemic agents – agents whose epistemic practice reflects their epistemic commitments – must uphold the epistemic norms that can be practiced and can flourish only within a democratic political framework. Anti-democrats surely hold anti-democratic beliefs, but such believers are deluded about their own implicit epistemic commitments; were their epistemic commitments made explicit to them, they would see that anti-democratic beliefs are inconsistent with their conception of themselves as truth-seekers. In this way, folk epistemology justifies democracy. There is no worry of circularity.

Let us next contrast the folk epistemic view with yet another kind of deliberative democratic theory. Some versions of deliberative democracy are decidedly *epistemic*. Epistemic deliberativisms are to be distinguished from *proceduralist* theories of deliberative democracy. Proceduralist views claim that political legitimacy accrues to a democratic outcome by virtue of the fact that the outcome was produced by a correct procedure. Proceduralist deliberative democrats maintain that only deliberative processes are procedurally correct. But proceduralist deliberativism confronts a difficult problem. Consider the question: what makes a decision procedure procedurally correct? Since proceduralists are democrats, they respond to this question by citing some characteristically democratic value that must be realized if a given procedure is to be procedurally proper. However, as David Estlund (1997) has convincingly argued, any such value can be realized – and perhaps *better* realized – by a non-democratic procedure. For example, let us suppose that *fairness* is the value that the proceduralist identifies as the criterion for proper procedure. The proceduralist argument, then, is that deliberative processes are necessary for fairness and, therefore, political legitimacy requires democratic deliberation. But if fairness is the value a decision procedure must realize if its outcomes are to be politically legitimate, why not make decisions by flipping coins (Estlund 1997: 176)? Coin flipping is the paradigm of fairness; surely it is fairer than any deliberative process. Yet coin flipping is not a particularly *democratic* way to proceed. So, on the proceduralist view, the decidedly *democratic* dimension of political decision-making seems ultimately dispensable. If this same form of argument can be applied to any other conception of the value that a decision procedure must manifest if it is to produce legitimate outcomes, then it seems that proceduralism fails.

Epistemic views, by contrast, hold that political legitimacy is primarily an *epistemic* property. That is, according to epistemic views, the legitimacy of a political decision has to do with its epistemic value. On the strongest version of epistemic deliberativism, political outcomes are legitimate only if they are true. One can find intimations of the strong epistemic view in Rousseau's *On the Social Contract* where he writes:

> When a law is proposed in the assembly of the People, what is asked of them is not precisely whether they approve the proposition or reject it, but whether or not it conforms to the general will which is their own: each in giving his vote states his opinion on that question, and from the counting of votes is taken the declaration of the general will. When the opinion contrary to mine prevails, that only proves that I was mistaken. (IV.ii)

The strong view is obviously non-viable in a large democratic polity, since for any outcome there will be some number of citizens who will reject its truth. On the strong view, citizens who regard a given democratic outcome as incorrect are justified in holding that outcome as illegitimate. Obviously this leads to instability.

Rousseau attempts to deal with this concern by appealing to the concept of the *general will*; on Rousseau's views, once the general will is revealed, it is to be taken as infallible. Hence, as we have seen in the quotation above, Rousseau thinks that once the general will has made its declaration, if one finds oneself in disagreement with it, one must regard oneself as mistaken, and hence change one's belief. But this seems too demanding, and perhaps not psychologically possible, especially in cases where deep and contentious moral issues are at stake. In such cases, people typically take themselves *to have powerful reasons* for thinking that their position is true or correct. For example, take the case of the pro-life advocate. Gaus correctly emphasizes that "To rationally believe that abortion is wrong must be to believe it for good, relevant reasons – *to see why it is wrong*" (2003a: 163) (original emphasis). Now, imagine that a vote was taken concerning the moral permissibility of abortion, and the pro-choice position won a decisive majority. On Rousseau's view, the pro-life advocate must see this as a kind of *proof* that her pro-life position is incorrect.

But it is difficult to see how one could take the results of a vote to be *epistemically* decisive. That a vast majority of people believe that *p* does not seem to constitute a proof of *p*. Of course, that a vast majority of people believe that *p* might, under certain conditions, be *evidence* of the truth of *p*. This is especially clear in cases where we epistemically defer to a relevant community of inquiry, such as when a vast majority of scientists working in the same field converge on a theory, *t*.[7] The important thing in these cases is that the convergence of opinion is not taken to *constitute* the truth of *t*; the convergence simply means that those who have seriously looked into the matter have found that the best reasons support *t*. Accordingly, when we defer in these cases, we do so because we take the convergence as *evidence* in favor of *t*, and we take it that were we to look seriously into the matter ourselves, we, too, would find that the best reasons support *t*.

Now, a citizen might take the outcome of a properly conducted vote to constitute *evidence* of the truth of the outcome. But, in cases like abortion in which deep moral commitments are at stake, it would be difficult to imagine a citizen in the minority taking the outcome as *conclusive evidence* against her view; the outcome would, at best, be taken as a relevant datum to be weighed against other relevant considerations, including the person's moral reasons (which, as we have already said, will in most cases prove overriding). However, Rousseau's view requires citizens to take the outcome to be *decisive*. It requires citizens to *abandon* their own moral reasons – the reasons on the basis of which the pro-life citizen *sees* the immorality of abortion – *simply* because a suitable majority disagrees. As Estlund (1997) and others have pointed out, this seems unacceptable. A citizen should not be required to epistemically defer her judgment to a collective decision; the distinction between outcomes that are *correct* and outcomes that are *legitimate* must be preserved. But Rousseau's view ultimately denies this distinction.

A more modest and viable version of epistemic deliberativism can be found in Estlund's "epistemic proceduralism." On Estlund's view,

---

[7] It also is worth mentioning – but only mentioning – the Condorcet Jury Theorem, which shows that under certain (seemingly) weak conditions, the collective judgment of modestly large deliberating groups is nearly infallible. The literature on this result is vast and the views about its relevance for democratic theory are varied. See, for example, Gaus 1997, List and Goodin 2001, Anderson 2006, Dietrich 2008, and especially Estlund 2008: ch. 12.

democratic outcomes are legitimate if they are produced by an epistemically reliable procedure (1997: 185). In this way, epistemic proceduralism can allow that a particular political outcome may be false and yet legitimate; yet legitimacy is, nonetheless, tied to epistemic value, since it is the epistemic value of the deliberative process that confers legitimacy upon its outcomes.

Epistemic proceduralism confronts the difficulty of showing why *democratic* deliberative procedures are epistemically most reliable. It seems likely that there are other, non-democratic procedures that are epistemically *more* reliable than deliberative democracy. Consider, for example, the epistemic elitism proposed by Mill (1991 [1861]), according to which political influence should be distributed not equally, but according to one's level of epistemic achievement. According to Mill, one who "labors with his head," or is a "graduate of a university" is in general more intelligent than the average citizen, and so is deserving of more political influence. Mill contends that "two or more votes might be allowed to every person who exercises any of these superior functions" (1991 [1861]: 336).

The task for epistemic proceduralism, then, is to find a way to "let truth be the guide without illegitimately privileging the opinions of any putative experts" (Estlund 1997: 183). In order to block the implication from epistemic proceduralism to a pernicious form of epistemic elitism, Estlund appeals to "a general criterion of legitimacy" according to which "the legitimacy of laws is not adequately established unless it can be defended on grounds it would be unreasonable to object to" (1997: 175). Hence, Estlund argues that "sovereignty is not distributed according to moral expertise unless that expertise would be beyond the reasonable objections of individual citizens," so "unless all reasonable citizens actually agreed with the decision of some agreed moral/political guru, no one could legitimately rule on the basis of wisdom" (1997: 183).

But here we must ask: what justifies the principle of legitimacy that Estlund appeals to? Surely, an epistemic elitist – the Plato of the *Republic*, for example – would reject such a principle, and would also reject the idea that it could be reasonable to object to rule by a true moral or political expert. So it seems that Estlund's view is open to the same kind of objection we raised against Gutmann and Thompson's view. At the heart of Estlund's view is the assumption that there is a moral principle of political legitimacy that is beyond reasonable contestation. That is, epistemic proceduralism invited the difficulties that confront the moral views of deliberative democracy we considered above.

The folk epistemic approach avoids this difficulty. It can "let truth be the guide" without thereby inviting epistemic elitism, since it contends that even the would-be Philosopher King or Millian ruling scholar has a reason to *reject* elitism. That is, the folk epistemic view has it that expertise can arise and persist only under the democratic conditions we have specified above. No one is born an expert, and expertise is itself something that must be *maintained*. Accordingly, the epistemic elitist claim that experts should rule is paradoxical. One's status as an expert depends precisely upon the continuing process of open reason-exchange and accountability that epistemic elitism seeks to foreclose.

Before proceeding, it should be emphasized that Estlund's epistemic proceduralism is addressed to a different question from the one we have been considering. Estlund aims to provide a theory of democratic *authority*, a theory of the moral bindingness of certain collective decisions, an account of why democratic citizens must obey properly produced outcomes even when they disagree with them. The folk epistemic view we have been developing is aimed at showing that, despite our deep moral differences, we each have a reason – importantly, the *same* reason – for upholding democratic commitments even in the light of democratic outcomes that strike us as morally unacceptable. Consequently, the folk epistemic view does not address the source of the legitimacy of particular democratic outcomes; there must be an account of why democrats who find themselves in the minority with regard to some specific democratic decision have an obligation to obey.

The folk epistemic view and Estlund's epistemic proceduralism are complementary. As we have seen, epistemic proceduralism raises the specter of rule by Philosopher Kings, what Estlund calls "epistocracy" (1997: 183). Epistemic proceduralism blocks this implication by adopting the moral premise that "citizens cannot be expected or assumed (much less encouraged or forced) to surrender their moral judgment" (1997: 183). The folk epistemic view provides an epistemic defense of this principle: the commitments that are internal to our folk epistemic practices compel us to take up the project of justifying ourselves to others and to regard others as fellow epistemic agents.

Having contrasted the folk epistemic view with the dominant styles of deliberative democracy, we are now able to characterize the conception of democracy entailed by the folk epistemic view. I have already noted that the folk epistemic view shares with the deliberativists the rejection of the aggregative or strictly proceduralist conception of democracy. With the deliberativists, the folk epistemic view holds that democratic legitimacy is tied to processes of public deliberation. Moreover, the folk epistemic view agrees with the epistemic deliberativists that it is the *epistemic* features of deliberation that matter for legitimacy. However, the folk epistemic view is skeptical of the more ambitious institutional proposals associated with deliberative democracy. For example, folk epistemology does not commit us to the view that proper democracy requires the creation of a new national holiday devoted to public deliberation (Ackerman and Fishkin 2004), or the staging of special "deliberative polling" (Fishkin 1993) events, or "citizen juries" (Gastil 2000). Similarly, the folk epistemic view resists the idea that democracies need to establish, by way of a constitutional amendment, a new "popular branch" of government devoted to deliberation (Leib 2004).

Of course, not all deliberative democrats endorse such drastic revisions of current democratic institutions. However, there does exist among most deliberative democrats a general tendency to reduce all properly democratic behavior to public deliberative behavior, to see public deliberation as the core democratic activity. And it is this commitment that encourages the more extravagant deliberativist institutional proposals. In this way, the folk epistemic view shares with Michael Walzer (2004) the general suspicion that deliberative democrats tend to exaggerate the role of public deliberation in democratic politics. Just as the market is not an apt model for the whole of democracy, neither is the jury. As Walzer recognizes, public deliberation does have "an important place" in democratic politics, but it does not have an "independent place"; that is, public deliberation does not enjoy a privileged place in the political economy of democracy that renders it the most basic kind of civic activity (2004: 106). There are other kinds of activity whose value does not derive primarily from the value of public deliberation, such as campaigning, educating, protesting, petitioning, fund-raising, and the like.

The folk epistemic conception of democracy shares with traditional non-deliberativist conceptions the view that the familiar institutions of democracy – voting in regular elections, representative bodies, and such – are sufficient for legitimacy. Rather than calling for a radical restructuring of existing democratic institutions, the folk epistemic conception calls for a more engaged and epistemically responsible democratic culture. The idea is that many of contemporary democracy's problems can be addressed and corrected by a reasoning citizenry. But the task of creating a reasoning citizenry cannot be accomplished by constitutional amendments and national holidays. If it is to be accomplished, there must be a change in the way citizens regard their disagreements and those with whom they disagree. The folk epistemic conception of democracy, then, is addressed primarily to the issue of motivating citizens to pursue a "culture of argument" (Walzer 2004: 107) and a "republic of reasons" (Sunstein 2001b: 239).

In this way, the folk epistemic conception of democracy works at a level that is analytically prior to that at which the deliberativists are working. On the folk epistemic view, the question of what policy and institutional arrangements best reflect and enable our democratic aspirations is one that can be settled only by democratic processes of reasoning and argument. As the view is aimed at making explicit the motivation each of us has to engage in dialogue across deep disagreements, we may call it, if it must have a name, *dialogical democracy*.

II FOLK EPISTEMOLOGY AND THE PROBLEM OF DEEP POLITICS

Now it is time to begin to evaluate the folk epistemic approach and the dialogical conception of democracy that it entails in light of the problem of deep politics. I will begin by considering a potentially serious objection to the effect that the folk epistemic approach is irrelevant to the problem of deep politics. With this objection defused, I will then consider the question of whether dialogical democracy can duly accommodate Rawlsian intuitions about reasonable pluralism. After showing that it can, I shall be in a position to state directly the folk epistemic solution to the problem of deep politics.

An objection: truth-seeking vs. truth-possessing

A critic might argue that the folk epistemic justification of democracy is unable to address the problem of deep politics due to the simple fact that dialogical democracy can be appealing only to those who take themselves to be truth-*seekers* rather than truth-*possessors*. The critic will argue that the problem of deep politics is *not* the problem of getting reasonable and open-minded inquirers to agree to be democrats; rather, it is the problem of getting morally and religiously *committed* individuals to take up democratic citizenship.[8] Were it the case that individuals deeply committed to their moral and religious doctrines were also likely to identify with the fallibilist and inquisitive spirit of folk epistemology, there would be no problem of deep politics in the first place. But, in fact, many citizens will say that folk epistemology is *incompatible* with their deepest religious or moral

---

[8] The criticism about to be developed resembles the arguments advanced by the plaintiffs in *Mozert* v. *Hawkins* to the effect that, in promoting critical thinking, the public school curriculum is incompatible with certain forms of religious commitment. The *Mozert* case will be discussed in Chapter 5.

convictions; according to many such doctrines, to admit that the doctrine could be wrong, or that it stands in need of justification, or that it could be improved upon, or even that one is in a position to evaluate such matters, is to concede that the truth of the doctrine is *negotiable* and thus to *betray* the doctrine.[9] So, the critic concludes, the folk epistemic approach is entirely beside the point: since most people regard their moral and religious commitments as *known to be true*, they *reject* the idea that their deep commitments need to be examined or debated any further. For such citizens, those who do not share their moral or religious view are *at best* tolerable; those with whom they profoundly disagree are certainly not epistemic peers or partners in any meaningful sense. Consequently, the problem of deep politics stands.

The challenge that this objection poses is to provide a motivation for those *convinced* of the final truth of their current moral and religious commitments to endorse a politics based on democratic processes of reason-exchange. To phrase the challenge directly: what good is a politics of truth-seeking to someone who already *knows* the truth?

The objection can be met by noting first that the claim to know the final truth of morality or religion is *consistent* with the thought that there are many matters about which one must inquire if one is to do the right thing. On any moral or religious view, doing the right thing requires *to some degree* that one should have true beliefs about mundane, but nonetheless complex, factual matters regarding the world we inhabit and the specific circumstances under which one is acting. For example, suppose that I am deeply committed to the view that euthanasia is always wrong. Suppose further that I take my reasons to be wholly conclusive and beyond revision, and for that reason see no point in engaging the issue with those who do not share my view. Moreover, suppose that I am *correct* both about euthanasia and about the strength of my reasons. It does *not* follow from these suppositions that I have no need of a political system designed to enable proper epistemic agency. My knowledge of the truth that *euthanasia is always wrong* does not *by itself* enable me to decide what cases count as cases of euthanasia. In order to know whether a particular case of killing is a case of euthanasia, I must assess a wide array of biological and neurological data. Furthermore, even if cases of euthanasia could be reliably detected, I must still confront the *moral* question of what is morally *permissible* in a wide array of cases involving

---

[9] *Cf.* Ian Shapiro's criticism of the deliberativist view of Amy Gutmann and Dennis Thompson: "The Gutmann–Thompson model works only for those fundamentalists who also count themselves fallibilist democrats. That, I fear, is an empty class, destined to remain uninhabited" (2003: 26).

patients in permanent vegetative states and various forms of untreatable chronic, debilitating illness. The knowledge that euthanasia is morally impermissible does not put all the moral questions to rest; one *still* needs to address the question of what is to be done.

It seems, then, that on any viable moral doctrine, religious or otherwise, right action will require a proper assessment of *both* the moral and non-moral data relevant to one's action. In other words, on any viable moral doctrine, even if one *knows* what is good and right, one must nevertheless *deliberate* about what action is morally required under a given set of circumstances. And this deliberation, if it is to be responsible, must be *informed* by accurate assessments of the relevant moral and non-moral facts of the given case.

I take it that this much is obvious. I next note that each of us is unavoidably dependent on others for many of our beliefs.[10] That is, when forming our own beliefs, we invariably rely to some extent, frequently large, on the testimony, argument, expertise, experiences, and observations of others. No man is an epistemic island. In fact, one may go further and claim that not only do we rely on others in forming our own beliefs, our general collection of epistemic habits are socially derived. That is, our sense of who the relevant epistemic authorities are, how and when they are to be consulted, to what degree we should defer to them, and when – if ever – they are to be distrusted is a product of our social upbringing. So, too, is the stock of our normative commitments. That one is a Christian rather than a Buddhist, for example, often owes much to one's cultural upbringing. To be clear, this last point is not a nod in the direction of cultural relativism. To say that the causal story about how one comes to hold that *p* is inevitably a social story is *not* to say that the story about *p*'s truth is inevitably a story about what is socially accepted. The general point is rather the simple descriptive one that we are epistemically subject to and dependent upon a range of social influences; our more specific point is that as epistemic agents we are invariably dependent upon others.

Our epistemic dependence is unavoidable because each individual has limited cognitive resources. Individually, we simply cannot inquire into every matter that is relevant to our beliefs; we must at some point rely on the epistemic capabilities of others, we must *defer*. This deference is in itself not a bad thing; great stores of knowledge and information that could not be produced by a single person are available to us precisely because of the

---

[10] The argument of the next several paragraphs builds on an illuminating discussion by Allen Buchanan (2004).

division of epistemic labor that epistemic dependence necessitates. But note that the division of epistemic labor upon which I rely is part of a complex system of epistemic dependence in that the epistemic authorities to which I defer themselves rely upon others for their expertise, and so on. Thus, we can say that we are epistemically dependent not only on the few others upon whom we immediately rely; rather, each of us epistemically depends on an entire *social epistemic system*. So, to return to our example, when I judge of a particular case that it is an instance of euthanasia, I am at least implicitly relying upon a complex epistemic network in which the work of various inquirers is coordinated. For instance, I am at the very least dependent on several medical professionals to report the relevant facts of the case at hand. In so doing, I place my trust in the institutions that trained them and the research that informs their practice. If I am unable to communicate with the medical experts directly, I count on various intermediaries – news media, for example – to report their findings. Without information of this sort, I cannot make a responsible moral judgment regarding the case at hand.

More important than the bare fact of epistemic dependence is the fact that it behooves us to have access to a social epistemic system that is epistemically *reliable*. Although epistemic dependence is unavoidable and not necessarily a bad thing, it inevitably involves certain serious risks, for we may grow to depend upon *unreliable* epistemic sources, or we may defer to the *wrong* epistemic authority in a given case. When forming a judgment about a given case that is potentially a case of euthanasia, I must rely on others to *accurately* report the relevant facts. If I am to do the right thing, as specified by whatever moral doctrine I may hold, I must get the *truth* about certain factual matters. For example, in our euthanasia case, I must be able to reasonably expect that the medical professionals are *accurately* reporting the facts about, say, the patient's brain activity. If I am *misinformed* about such facts, I am unlikely to form the correct judgment and, therefore, unlikely to do the right thing.

Consequently, even if I am absolutely certain about the truth of my moral doctrine, it is nonetheless necessary to my success as a moral agent to have access to a social epistemic system that is *reliable* and not corrupt. Now let us press the question: what conditions are necessary if there is to be a reliable and stable social epistemic system? I contend that a reliable system of social epistemology can exist and persist only within the kind of democratic political context that we have outlined above. To be more specific, in order for a reliable social epistemic system to exist and persist, there must be institutions and norms that enable the open exchange of reasons, arguments, and information. Additionally, individuals must enjoy freedom of thought and expression, and must be protected in cases in which their reasons lead them to adopt unorthodox, heretical, or unpopular views. This in turn suggests the kind of epistemic egalitarianism discussed above, according to which there are no authorities beyond question, no fixed epistemic hierarchies, and no expertise except that which comes from the ability to demonstrate the strength of one's reasons. That is to say, a reliable social epistemic system can exist only under democratic political conditions.

Hence, we have arrived at a response to the objection. Despite the ways in which citizens are otherwise deeply divided, all can be expected to countenance the fact of epistemic dependence, and will recognize that a well-functioning and reliable social epistemic system is necessary for proper moral judgment. Such a system can exist and flourish only under democratic political conditions. Thus, even those who take their own moral doctrines to be beyond revision and not in need of examination or justification have reason to endorse the kind of democratic politics entailed by folk epistemology.

A proponent of the kind of objection we have been considering could reply as follows: surely one can accept the need for a reliable social epistemic system in order to establish and assess the non-moral facts in particular cases that call for moral judgment, and surely one can accept the claim that such a system requires a broadly democratic set of political conditions. However, one may yet deny that the folk epistemic practice of open reason-exchange should apply to one's deepest *moral* or *religious* commitments. In fact, the lesson one should draw from the response to the original objection is that one should seek democratic society only with those who share one's deep commitments. Thus, our critic concludes, the problem of deep politics remains.

I begin by granting the terms of the criticism. Consider, then, that you believe some moral or religious proposition p, and let us stipulate not only that p is true, but also that you *know* that p. The folk epistemic view prescribes a politics according to which you must, despite your knowledge that p, keep open the channels of reason-exchange and criticism regarding p. The objection under consideration challenges the folk epistemologist to motivate this commitment. By way of response, recall the discussion in Chapter 2 of the phenomenon of group polarization. The data show that when doxastically homogenous groups deliberate, each member comes to hold a more extreme version of the belief she held prior to discussion. Thus, if you hold that p, but insulate p from critical discussion, you are likely to lose the belief that p and adopt some more extreme relative of p. That is, a politics based upon the idea that we must all agree to some moral truth, p, which then attempts to secure this agreement by prohibiting critical discussion of *p* actually *obstructs* the goal of believing the truth. Under such conditions, we will gradually drift away from the belief that *p* and adopt some more extreme relative, say, *p'*; however, *ex hypothesi*, *p'* is not true. Accordingly, the lesson of the group polarization phenomenon is that true beliefs, *qua* beliefs, must be *maintained*. This maintenance is achieved by keeping the logical space of giving reasons open to those with whom we disagree. It seems, then, that Mill was correct: truth needs contestation.

Thus, the thought driving the criticism we have been considering is deeply mistaken. Recall that the critic suggested that those who *know* the truth have no need for a politics that allows for contestation of that truth. In light of the group polarization phenomenon, however, we now see that the critic has matters exactly backwards. It is precisely for the sake of the *truth* of our deepest commitments that we must remain open to the kind of epistemological engagement that is possible only within a democratic political order. Put another way, by engaging in democratic processes of reason-exchange, we express our commitment to the truth of our beliefs. The more deeply one is committed to *p*, and the more one regards the truth of *p* to be a matter of importance, the more ready one should be to engage others.

Freestandingness and reasonable pluralism

Thus far I have argued that, despite the many respects in which we are deeply divided, there is a set of epistemic considerations that we share which can compel each of us to endorse a democratic politics. It is important to note at this point that the kind of justification for democracy that has been offered is precisely what contemporary theorists influenced by the later work of John Rawls insist is not available to the democratic theorist. As we saw early in Chapter 2, the Rawlsian account has it that any attempt to provide a substantive justification of democratic politics – that is, a justification that is not "freestanding" but "comprehensive" (2005: 145ff.) – will fail to accommodate adequately the fact of reasonable pluralism. As reasonable pluralism is taken by Rawls to be a "permanent feature" of any free society (2005: 36), the attempt to justify democracy by way of a substantive philosophical doctrine is at odds with the very idea of a free society. Hence, Rawls claims that "a continuing shared understanding on one comprehensive doctrine can be maintained only by the oppressive use of state power" (2005: 37). On the Rawlsian picture, justification consists in developing a freestanding conception of our democratic commitments that can be the focus of an overlapping consensus among reasonable citizens.

The folk epistemic conception is not freestanding for at least two reasons. First, a freestanding justification is addressed to individuals in their capacity as citizens of a liberal-democratic political order; that is, as Rawls says, political justification starts "within the tradition of democratic thought" (2005: 18) and presumes only a "political conception of the person" (2005: 29). The folk epistemic approach, by contrast, addresses political justification to each of us in our capacity as epistemic agents, as cognitive beings who hold beliefs. It does not, therefore, begin from the concept of the citizen that derives from within the tradition of democratic thought. Second, a freestanding justification understands political agreement on the model of an overlapping consensus. That is, when political justification is successful, each person endorses the political conception for reasons drawn from *his own* comprehensive doctrine; accordingly, where a political conception is endorsed as an overlapping consensus, individuals agree to endorse the conception but do not agree about the *reasons* why that conception should be endorsed. By contrast, the folk epistemic justification attempts to show not only that we all have reason to endorse a democratic political order, but that we all have the *same* reason to do so, namely, that democracy is the political manifestation of our epistemic commitments.

Given that the folk epistemic justification is not freestanding, the Rawlsian is committed to the claim that our view is unable to duly acknowledge reasonable pluralism. Let us see whether this is so.

To begin, let us consider what makes the fact of reasonable pluralism *worth* accommodating in our political theorizing. Rawls himself points in a direction that is consonant with the folk epistemic approach. Rawls acknowledged that it is not the "fact of pluralism as such" that is worth accommodating, but the fact that there is a plurality of distinct and conflicting doctrines that are *reasonable* (2005: 36).[11] Rawls explains this plurality of reasonable doctrines by appealing to a catalogue of the "many hazards involved in the correct (and conscientious) exercise of our powers of reason and judgment" (2005: 56), which he collectively refers to as "the burdens of judgment" (2005: 54). Rawls provides an incomplete list of the burdens which obstruct deep moral consensus among reasonable persons (2005: 56–57), which we can follow Larmore (1996: 170) in paraphrasing as follows:

---

[11] Thus, the requirement of recognizing the fact of reasonable pluralism is not an instance of a more general imperative to recognize the liberty, autonomy, or equality of *persons* more generally. On Rawls's view, some persons (i.e., the unreasonable ones) may be legitimately coerced, and some doctrines (i.e., the unreasonable ones) may be legitimately suppressed (2005: xvi, 64 n. 19).

(1) the empirical evidence may be conflicting and complex;
(2) agreement about the kind of considerations involved does not guaran-
     tee agreement about their weight;
(3) key concepts may be vague and subject to hard cases;
(4) our total experience, which shapes how we assess the evidence and
     weigh values, is likely in complex modern societies to be rather disparate
     from person to person;
(5) different kinds of normative considerations may be involved on both
     sides of a question; and
(6) being forced to select among cherished values, we face great difficulties
     in setting priorities.[12]

These burdens account for the fact that, although reasonable persons "share
a common human reason" and have "similar powers of thought and judgment" (Rawls 2005: 55) they may, nonetheless, come to hold conflicting and
irreconcilable moral views.

Now let us draw out a further point that Rawls does not address. The
burdens of judgment not only explain why otherwise intelligent and
rational persons disagree with us; there is in addition a self-reflexive component to the recognition of these burdens. By appealing to the burdens of
judgment as an explanation for why others disagree with us, we come to see
that we too are subject to those same burdens. It is important to note that to
admit that the burdens of judgment apply in one's own case is *not* to
succumb to skepticism or relativism. The burdens of judgment entail
only that we recognize that getting moral matters right is a complex and
difficult business, perhaps a Herculean – but not necessarily impossible –
task that requires a considerable degree of exactness and sophistication.

Accordingly, recognition of the burdens of judgment compels each of us
to acknowledge that there is a plurality of *philosophically respectable* positions
in moral theory, an abundance of *live options*[13] for reasonable persons at the
level of comprehensive doctrines. Thus, one can recognize that the utilitarian's position is *reasonable* even if one denies its *truth*; similarly, one can

---

[12] Compare Stephen Mulhall and Adam Swift's encapsulation:

[With regard to any particular moral judgment,] the evidence bearing on the case is complex and
conflicting; the weight to be attached to any given piece of evidence is contestable; our concepts are
vague and subject to hard cases; and our judgments are imponderably but decisively influenced by the
whole course of our moral experience. (1996: 177)

[13] I here appropriate a term introduced by William James in his "The Will to Believe" (1977: 717). James
used the term in a *subjective* sense: the liveness of a proposition has to do with the subjective feeling
that it could be true. I here use the term to denote what I think of as an *objective* sense: the liveness of a
proposition need not involve one's own feeling that it could be true, but only that it is understandable
how another rational person doing his epistemic best may believe it.

hold that the utilitarian is *mistaken* without judging that she is *stupid, ignorant,* or *irrational.* More generally, when we acknowledge the burdens of judgment, we come to see that competing reasonable doctrines are structured in an intellectually respectable way – we come to understand the set of premises from which they begin and the moral intuitions they most wish to accommodate – and so we can describe the ways in which competing views differ from our own in a way that proponents of those competing views can accept, or at least we can sincerely try to do this.

The point is that when we engage in serious moral reflection, we quickly discover that there is a plurality of philosophically respectable, well-developed perspectives on offer. And we discover that for each of these positions, there can be found an intelligent, sincere, and responsible proponent who is able to provide powerful reasons and arguments in favor of his position. The evaluation of the arguments and reasons offered by competing moral doctrines is a difficult project, and there is good reason to think that there should be more than one reasonable and responsible way to judge such matters. In this way, serious moral reflection leads us to the view that was characterized earlier as moral pluralism. To be sure, let me stress again that this is not to say that moral reflection leads to moral skepticism. The moral pluralist claims that, since it is extremely difficult to get the most important matters correct, there are several reasonable and defensible moral theories. This thesis is manifestly *consistent* with the view that only one such theory is, ultimately, correct. Moreover, moral pluralism is consistent with the view that one's own position is, indeed, the correct one. What moral pluralism precludes is the view that all who disagree with one's own moral position are *ipso facto* irrational, irresponsible, benighted, wicked, or in some other way intellectually inept or defective. Of course, some of your moral opponents *may* be irresponsible and evil, but it is not *by virtue* of the simple fact that they disagree with you that they are so. The judgment that someone is irrational, naïve, or wicked has to do with the character of his positive commitments rather than with the fact that his commitments are not yours.

Once we recognize that at least some of those with whom we disagree fundamentally are reasonable, responsible, and sincere epistemic agents, we are led to the view that these others must be making some kind of mistake. However, we are also led to recognize that, insofar as they are *reasonable*, our opponents' mistakes could be identified and corrected, at least in principle. Hence, if we are committed to the truth of our moral doctrines, we are committed to the view that reasonable dissenters from the moral truth are in need of *instruction*, not *persecution*.

Let us pause to recapitulate the argument thus far: proper regard for the truth leads us to recognize that there is a plurality of defensible moral positions. This in turn leads us to see many of those with whom we deeply disagree as reasonable and sincere participants in the common moral task of trying to do the right thing despite the many hazards and obstacles this task involves. Thus, the recognition of reasonable pluralism carries with it the recognition of those with whom we reasonably disagree as subject to the same epistemic norms that we take ourselves to uphold. That is, a proper recognition of the fact of reasonable pluralism not only involves respecting the plurality of live options in moral theory among reasonable persons, it also calls us to engage our differences.

It is precisely because the project of reason-exchange constantly brings into view the rationality of those with whom we disagree that we come to respect and non-repressively tolerate deep differences. Put otherwise, it is in the processes of exchanging arguments, voicing criticisms, and responding to objections that we come to see each other as reasoning and reasonable agents. By contrast, as I argued in Chapter 2, where processes of reason-exchange are *disengaged*, straw-men, as well as other, more pernicious distortions, thrive. From this, it follows that only when our implicit shared commitment to folk epistemology is made explicit are we able to properly recognize the fact of reasonable pluralism.

There is no doubt that this will strike the Rawlsian as a most surprising conclusion. To repeat, the core premise of Rawls's freestanding approach is that comprehensive democratic theory is incompatible with the fact of reasonable pluralism. But the premise holds only if we think of comprehensive doctrines as *essentially* moral doctrines. However, as I have argued, there is a philosophically substantive *epistemic* doctrine that can serve as the basis for democratic justification. As I have argued above, although the folk epistemic justification is not freestanding, it nonetheless does not run afoul of moral pluralism: the folk epistemic doctrine is consistent with a wide range of reasonable comprehensive doctrines, perhaps the full range. To see this, consider that adherents of the comprehensive doctrines that Rawls himself discusses as paradigmatically reasonable – utilitarianism, Kantianism, familiar religious doctrines, and various other conceptions (2005, 145) – will generally agree that in order to get moral matters right, we need to be able to exchange reasons, criticize each other's and our own judgments, gather information, and so on. Consequently, otherwise opposed but reasonable parties can agree that it morally pays to live under a social order in which it is possible to engage in proper epistemic practice. We have argued that proper epistemic practice can be exercised only under democratic political conditions.

And so we have developed a non-freestanding justification for democratic politics that can duly accommodate the fact of reasonable pluralism.

The problem of deep politics resolved

At last I am able to draw together the considerations developed in the previous two sections and state directly the folk epistemic response to the problem of deep politics. We have seen that the dominant strategy for addressing the problem of deep politics consists in trying to erect a wall of separation between our shared political lives as citizens and our supposedly personal or private moral and religious commitments. As I argued in Chapter 2, this strategy must fail because the very idea that politics is separable from our deepest commitments is one of the matters about which we are profoundly divided. Another matter about which we deeply disagree is where the wall of separation, if indeed there must be one, should be erected. Any proposed boundary between the political and the non-political will be contested. Hence, such responses to the problem of deep politics simply reinstate the problem.

The point to keep in mind is that such deep divisions exist because of the commitment to truth that we share in common. We experience disagreement over fundamental matters of religion and morality as *conflicts* because we are implicitly committed to the idea that our own commitments are *true*. Since we take our own commitments to be true, we hold that doctrines that are inconsistent with our own are *false* and stand in need of correction. Hence, at the heart of the problem of deep politics is the shared commitment to truth. Were it not for our commitment to the truth of our beliefs, there would be no problem of deep politics, for there would be nothing that would count as *disagreement*. Indeed, under such conditions, there would be no politics at all.

The problem of deep politics arises precisely because we are deeply committed not simply to our moral and religious doctrines, but to their *truth*. I have argued that the commitment to the *truth* of a belief compels us to engage in certain epistemic activities that can exist and thrive only within a democratic political context. Moreover, I have argued that the exercise of proper epistemic agency leads us to discover the fact that there are several live options in moral and religious philosophy, a plurality of reasonable doctrines regarding the "Big Questions" of life. From this, it follows that at least some of those with whom we deeply disagree are reasonable and intelligent epistemic agents doing their epistemic best. In light of such *reasonable* disagreement, it would be *unreasonable* to attempt to quell debate or to *impose* a single doctrine upon all; the proper response is to keep open the channels by which reasoned debate can continue. Hence, the strength of our commitment to our moral and religious doctrines should be *directly* proportionate to the strength of our commitment to democratic politics. Accordingly, democracy does not stand in need of a solution to the problem of deep politics; democracy, understood dialogically as that mode of political organization designed to preserve and enable proper epistemic practice *is the solution.*

Towards a politics of engagement

According to the view I have been developing, a proper commitment to the truth of our own beliefs requires us to keep before us the manifest reasonableness of those with whom we deeply disagree. This in turn requires that we open ourselves up to *engagement* across the deep differences which divide us. And such engagement is possible only because we are already implicitly committed to folk epistemic principles that specify proper norms of belief, assertion, dialogue, and argumentation. Hence, we see that the politics of omission has matters exactly backwards. It is not by omitting or bracketing off our deep disagreements that we respect the fact of reasonable pluralism and recognize the reasonableness of those with whom we disagree; rather, reasonable pluralism calls us to practice a *politics of engagement*.

In this way, the dialogical conception of democracy leads us back to Jeffrey Stout's model of immanent criticism, which was criticized in Chapter 2. Recall that Stout's approach to the problem of deep politics involves the premise that democratic citizens divided at the level of basic moral and religious commitments already share in the common moral tradition that is democracy itself. The democratic moral tradition prescribes a mode of public dialogue that rejects Rawlsian *ex ante* omissions, proposing instead that citizens engage in what Stout calls immanent criticism or "conversation" (2004: 10). Stating the nub of problem of deep politics in its decidedly religious manifestation, Stout (2004: 10) writes:

It is true that the expression of religious premises sometimes leads to discursive impasse in political debate. But there are many important issues that cannot be resolved solely on the basis of arguments from commonly held premises. So if we are going to address those issues meaningfully, we had better find a way to work around the impasses when they arise.

He continues:

One name for the way I propose is conversation. By this I mean an exchange of views in which the respective parties express their premises in as much detail as they see fit and in whatever idiom they wish, try to make sense of each other's perspectives, and expose their own commitments to the possibility of criticism. (2004: 10–11)

Stout recommends this conversational mode because:

It is precisely when we find ourselves in an impasse … that it becomes most advisable for citizens representing various points of view to express their actual reasons in greater detail. For this is the only way we can pursue the objectives of understanding one another's perspectives, learning from one another through open-minded listening, and subjecting each other's premises to fair-minded immanent criticism. (2004: 90)

I have already argued that Stout's presumption that democratic citizens already share the above "objectives" of understanding and learning from each other's "perspectives" begs the question of the problem of deep politics. If citizens were already disposed to regard the views of those with whom they deeply disagree as "perspectives" from which one could learn, rather than perversions that can only corrupt or exhibit wickedness, there would be no problem of deep politics. Again, the problem facing Stout is that he offers no reason why deeply divided citizens should adopt this open-minded attitude toward each other, except to say that as democratic citizens they are already committed to such inclusive and experimental conversational norms.

The same kind of difficulty plagues an otherwise powerful proposal by Christopher Eberle (2002). Like Stout, Eberle rejects the politics of omission and promotes an "ideal of conscientious engagement" (2002: 104). According to Eberle, a citizen meets all the requirements of responsible democratic citizenship when she offers her reasons to her fellow citizens in a way that satisfies the following six principles:

(1) she will pursue a high degree of rational justification[14] for the claim that a favored coercive policy is morally appropriate;
(2) she will withhold support from a given coercive policy if she cannot acquire a sufficiently high degree of rational justification for the claim that that policy is morally appropriate;
(3) she will attempt to communicate to her compatriots her reasons for coercing them;
(4) she will pursue public justification for her favored coercive policies;

---

[14] As Eberle uses the term, rational justification is a "radically *perspectival* phenomenon" in that "whether a citizen is rationally justified in adhering to [some belief] B depends, at least in part, on his point of view – on the evidence to which he has access by pursuing the appropriate procedures, on the assumptions with which he conducts his inquiry, and so on" (2002: 62) (original emphasis).

(5) she will listen to her compatriots' evaluation of her reasons for her favored coercive policies with the intention of learning from them about the moral (im)propriety of those policies; and

(6) she will not support any policy on the basis of a rationale that denies the dignity of her compatriots. (2002: 105)

Roughly, then, Eberle's view is that democratic citizens owe to each other the *attempt* to provide Rawlsian public reasons, but may nonetheless persist in advocating policy that cannot be defended on such a basis provided that their non-public reasons meet certain broad standards and have been offered in a spirit that invites critical evaluation from fellow citizens. But, like Stout, Eberle offers no *reasons why* citizens should adopt the model of conscientious engagement. Why, for example, should religiously committed citizens endorse Eberle's fifth principle, which, as Eberle contends, requires that religious citizens adopt a "fallibilist" attitude toward their political commitments (2002: 102)? The question is especially pertinent when it is recognized that such an attitude calls on religious believers to "be willing to learn" (2002: 102) from their fellow citizens, even citizens who explicitly reject their religious views. Why shouldn't a religiously committed citizen see those who reject her religious view simply as fallen, failed, and irrational?

Hence, Stout and Eberle both call for democratic engagement across deep moral divides as a response to the problem of deep politics. But they cannot *justify* the call. Neither can offer reasons why citizens must engage in this way. The folk epistemic approach supplies the justification. Citizens are compelled to democratically engage their deep differences by their own *epistemic* commitments. That is, on the folk epistemic view, citizens must engage their differences, not because they are already committed to a shared democratic morality that prescribes mutual engagement, but rather because they are committed to the truth of their beliefs. So, Stout's conception of the "objectives" of paradigmatically democratic citizens as "understanding one another's perspectives, learning from one another through open-minded listening, and subjecting each other's premises to fair-minded immanent criticism" (2004: 90) is on our view given a decidedly epistemic gloss. Our paradigmatic objective is having true beliefs, and in order to pursue the truth properly, we must allow our own beliefs to be scrutinized and criticized by those with whom we disagree. Thus, to refuse to engage in this way is not simply to violate the norms of a traditional democratic ethos to which we are supposedly committed, it is to violate the very epistemic norms that account for the depth of our moral and religious commitments. It is, in a sense, to *disrespect* that which we profess to take most seriously and that which we demand that others respect.

Importantly, this thought leads us to acknowledge the truth in the Rawlsian position as well. Our dialogical model shares with the Rawlsian, Stoutian, and Eberlean views the idea that democratic arrangements call for citizen participation in political decision-making, and that one of the central modes of citizen participation is public discourse. However, democratic polities must make political *decisions*; they must act, make laws, institute policies, distribute goods and burdens, educate children, care for the infirm, and so on. Rawls's critics are correct to object to the politics of omission on the grounds that many of the most pressing issues about which democracies must decide policy are too morally rich and complex to be treated within the confines of public reason (Reidy 2000). However, the sentiment that in large part drives the Rawlsian program is sound as well. Democratic politics cannot proceed from a settled consensus on a comprehensive moral doctrine because no such consensus is likely to exist among free and reasonable persons. Pressing questions of policy cannot wait for a consensus on the answers to the "Big Questions" of the universe. The Rawlsian contention is that unless we employ a strategy of avoidance, democracy will be at best paralyzed and at worst dissolved altogether. The Rawlsian call for a mode of political decision-making that in public debate countenances only those premises that can be reasonably expected to be acceptable by all democratic citizens follows.

When read as an *appeal* to democratic citizens to put aside their deepest differences and seek common ground when articulating their proposals for political decisions on fundamental issues rather than as a *stipulation* of the content of that common ground, the Rawlsian public reason model seems much more palatable. What this means in practice is that omission is taken as a merely *pragmatic* requirement of dialogical democratic politics. To explain: each of us is committed to the truth of our comprehensive doctrine, but we find by dialogically engaging with others that our best arguments and reasons do not move all of those who disagree; moreover, we find that those who hold beliefs that run counter to our own can formulate good responses to our best criticisms. As I argued above, the conclusion to draw is not the skeptical or relativist one that no doctrine is true, but rather the modest view that *some*, perhaps many, of those who disagree with our most fundamental moral or religious commitments are sincere, intelligent, and reason-responsive. But to see those with whom one disagrees in this way is to admit that, given further opportunity to argue and reason together, they can be *convinced* of the truth of one's own doctrine. However, again, it is often the case that democratic decisions simply cannot wait until all the relevant arguments have been aired. Democracies must decide *despite* the lack of consensus on fundamental matters.

Given this, the dialogical view of democracy that I have been developing recognizes that under certain circumstances, one should recognize the kind of conversational restraints that the Rawlsians propose. Yet this call for omission differs importantly from the Rawlsian model. For one thing, our dialogical view attempts to show that each of us has a reason to *self-impose* conversational restraints. That is, the motive for self-imposed omission is *not* the Rawlsian one of securing political stability by inoculating politics against deep moral and religious conflict. On the contrary, our view contends that one should omit reference to controversial premises in order to facilitate democratic decision and *so that* argument over fundamental value commitments can continue in the future. In this way, the omission of controversial premises and the correlative appeal to common ground falls out of our commitment to the truth of our most deeply held beliefs. It is by omitting reference to controversial premises that we preserve democracy and thereby secure the conditions under which proper epistemic practice can continue.

Consequently, although the dialogical view does indeed call for acts of discursive restraint, it is not a full-blown *politics of omission* because it rejects the idea that proper politics is *necessarily* conducted in the absence of reference to deep commitments. Moreover, the folk epistemic view rejects the idea that omission is a final or all-or-nothing affair. The view holds that the questions of when to omit certain premises and what premises are controversial enough to warrant omission are continually *open* questions; the line between the admissible and the inadmissible is not fixed but *negotiable*. In this way, dialogical omission is not part of a policy of non-entanglement or avoidance, but a pragmatic requirement for a politics of engagement.

III CONCLUSION

If the foregoing arguments go through, the problem of deep politics is resolved: citizens have compelling reasons rooted in the folk epistemic commitments they already endorse to support a democratic political order, even in light of the fact that doing so preserves the possibility that their core moral values might fail to win expression in political policy and law. In addition, I have argued that folk epistemology fixes a particular conception of democracy, what I have called *dialogical democracy*. Dialogical democracy in turn requires that we reject the politics of omission in favor of a politics of engagement. To be sure, more needs to be said about the politics of engagement. In particular, something must be said about the institutional requirements for citizen engagement. I begin to take up these issues in Chapter 5.

Epistemic perfectionism

The argument thus far has been focused on highly theoretical questions concerning the reasons that can be given to citizens living in a morally divided society to sustain their commitment to a democratic political order, even in cases where such a commitment seems to conflict with their core moral convictions. In this final chapter, I begin by taking up a series of issues of a slightly more concrete nature concerning the state of contemporary democratic politics. With these issues addressed, I will make a case for thinking that a dialogically democratic society requires an *epistemically perfectionist* state. In the discussions with which the book concludes, I evaluate a few policy suggestions proposed by Ronald Dworkin.

I DEMOCRACY AND PUBLIC IGNORANCE

The dialogical view of democracy that I have been developing expects a lot from democratic citizens. Dialogical democracy seems even more demanding than many of the deliberativist views, since it emphasizes the activities associated with truth-seeking and reason-exchanging. On the dialogical model, political decision is to reflect ongoing rational deliberation; thus, the dialogical view presupposes that citizens are epistemically capable of rational discourse. The kind of rational deliberation envisioned requires, at the very least, that citizens are able to draw correct inferences from given premises.[1] More importantly, the dialogical conception of democracy presumes that citizens are capable of recognizing and understanding the basic political facts from which their deliberations are to begin. Hence, if citizens prove to be incapable of drawing correct inferences, or if they prove to be unable to understand the basic political facts from which such inferences are

---

[1] Public deliberation arguably requires more, including certain traits of character such as the willingness to listen respectfully to opposing views, the readiness to admit one's errors, and the preparedness to set aside one's own interests for the sake of a common good.

to be drawn, then they are unfit for democracy as folk epistemology conceives of it.

Is it naïve to presume that citizens are possessed of the epistemic capabilities requisite to dialogical democratic citizenship? Does dialogical democracy as we have described it demand too much of citizens? Let us consider a line of argument that attempts to establish that, indeed, dialogical democracy is too demanding.

Dialogue and demandingness

In recent work, Richard Posner (2002; 2003; 2004) and Ilya Somin (1998; 2004) have promoted a forceful argument against deliberative democracy according to which deliberative democracy, even in its modest forms, is epistemically too demanding. Since the dialogical view is more epistemically demanding than many deliberativist views, the success of the criticisms offered by Posner and Somin defeats dialogical democracy.

The argument posed by Somin and Posner turns on the claim that citizens are subject to high levels of public ignorance and, hence, are demonstrably lacking in the cognitive abilities requisite for rational public deliberation. In a comprehensive review of the research concerning public ignorance, Somin (1998: 417) finds that ignorance of even the most basic political facts is so pervasive that "voters not only cannot choose between specific competing policy *programs*, but also cannot accurately assign credit and blame for highly visible policy *outcomes* to the right office-holders." Noting that deliberative democracy "imposes a substantial ... knowledge burden" (1998: 440) upon citizens, Somin laments that "deliberative democrats have generally overlooked the widespread ignorance that prevents most voters from achieving even ... modest levels of political knowledge" (1998, 440–441). Hence, Somin concludes that deliberative democracy is naïve.

Posner (2003: 151–152) agrees with Somin on the fact of public ignorance, and contends that the extent of such ignorance renders deliberative democracy a "pipe dream hardly worth the attention of a serious person" (Posner 2003: 163). However, Posner pushes the argument further than Somin. On Posner's view, the utopian nature of deliberative democracy renders it potentially dangerous. According to Posner (2003: 135, 166), the deliberativists' requirement that citizens engage each other on controversial political issues can only bring to the surface, and thus exacerbate, deep moral differences among citizens, thereby making for an increasingly antagonistic and volatile politics.

Although Somin and Posner differ in nuance, they propose roughly the same objection to deliberative democracy, which I shall call the Public Ignorance Objection. Stated roughly, their argument runs as follows:

(1) Deliberative democracy, in whatever form, expects citizens to be highly informed with regard to basic political facts and emerging data relating to complex policy questions;

(2) Citizens are, in fact, highly ignorant of even the most basic political facts;

(3) therefore, deliberative democracy is "both unrealistic and, as a result, potentially dangerous" (Somin 2004: 8).

The Public Ignorance Objection admittedly has an intuitive appeal. If citizens are in general highly ignorant of the facts relevant to their beliefs, and moreover are unable to reason competently, the folk epistemological call for political engagement seems rather silly. However, it is not clear that the premises in the above argument warrant its conclusion. That is, it is not clear that the fact of widespread public ignorance defeats deliberative or dialogical democracy as models of democratic politics.

Two concepts of ignorance

Despite its straightforward and confident air, the Public Ignorance Objection trades on an ambiguity regarding the term *ignorance.* To see this, suppose there is a policy question, Q, facing a given democratic population. Suppose further that a factual proposition, *p*, is true and bears so significantly upon Q that unless deliberators hold that *p*, they are unlikely to reach a rationally justifiable response to Q. Let us say that a typical citizen, Alfred, holds instead of *p* some instantiation of *not-p*. Now, what are we to say about Alfred? Surely, Alfred has a false belief, and, ex *hypothesi*, is unlikely to reach a justifiable position with regard to Q. But is he *ignorant*?

In one sense of the term, Alfred is certainly ignorant. He holds the false belief that *not-p*, and consequently is ignorant of the fact that *p*.[2] Ignorance in this sense is equivalent to false believing; hence, we shall call it *belief ignorance*. However, imagine that Alfred's belief that *not-p* was generated by correct inferences from popularly held and socially reinforced (but nevertheless false) premises. More specifically, let us suppose that *not-p* is a justified inference from premises, *a* and *b*, that are false but, nonetheless, are promoted by sources of political information that are otherwise justifiably held to be reliable, such as, say, *The New York Times, All Things*

---

[2] I am here excluding the complicating possibilities of self-deception and other forms of irrational belief.

Considered, or CNN. Now, in this case, Alfred is still guilty of *belief ignorance*; however, since his belief that *not-p* follows from other premises he acquired from sources that he was justified in believing to be reliable, his false belief is, in a sense, not his fault. In this case, we would be correct to say that Alfred is *misinformed*.

Contrast Alfred with Barbara. Like Alfred, Barbara believes that *not-p*; however, unlike Alfred, Barbara believes that *not-p despite* the fact that she has had regular exposure, from sources that are justifiably believed to be reliable, to the true premises which warrant the inference to *p*. That is, Barbara's belief that *not-p* is the result either of an incorrect inference or of some type of carelessness with respect to her premises. Like Alfred, Barbara is guilty of *belief ignorance*; but, unlike Alfred, since she had access to the true premises from which *p* follows, Barbara is *culpable* for her false belief. Thus, in addition to saying that *Barbara is ignorant of the fact that* p, we might say simply that *Barbara is ignorant*. To claim that *Barbara* is ignorant is to accuse her not only of false believing, it is to charge her with a kind of *cognitive failure*, it is to say that her *belief ignorance* is *her fault*. In cases where the cognitive failure is particularly egregious, we might say that Barbara is *incompetent*. In any case, as it involves an evaluation of the *believer* in addition to the evaluation of the *belief*, we shall call ignorance in this sense *agent ignorance*.

Keeping this distinction in mind, let us now evaluate the argument presented in the Public Ignorance Objection.

Is the argument valid?

The public ignorance literature endorsed by Posner and Somin, among others, aptly demonstrates a disturbingly high degree of *belief ignorance* among citizens of the United States. However, if the Public Ignorance Objection is to succeed, what must be demonstrated is that there is a high degree of *agent ignorance*. Put otherwise, the public ignorance literature reveals significant public *misinformedness* about fundamental political facts, but the Public Ignorance Objection requires the premise that the public is not simply *misinformed*, but *incompetent* and, hence, *unable* to muster the cognitive resources necessary for deliberative democracy. Without such a premise, the argument is formally invalid: the conclusion does not follow from the premises.

To see this, consider that, unless it could be shown that *agent ignorance* is widespread, the deliberative democrat can respond that the high degree of *belief ignorance* indicates the extent to which fundamental democratic institutions, such as the Press or the public education system, are failing. Deliberative and dialogical democrats could say that the public ignorance data show only that the public is in a state much like Alfred's, not Barbara's, and as such, the proper response is to *criticize* and attempt to *repair* the civic institutions that are responsible for enabling deliberation, such as the sources of political information, analysis, and commentary.

In fact, many deliberative democrats make precisely this kind of argument.[3] To take one example, Bruce Ackerman and James Fishkin agree with Somin's and Posner's assessment of the state of the general population with respect to knowledge of public affairs; they write, "If six decades of modern public opinion research establish anything, it is that the general public's political ignorance is appalling by any standard" (Ackerman and Fishkin 2004: 5). However, they lay the blame for such ignorance upon a failing civic system:

We have a public dialogue that is ever more efficiently segmented in its audiences and morselized in its sound bites. We have an ever more tabloid news agenda dulling the sensitivities of an increasingly inattentive citizenry. And we have mechanisms of feedback from the public, from viewer call-ins to self-selected internet polls that emphasize intense constituencies, unrepresentative of the public at large. (Ackerman and Fishkin 2003: 8)

Ackerman and Fishkin (2004: 7) contend that experiments with Deliberative Polling and citizen juries demonstrate that "When the public is given good reason to pay attention and focus on the issues, it is more than capable of living up to the demanding democratic aspirations." Thus, the reformation of existing civic institutions is central to the deliberativist program.

Hence, Ackerman and Fishkin are able to accept the premises of the argument presented in the Public Ignorance Objection, but deny the conclusion. Accordingly, the argument as it stands is invalid. Of course, showing that the objection fails is not sufficient to vindicate deliberative democracy; it is merely to demonstrate that the Public Ignorance Objection is by itself insufficient to defeat the deliberativist program.

Uninterested citizens?

One of the thoughts explicitly driving Posner's criticism of deliberative democracy is that citizens are *ignorant* of politics because they are inclined

---

[3] See Sunstein 2001a and 2003b; Page 1996; and the essays collected in Chambers and Costain 2000.

to *ignore* politics. According to Posner (2003: 164), the United States is a "tenaciously philistine society," and its citizens have "little appetite" for the kind of "abstractions" and arguments that deliberation involves; accordingly, they tend to disengage from politics to the greatest extent possible, preferring to pursue "other, more productive activities" (Posner 2003: 172). Posner takes this tendency to be a good thing, and thus criticizes deliberative democracy on the grounds that it "hopelessly exaggerates" (2003: 144) the degree to which it is reasonable to expect citizens to care about politics. Hence, with his characteristic frankness, Posner (2004: 41) presses the following objection against Ackerman and Fishkin's proposal for Deliberation Day: "If spending a day talking about the issues were a worthwhile activity, you wouldn't have to pay voters to do it."[4]

Let us then revise the Public Ignorance Objection in light of this. It would seem now that the objection to deliberative democracy has it that widespread *belief ignorance* indicates the extent to which citizens are *uninterested* in politics. If citizens generally do not care much about political issues, then any participatory theory of democracy, including deliberative democracy, must fail. Thus, although public ignorance does not itself *constitute* an objection to deliberative democracy, it provides *evidence* to the effect that in general citizens are unfit for deliberative democracy.

But the claim that citizens are uninterested in politics is difficult to square with the fact that political commentary is now a billion dollar business. The prevalence of political talk shows and call-in forums on television, radio, and the Internet, as well as the success of books offering popular political analysis, suggests that citizens are *not* uninterested in the way in which Posner suggests. More importantly, as I have already noted, these forums explicitly stress the need for rational deliberation and reason-exchange. And this suggests that citizens are not only interested in politics, but are also interested in the kind of engagement that our model advocates.

Thus, Posner and Somin have overestimated the force of their argument. In order to pose a serious challenge to deliberative democracy, the public ignorance evidence must show that citizens are highly susceptible to *agent ignorance*. Moreover, in order to fully defeat dialogical democracy, the evidence must show that the high levels of *agent ignorance* are irremediable, that citizens are *inherently* or *necessarily* epistemic incompetents. As they stand, the data show neither. The public ignorance results show only that

---

[4] Ackerman and Fishkin (2003; 2004) have recently proposed a new national holiday on which citizens would be paid a modest honorarium for voluntary participation in a day-long deliberative polling event they call "Deliberation Day."

there are high levels of *belief ignorance* among contemporary democratic citizens.

To be sure, *belief ignorance* is something about which we should be concerned. However, existing levels of *belief ignorance* pose a problem for *any* conception of democracy, whether deliberative, dialogical, or otherwise. Even those who adopt a maximally prodecuralist conception of democracy – such as Posner or neo-Hayekians like Jeffrey Friedman (2005) – must attribute to citizens both knowledge of their own interests and of the workings of government sufficient to hold the right government agencies responsible when they fail to satisfy those interests. Accordingly, the problem of *belief ignorance* cannot be laid at the door of deliberative and dialogical conceptions of democracy alone. As Plato understood, it is a problem for democracy in any form. Perhaps it is a problem for politics as such.

II DISCOURSE FAILURE

The success of the foregoing response to the Public Ignorance Objection gives rise to a further difficulty that we must confront. Roughly the difficulty is this: why does *belief ignorance* persist despite increased access to and participation in public deliberative activity?

One answer has it that popular news outlets are failing in their social mission. This view contends that people are misinformed because their sources of news increasingly tend to focus on topics and events that are not actually newsworthy. To be sure, there is evidence to support this. For example, a recent study conducted by the Project for Excellence in Journalism finds that, in the first quarter of 2007, Fox News Channel devoted 15 percent of its daytime news reporting to the Iraq war, 9 percent of its programming to the 2008 Presidential election, and a full 10 percent to the exploits and death of the celebrity Anna Nicole Smith.[5] By contrast, CNN devoted 25 percent to Iraq, 7 percent to the election, and merely 4 percent to Smith, and MSNBC devoted 31 percent to Iraq, 14 percent to the election, and 6 percent to Smith. Even if we accept Jack Beatty's analysis that these data show that Fox News is "comparable to a party-run medium like *Pravda*" (2007), the prevalence of unworthy content does not explain the phenomenon with which we are concerned. Regardless of how much time is given to Anna Nicole Smith, why is it that *belief ignorance* is so prevalent despite greatly increased access to news and information? To

---

[5] www.journalism.org/node/5719.

appropriate a term proposed by Guido Pincione and Frenando Teson (2006) in a different context, what is needed is an account of *discourse failure*.[6]

The phenomenon of discourse failure

We have seen that deliberative democrats such as Ackerman and Fishkin agree with proponents of the Public Ignorance Objection that public ignorance is rampant and needs to be addressed. But since the deliberativists are committed to the view that public ignorance is *belief ignorance*, they attribute rampant public ignorance to a failure of the institutions that are supposed to enable proper public deliberation. Accordingly, the deliberativist response to public ignorance is to criticize the current state of the educative institutions of civil society, especially the press and the media in general.

However, in response to Posner's charge that citizens are uninterested in political deliberation, I argued that the fact that popular political commentary is a billion dollar business suggests that democratic citizens are *not* uninterested in democratic politics. It is important to note that the popular political commentary industry is now thoroughly *interactive* and *participatory*. News and opinion are now disseminated on the Internet in ways that allow for – and in fact often encourage – real-time public commentary; through blogs, list-servs, newsgroups, and other kinds of Internet fora, ordinary citizens can now interact and engage directly and instantly not only with each other, but with policymakers, politicians, pundits, best-selling authors, and nationally syndicated journalists. Even a cursory examination of the Internet presence of mainstream media channels, such as *The New York Times*, *The Washington Post*, CNN, and the Associated Press is sufficient to demonstrate that public participation in political commentary, discussion, and debate has spread beyond what even the most enthusiastic participatory democrat could have envisioned just three decades ago. One might expect that increased participation and interaction with political analysts and commentators – even if the engagement is highly partisan – would result in a *decrease* of political ignorance. But the trend does not work

---

[6] Pincione and Teson use the term *discourse failure* to refer very generally to instances in which political positions retain popular support despite conclusive and widely-known social scientific evidence to the contrary (2006: 17ff.). I am using the term to refer specifically to the concurrence of heightened participation in ostensibly deliberative activities and increasing public ignorance. Pincone and Teson's general criticism of deliberativist conceptions of democracy is formidable, but cannot be taken up here.

this way. A widely publicized 2003 study by the Univeristy of Maryland's Program on International Policy Attitudes (PIPA) titled "Misperceptions, the Media, and the Iraq War" has found that increased attention to the media fora that tend to feature more by way of real-time argumentation – namely, television and radio, as opposed to print sources – is *positively* correlated with political ignorance.[7]

To explain: the PIPA study found that in 2003, 48 percent of Americans falsely believed that the United States had found clear evidence linking Iraq and al-Qaeda – despite the fact that no evidence of such a connection had been found and that the official position of US intelligence agencies was that there was no connection. As recently as September 2003, 22 percent of Americans *still* believed that evidence of WMDs had been found in Iraq, even though during the invasion, US military forces produced not even a shred of evidence. Lastly, in March 2003, only 35 percent of Americans correctly perceived that the majority of people in the rest of the world were opposed to the war in Iraq. According to this by now infamous poll, only 30 percent of Americans turned out to be correctly informed about all these subjects (the Iraq/al-Quaeda link, WMDs in Iraq, and international support for the Iraq war). Perhaps unsurprisingly, domestic support for the Iraq war was proportionally greater among those who held false beliefs about these matters. For example, 86 percent of respondents who had all of these misperceptions favored war in Iraq, whereas only 23 percent of the respondents who had no misperceptions did so.

To be sure, it might be thought that these results suggest that the American public is, as Posner alleges, simply uninterested in the Iraq war. One might hold that if people only paid closer attention to the news, there would be fewer people with these misperceptions. But the PIPA study suggests that this is only partly true. Those who primarily consulted the print media for their news, *and* who paid careful attention, did indeed have fewer misperceptions compared with those who did not closely follow the news. Similar results were obtained for viewers of the 24-hour news channel, CNN. But the study also showed that in the case of viewers of Fox News, the number of those polled who paid careful attention to the news broadcasts and who had misperceptions was nearly *double* that of those who claimed to not pay careful attention and who had misperceptions. Regarding the supposed link between al-Qaeda and Saddam Hussein, for example, only 42 percent of Fox viewers who did not follow the news closely

[7] www.pipa.org/OnlineReports/Iraq/ Media_10_02_03_Report.pdf.

thought there was a connection between the two, whereas 80 percent of those who followed the news very closely did.

In short, the data suggest that paying *closer* attention to Fox News seems to *result* in ignorance. Yet when we examine the programming on Fox News, we find an abundance of ostensibly deliberative fora in which representatives of opposed viewpoints appear together to engage their disagreements. This format is not found only on programs designed around debate, such as *The O'Reilly Factor* and *Hannity and Colmes*; even the straightforward news reporting features a high instance of ostensibly deliberative episodes.

The question to be pressed, then, is this: if indeed the folk epistemic norms I have identified are deeply embedded in our epistemic practice, then why should it be the case that actual deliberative encounters concerning pressing political matters turn out to be so epistemically corrupt? Why is it that, despite the fact that citizens are already committed to proper folk epistemic norms, increased deliberation seems to have led to increased public ignorance? More people with greater frequency are engaging in public discourse about political issues of shared concern, but they are no less ignorant about fundamental political facts. Democratic discourse seems to be failing. What is going wrong?

Pseudo-deliberation

One could try to explain discourse failure by charging that the public deliberative processes are epistemically corrupt. This response would have it that popular fora of public deliberation, including Internet blogs, talk radio, debate-based television, and the rest are improperly deliberative. But we must be careful, because this response only pushes the question back one step: how could such epistemically corrupt deliberative processes persist – and indeed thrive – among contemporary democratic citizens, who, *ex hypothesi*, are committed to the folk epistemic norms that we have identified? It would seem that citizens committed to folk epistemic norms would not abide corrupt deliberative processes.

I think the correct response to discourse failure is to adopt a more subtle critique of prevailing modes of public discourse. Specifically, the charge must be that popular deliberative fora of the sort identified above are most often *pseudo-deliberative*. The concept of a pseudo-deliberative forum must be carefully elaborated, but the general idea is that standing fora in which citizens engage in political discussion and exchange *merely mimic* rather than instantiate deliberation.

The thought is not as foreign as it may seem. Consider a puzzle, analogous to that of deliberative failure, which arises in informal logic. The most obvious rules of valid inference are often thought to be in some sense embedded in either our minds or our language, or both. But this makes a puzzle of our propensity to commit certain types of fallacious inference: if deductively valid inferential patterns are deeply embedded, why do we so often make inferential errors? One way of addressing this question is to point out that the most common logical fallacies are so frequently committed because they *mimic* common deductively valid inferences. Consider, for example, the fallacy of *affirming the consequent*, which clearly involves the conflation of the two fundamental deductively valid forms involving if–then statements (which logicians call *conditionals*), *modus ponens* and *modus tollens*. To wit:

Modus ponens:
   (1) If it is raining, the game is cancelled.
   (2) It is raining.
   (3) Therefore, the game is cancelled.

Modus tollens:
   (1) If it is raining, the game is cancelled.
   (2) The game is not cancelled.
   (3) Therefore, it is not raining.

Affirming the consequent:
   (1) If it is raining, the game is cancelled.
   (2) The game is cancelled.
   (3) Therefore, it is raining.

Both *modus ponens* and *modus tollens* are deductively valid because the truth of the premises guarantees the truth of the conclusion. Accordingly, in both cases, there is no way to affirm the premises but deny the conclusion (without contradicting yourself). The case of *affirming the consequent* is different – one can affirm the premises while denying the conclusion (without contradiction). Therefore, the truth of the premises does not guarantee the truth of the conclusion; the inference is deductively invalid. For example, the game might have been cancelled due to the fact that the umpire had been kidnapped, or maybe every player was sick, or maybe the field was flooded due to a water-main break, and so on. The logic is elementary and obvious, but somehow the fallacy is common. The point is this: it is the very naturalness, the manifest intuitiveness, of the valid inferential forms that allows us to be careless enough to *mistake* them for their fallacious counterparts.

I should like to propose a similar analysis of discourse failure. On such an analysis, the problem is not that citizens committed to proper epistemic norms deliberating together nonetheless fail to reach epistemically sound conclusions; rather, the failure is that our ostensibly discursive fora in fact *fail* to be discursive in the relevant or proper sense, but they nonetheless imitate proper epistemic processes successfully enough to pass for proper deliberation. I cannot make a full case for this analysis here; in fact, a proper case would require a good deal of empirical work that is best left to social scientists and theorists of argumentation. But consider that our vast communicative environment is in large measure organized according to the standard political categories of liberal and conservative, Democrat and Republican. Blogs, news groups, talk radio shows, and even television news programming all feature more or less overt cues which indicate who their target audience is. The media outputs of, say, Michael Savage and Sean Hannity are pro-conservative and anti-liberal, and this is made explicit.[8] By means of his books and his radio show, Al Franken seeks to communicate mostly with liberals.[9] The same is true of political blogs and news groups: they are easily classified as conservative or liberal, Left or Right. Accordingly, many of our most active deliberative spaces are aimed at a self-selected audience and already claimed for a particular political perspective.

I will not rehearse the ways in which deliberative encounters with a self-selected group of like-minded interlocutors tend to be *epistemically* deficient; the problems associated with group polarization and crippled epistemology were taken up in previous chapters. For present purposes, the pseudo-deliberative feature of such encounters must be emphasized. That is, although prevailing modes of political discourse are, in fact, occasions for galvanizing an audience by confirming the beliefs the audience already holds, they *present themselves* as forums in which reasons are judiciously weighed, objections are carefully considered, and dissenters are respectfully engaged. Accordingly, popular forums of political discussion are saturated with the *rhetoric* and *appearance* of deliberation; as we observed earlier, folk epistemic norms are constantly appealed to in the popular political media. More importantly, pseudo-deliberative modes of reason-giving have arisen.

---

[8] Recall again the titles of Savage's and Hannity's books: *Liberalism is a Mental Disorder* (Savage 2005), and *Deliver Us from Evil: Defeating Terrorism, Despotism, and Liberalism* (Hannity 2004).
[9] Hence, Franken's books of political commentary: *Rush Limbaugh is a Big Fat Idiot* (1996) and *Lies and the Lying Liars Who Tell Them: A Fair and Balanced Look at the Right* (2003).

An example: the weak-man fallacy

Again, I cannot here develop a complete analysis, but I will mention one form of pseudo-deliberation that is especially prevalent in popular political commentary.[10] I shall call it the *weak-man fallacy*.[11] The weak-man fallacy is a close cousin of the common *straw-man fallacy*. One commits the straw-man fallacy when one deliberately misrepresents an opponent's position in a way that imputes to it implausible commitments, and then refutes the misrepresentation instead of the opponent's actual view; consequently, in cases of the straw-man, no one's actual position is refuted. One commits the weak-man fallacy, by contrast, when one selects an especially weak version of the kind of view one wants to criticize and then presents a successful refutation of *that version* of the view as if it were sufficient to refute *all* versions. When the weak-man fallacy is committed, an actual interlocutor's actual view is taken up and refuted; the fallacy, however, consists in presenting a weak instantiation of a view as if it were a representative articulation. In short, the essence of this fallacy is to cast the *entirety* of one's opposition in the terms adopted by one's *weakest* opponent.

Paradigmatic instances of the weak-man fallacy can be found in the work of the likes of David Horowitz. For example, in an essay titled "Ward Churchill is Just the Beginning," Horowitz engages the admittedly absurd views of Churchill, and then declares that "Churchill's views, which are both hateful and ignorant, represent the views of a substantial segment of the academic community ... on campuses generally."[12] Horowitz never explains what he means by the notorious weasel word "substantial," and never engages the likes of Ronald Dworkin, Amy Gutmann, or Martha Nussbaum, people who are easily among the most argumentatively forceful representatives of the liberal academy. Or consider Michael Moore's *Bowling for Columbine*, which features a scene in which Moore confounds a hapless Charlton Heston (then president of the National Rifle Association), and takes himself to have defeated the anti-gun control position. Policy experts who agree with the NRA's position are never consulted, much less engaged with. For another example, consider

---

[10] Scott Aikin and I have begun more detailed work on the tropes of what I am here calling pseudo-deliberation. See Talisse and Aikin 2006; 2008.

[11] The argument of this section draws heavily from Talisse and Aikin 2006. There, we refer to the "selection" form of the *straw-man* fallacy. Following a very helpful suggestion from Steven Cahn, I here use the term *weak man* to characterize the fallacy.

[12] Horowitz, "Ward Churchill is Just the Beginning" (February 9, 2005) at: www.frontpagemag.com/ Articles/ReadArticle.asp?ID=16946 (accessed June 1, 2007).

President Bush's statement in November of 2005 in response to the idea that US military forces should be withdrawn from Iraq:

We've heard some people say, pull them out right now. That's a huge mistake. It'd be a terrible mistake. It sends a bad message to our troops and it sends a bad message to our enemy and it sends a bad message to the Iraqis.[13]

It is important to notice that Bush did not attribute to any *particular* opponent of his Iraq policy the position that the United States should pull out of Iraq "right now." He claims only to have "heard some people say" this. Bush was right not to make any such attributions, for even the most extreme proposals from the Congress for withdrawal from Iraq do not suggest that it be done immediately, but rather over a period of several months. The position that troops should be withdrawn "right now" was held only by the least sophisticated critics of Bush's war policy. But Bush's response suggests that his opposition's alternative to his Iraq policy is the admittedly foolish one of instantaneous and immediate withdrawal.

The weak-man fallacy is especially poisonous to proper deliberation because its success *relies on* and then *further entrenches* the ignorance of one's audience. That the weak-man fallacy relies upon ignorance should be clear: for the weak-man fallacy to be successful, one's audience must be unfamiliar with the best arguments made by one's opposition. The weak-man fallacy further entrenches ignorance because, when successful, one's audience is convinced that *there is no intelligent opposition* to one's view and thus *no forthcoming rejoinder from the opposition that could be worth attending to.* Only a narrow and distorted view of contemporary political disputes can result. That is, when it succeeds, the weak-man fallacy convinces one's audience not only of the correctness of one's view, but also of the absence of reasoned and intelligent opposition to it. The result of the widespread use of the weak-man fallacy is a popular public discourse of heightened passion and outrage that grows increasingly ignorant of what is actually in dispute. Under such conditions, a premium is placed on holding one's ground without regard for the reasons and arguments of those who disagree; for where the weak man prevails, one sees one's opposition as utterly *dismissible*. In short, the result is an undermining of deliberation by means that *appear* to instantiate all of the proper deliberative norms.

Now we can state in a general way the essence of pseudo-deliberation. Pseudo-deliberation consists in ostensibly deliberative speech acts that are

---

[13] www.whitehouse.gov/news/releases/2005/11/20051129–2.html. I thank Yvonne Raley for calling this particular example to my attention.

aimed not at critically engaging the reasons of one's interlocutor, but rather at convincing onlookers that one's interlocutor is silly, benighted, foolish, or wicked, and, accordingly, that his position is not worth engaging. But all proper deliberation proceeds from the assumption that there is a disagreement to be engaged, reasons to be articulated, evidence to be weighed; this assumption in turn presupposes that one's interlocutor is at the very least a competent dialectical partner, capable of giving, evaluating, and responding to reasons. Hence, pseudo-deliberation is *pseudo*-deliberative because it invokes all the norms and rhetoric of proper deliberation for the purpose of *denying* that a properly deliberative encounter is possible; that is, pseudo-deliberation aims to show that there is no reasonable opposition to one's view, that all opponents are ignorant or depraved and, therefore, do not deserve arguments but are in need of instruction.

The weak-man fallacy is but one pseudo-deliberative trope that is prevalent in current political discussion. There are many others. Recall that my hypothesis is that our contemporary fora of political discussion are infused with a wide array of pseudo-deliberative phenomena.[14] As I have said, more empirical work needs to be done on the communicative dynamics that prevail in contemporary discursive fora. But if my hypothesis is roughly correct, we will have provided an account of discourse failure.

III EPISTEMIC PERFECTIONISM

The upshot of the preceding two sections is that it is not enough for deliberative and participatory democrats to call for more public deliberation or civic engagement. Under contemporary conditions, neither *access* to sites of political discussion nor *participation* in processes of public deliberation is at issue; citizens are perhaps more than ever engaged in these ways. The preceding arguments show, instead, that the well-functioning social epistemic system upon which dialogical democracy depends requires *maintenance*. Specifically, dialogical democracy requires that sites of public deliberation be designed to call forth or cultivate the kind of epistemic abilities requisite to the manner of engagement identified at the end of Chapter 4. This is to say that the folk epistemic view of democracy entails a commitment to an *epistemically perfectionist* state. The claim that democracy requires a kind of perfectionist state will undoubtedly raise red flags among

---

[14] *Cf.* Bernard Williams's claim that contemporary political discourse involves a kind of "collective self-deception" (2005: 163f.)

many contemporary political theorists; consequently, the idea of epistemic perfectionism stands in need of clarification.

Perfectionism and neutralism

In its most common forms, *perfectionism* is the view that "the state should promote excellence and/or assist its citizens in their efforts to lead worthwhile lives, even if doing so requires it to undertake political action that is reasonably controversial" (Wall and Klosko 2003: 13). Perfectionism is thus often associated with the Aristotelian claim that political associations, including the state, exist for the sake of inculcating virtue or promoting the good life; on such views, the state is an agent of moral instruction and thus may enact policy designed to make its citizens morally good or enable them to "lead valuable and worthwhile lives" (Wall 1998: 8).

Most contemporary democratic theorists vehemently reject perfectionism. These theorists reason that since reasonable persons can disagree about the good life the state must adopt a stance of neutrality with regard to the moral good of its citizens; in other words, these theorists endorse what is known as the *principle of neutrality*, which holds that "the state should not favor, promote, or act on any particular conception of the good" (Sher 1997: 1).[15] Following John Stuart Mill in holding that "the only freedom which deserves the name is that of pursuing our own good in our own way" (1991 [1861]: 17), neutralists see perfectionism as a serious violation of individual liberty.

The precise meaning of the principle of neutrality is something about which its proponents disagree; however, it is most frequently understood as a principle of political justification, "a constraint on what factors can be invoked to justify a political decision" (Larmore 1987: 44).[16] This constraint has it that the *justification* for a political policy, institution, or decision must not rely upon any particular conception of the good. Of course, this is not to say that political decision and policy must not *in fact* favor some visions of the good over others – "neutrality of effect" (Rawls 2005: 194) is impossible. Rather, it is to say that the state must avoid instituting policy *for the sake of* some such conception; that is, the liberal state must be neutral in *aim* (Rawls 2005: 193). To employ a simple

---

[15] Although Sher rejects neutralism, his is a standard articulation of the neutralist thesis. Compare similar articulations in Dworkin 1985: 191; Nozick 1974: 33; and Barry 1995: 160.

[16] For influential discussions, see Nagel 1987, Ackerman 1989, and Waldron 1993. See Gaus 2003b and Arneson 2003 for more recent treatments.

example, neutralists hold that the state cannot invoke as a justification for a coercive policy prohibiting, say, smoking in enclosed public spaces the claim that public smoking is unhealthy for the smokers. Such a justification violates the principle of neutrality because it commits the state to a particular moral view, namely, one that holds that it is better to be healthy rather than unhealthy and thus it is better not to run certain risks with one's health. A *neutral* justification for such a policy appeals to the right of non-smokers to regulate the risks they take with their health; since second-hand smoke has been proven to be hazardous to non-smokers, the state may regulate the behavior of smokers, at least in those contexts where their smoking impacts on others.

It is not my aim at this point to take a stand on the principle of neutrality. It does seem, however, that advocates of neutralism are correct to bristle against standard varieties of perfectionism, especially in light of the fact of reasonable pluralism. But, as I shall argue in the next section, the kind of perfectionism that I contend follows from our folk epistemology does not founder on the fact of reasonable pluralism.

Why epistemic perfectionism is different

Epistemic perfectionism is different from common varieties of perfectionism in the following important respect: the good it calls upon the state to promote is an *epistemic* good rather than a *moral* one. That is, the dialogical democratic state does not *directly* promote or attempt to codify a vision of the moral good. Rather, it seeks to promote habits and capabilities that enable citizens to engage fruitfully in moral and political deliberation. To recall a discussion from Chapter 4, the dialogical democrat holds that, on any reasonable moral doctrine, a proper social epistemic system is *necessary* to proper moral judgment. The maintenance of a proper social epistemic systemic involves the promotion of certain epistemic practices among citizens. Hence, the democratic state must promote those practices *for the sake of* enabling proper moral judgment. In this way, the democratic state is involved in what perfectionist Michael Sandel calls a "formative project" (1996: 321); however, again, this project is *epistemic* rather than *moral*. Consequently, epistemic perfectionism avoids the principal objection of neutralists: epistemic perfectionism calls upon the state to promote an epistemic good that does not conflict with the fact of reasonable pluralism concerning comprehensive moral commitments.

To be sure, the most strident versions of neutralism reject the idea that the state should act for the sake of *anything* other than the protection of individual freedom.[17] Neutralists of this sort will accordingly reject dialogical democracy. However, many prominent strands of democratic theory – including those associated with Rawls – endorse a more moderate version of neutrality. Moderate versions of neutralism hold that "governments should not base their actions on grounds that can be reasonably rejected" (Klosko 2003: 168), and hence justify neutralism by way of a "norm of rational dialogue" (Larmore 1987: 53). In this respect, then, moderate neutralists are committed to a politics in which the "public realm" functions as a "forum in which we try to convince others of the worth of our views so that they can become part of the shared allegiances the state should promote" (Larmore 1996: 135). Such a forum is important because "a liberal polity benefits greatly from people coming to know the full extent of their reasonable disagreements"; such recognition is "necessary for exercising the equal respect we owe one another" (Larmore 1996: 136). The claim of the dialogical democrat – which enjoys the empirical support of the group polarization findings that we discussed in Chapter 2 – is that the epistemic capabilities requisite to acknowledging reasonable disagreements and engaging in rational dialogue cannot be taken as given, but must be socially cultivated and maintained. This cultivation and maintenance is achieved by political institutions and state policy designed for that purpose. Thus, the mode of epistemically formative politics called for by dialogical democracy should be unobjectionable from the point of view of any theory that draws upon the concept of reasonable rejectability as a criterion of unjustifiable state coercion. Indeed, it would seem that this brand of epistemic perfectionism is actually a *complement* to the standard view of neutrality.

Epistemic capabilities

I have said that an epistemically perfectionist state seeks to cultivate the capabilities that enable citizens to engage fruitfully in moral and political deliberation. I have employed the language of *capabilities* deliberately in order to call to mind recent work by Martha Nussbaum (2000; 2006; 2007).[18] As Nussbaum notes, the idea of capabilities was introduced by Amartya Sen as part of a criticism of John Rawls's theory of justice, which posited a short list of "primary goods" shared by all that could serve as the

---

[17] See Kukathas 2003 for an extended defense of this kind of position.

[18] Nussbaum's "capabilities approach" to justice derives in large measure from Amartya Sen's (1975; 1999) work. For a discussion of the differences between Nussbaum and Sen, see Nussbaum 2000: 11ff. Here I am concerned with Nussbaum's development of the idea.

basis for interpersonal comparisons of well-being.[19] Sen's objection, as Nussbaum relates it, is that the Rawlsian primary goods of wealth and income are inadequate to measure comparative well-being: "the person in the wheelchair may have the same income and wealth as the person of 'normal' mobility and yet be unequal in capability to move from place to place" (2006: 164). Yet Nussbaum expands Sen's employment of the concept of capabilities; according to Nussbaum, the idea of capabilities forms the core of an entire conception of justice and the good society more broadly.

Nussbaum provides a list of ten "central human capabilities"; among them are the abilities to live a normal lifespan, to achieve a level of health, to develop requisite reasoning capacities, to enjoy recreational activities, to participate in "political choices that govern one's life," and to hold property (2006: 76ff.). The reason for appealing to Nussbaum is that her capabilities approach aspires to establish that the state must promote the development of certain capacities among all citizens. Her view is, hence, mildly perfectionist, yet, she contends, compatible with liberal neutrality. It is not my aim at present to evaluate Nussbaum's position, except to say that many theorists have argued, compellingly in my judgment, that her capabilities list is more controversial and less universal than she claims.[20] Does an epistemic perfectionism rooted in a conception of epistemic capabilities fare any better?

Thus far we have said little if anything specific about what those capabilities are and how they may be cultivated. This lacuna is remedied easily, since a short list of capability types can be neatly read off our folk epistemic commitments. Following Nussbaum, we think of capabilities as abilities to function in the relevant respects to an "appropriate threshold level" (Nussbaum 2006: 167). Of course, the concept of an *appropriate* level of ability is necessarily imprecise, but, especially in the case of *epistemic* capabilities we can rely upon rough and ready standards of competence, keeping in mind, of course, that such standards are contestable and may need to be revised.

To begin, let me restate the five principles of folk epistemology:

(1) to believe some proposition, p, is to hold that p is true;

(2) to hold that p is true is generally to hold that the best reasons support p;

---

[19] Rawls characterizes the primary goods as those which "normally have a use whatever a person's rational plan of life" (1999: 54); they are things that "every rational man is presumed to want" (1999: 54), whatever else he wants" (1999: 79).

[20] For example, see Williams 1995: 196f.; Wolf 1995; and Ackerly 2000: 94ff.

(3) to hold that p is supported by the best reasons is to hold that p is *assertable*;

(4) to assert that p is to enter into a social process of reason *exchange*; and

(5) to engage in social processes of reason exchange is to at least implicitly adopt certain cognitive and dispositional norms related to one's epistemic character.

Without rehearsing the elaboration offered in Chapter 3 of these principles, I think it should be clear that roughly five types of epistemic capabilities follow from them. To satisfy their folk epistemic commitments, individuals must embody the following capabilities:

Communicative capabilities. Individuals must be able to read competently, listen carefully, interpret charitably, speak precisely, and write clearly.

Formal capabilities. Individuals must be able to make valid or cogent inferences from accepted premises, competently track arguments and chains of reasoning, detect, diagnose, and correct fallacies, and distinguish and keep distinct the formal or logical properties of arguments from their affective or emotional content.

Informational capabilities. Individuals must have at their disposal knowledge of fundamental facts about history, politics, the Constitution, international relations, mathematics, geography, natural science, and social science. Where the fundamental facts are in dispute, they must be aware of this fact.

Methodological capabilities. Individuals must be able to evaluate methods of arriving at, confirming, and testing beliefs, identify appropriate sources of information and data, suspend judgment appropriately, weigh evidence competently, revise commitments responsibly, and engage in processes of self-criticism.

Interpersonal capabilities. Individuals must be able to keep separate their personal relations with fellow citizens and their dialectical relations with interlocutors, respectfully engage with those with whom they disagree, respond directly to questions, criticisms, and challenges, gracefully accept criticism and even correction, honestly evaluate their arguments and those of others, and tolerate persistent disagreement.

These articulations are admittedly very rough, and may prove to be in need of revision. However, they capture the capabilities requisite to responsible epistemic agency. Deficiency in any of them below a certain threshold of competence renders an individual incapable of accepting, rejecting, asserting, and revising beliefs in an epistemically responsible way.

The cultivation of these epistemic capabilities among citizens undoubtedly requires, at the very least, that an efficient and effective system of free public education be in place. Importantly, the curriculum of our educational institutions must be focused not merely on developing communicative and informational competence, it must also aim to develop capability in the methods and dispositions associated with inquiry, argumentation, and disputation. How these abilities are most effectively developed is an empirical question about which I will not here speculate. The important point is that, in a democratic society, acquiring information and mastering basic reading and writing skills are not enough. The schools must endeavor to cultivate the abilities associated with *finding things out*, *articulating reasons*, *dealing with disagreement*, and *living with reasoned conflict*.

Yet the cultivation of the epistemic capacities is not only the task of the school. Even well-educated citizens are vulnerable to group polarization and the related epistemic hazards discussed above. Again, what is required is a well-functioning *social epistemic system*, and this requires what Cass Sunstein has called "a *culture* of free speech" that "encourages independence of mind," imparts "a willingness to challenge prevailing opinion through both words and deeds," and engenders "a certain set of attitudes in listeners, one that gives a respectful hearing to those who do not embrace the conventional wisdom" (2003b: 110). On Sunstein's view, which is in agreement with the view we are elaborating, these attitudes and traits are to be promoted by means of certain institutional arrangements that guarantee their *exercise*. Hence, Sunstein calls for a series of free speech interventions designed to ensure sound epistemic practice. Such interventions require a "New Deal" for free speech (1996: 17ff.) and a "two-tiered" first amendment (1996: 124ff.). Among his most well-known policy suggestions is that politically partisan websites should be required by law to carry links to sites espousing opposing viewpoints (2001a: 169f.). More recently, he has proposed that society should take special care to protect, and even *reward* dissent (2003: 93). Such measures are designed to promote proper epistemic practice by increasing "society's total stock of argument pools" (2003: 157).

Indeed, the idea that society should actively promote certain epistemic ends informs Sunstein's entire line of constitutional interpretation. He holds that:

The American constitutional system is emphatically not designed to protect private interests and private rights. Private interests and private rights are of course protected; but this is not the entire point of the system ... Instead, a large point of the system is to ensure discussion and debate among people who are genuinely different in their perspectives and position, in the interest of creating a process through which reflection will encourage the emergence of general truths. (1996: 241)

The dialogical democrat follows Sunstein in seeing our Constitution as not simply a fair procedure for resolving conflicts and protecting rights, but rather a system designed to "protect the process of reason-giving, ensuring something like a 'republic of reasons'" (Sunstein 2001b: 239). It follows that dialogical democrats are bound to endorse policies and institutions that can reasonably be expected to further those epistemic goals. In short, if folk epistemology entails dialogical democracy, it also entails epistemic perfectionism.

The case of Mozert *v.* Hawkins

Neutralists will perhaps endorse the programmatic features of epistemic perfectionism that I have identified. Why then, they may ask, should one think that epistemic perfectionism is indeed distinct from neutralism? I think the two positions can be distinguished by means of a discussion of the well-known case of *Mozert* v. *Hawkins*.

Eamonn Callan (1997: 157) is correct to observe that the *Mozert* case is complicated in part because the plaintiff's complaint "confounded reasons of extremely uneven merit." I do not intend, therefore, to engage in an extended analysis of the details of the case. Rather, I want to contrast Stephen Macedo's (1995; 2000) neutralist analysis with what I take to be an epistemic perfectionist one. To this end, I will follow Macedo in focusing on one particular issue raised by the case.[21]

First, a few details about the case must be put forward. In *Mozert*, several born-again Christian families brought the complaint against the public school board of Hawkins County, Tennessee, that the primary grade reading curriculum violated the families' free exercise of religion because the textbooks used in that curriculum exposed their children to stories told from a wide variety of religious points of view, including Buddhist, Native American, Islamic, and Christian. One of the plaintiffs, Vicki Frost, objected to the even-handedness with which the non-Christian views were presented on the grounds that a proper Christian must refuse to see other religions as "equal" to Christianity (Macedo 2000: 168); as Macedo indicates, according to Frost, the "exposure to diversity" of religious worldviews itself constitutes a violation of the free exercise of her religion, which commands her to raise her children to be Christian (1995: 471).

---

[21] Since I want to avoid raising disagreements concerning the facts or most salient features of the case, I shall also draw my account of the case from Macedo's discussions. See Bates 1993 for a comprehensive account of *Mozert*.

What makes the case compelling from the point of view of democratic theory is that the *Mozert* parents were not attempting to have the reading curriculum abolished or the textbooks in question replaced. Rather, the parents sought an *exemption* for their children from the classes that employed the textbooks. The parents agreed that their children needed reading instruction, and proposed that their children would be taught to read at home and would sit for the same standard reading examinations as the other students in the class. That is, the *Mozert* parents did not attempt to impose their own religious convictions on other students; they simply claimed their right to control the kind of worldviews to which their children were exposed.

The Hawkins County School Board initially allowed the proposed exemption, but quickly reversed its decision and declared participation in the reading curriculum mandatory for all students, vowing to suspend any student who refused. Although many of the concerned parents withdrew their children from the public school system, others brought a case against the school board. The case was dismissed by a federal court, but this dismissal was reversed by a higher court, which decided to uphold the parents' complaint. However, this decision was eventually reversed by a federal appeals court, which found in favor of the Hawkins County School Board.

Macedo does a good job of framing the philosophical issues raised by *Mozert*:

Can respectful exposure to diversity interfere with the free exercise of religious beliefs? And if so, do state officials – operating on the basis of their democratic mandate – have the authority to condition a benefit such as public schooling on the willingness of parents to have their children exposed to diversity, or does doing so violate fundamental rights or run afoul of some other principled limit on public authority? (2000: 161)

Furthermore, Macedo gives what seems to me to be the right response. Macedo concedes that the reading program interferes with the *Mozert* parents' ability to "teach their children their particular religious views," but he denies that this constitutes a violation of their moral or constitutional rights (2000: 162). Macedo writes:

While it is true enough that our liberal Constitution protects freedom to proclaim that the religious doctrines of others are heretical, a more complex dynamic is at work here. A liberal democratic polity cannot endure without citizens willing to support its fundamental institutions and principles and to take part in defining those principles … Liberal citizenship carries with it not only privileges but also obligations, including the obligation to respect the equal rights of fellow citizens, whatever their faiths … Our constitutional order must shape citizens, and not only establish political institutions. Citizens, not courts or legislatures, are the ultimate custodians of our public morality. We have every reason to take seriously the political project of educating future citizens with an eye to their responsibilities as critical interpreters of our shared political traditions – that is, as participants in a democratic project of reason giving and reason demanding. (2000: 164–165)

The epistemic perfectionist, of course, endorses Macedo's appeal to public education as an institution aimed in part at shaping citizens in order to enable them to become partners in the democratic project of "reason giving and reason demanding." On the view I have been developing, the cultivation of these epistemic skills is a necessary part of genuine believing, regardless of what comprehensive moral doctrine one might adopt. Macedo, however, sees the democratic project he describes as part of his broader "civic liberalism" (2000: 169). According to Macedo, civic liberalism is a species of Rawlsian political liberalism that "goes beyond" Rawls's version and "includes an account of the political institutions and social structures that help promote a publicly reasonable liberal community" (2000: 169). The issue to be considered is whether Macedo's civic liberalism can be supported by neutralism.

The principal move that Macedo makes is to offer his civic liberalism as a proposal that is strictly "political" in the Rawlsian sense; Macedo claims that his civic liberalism "focuses our attention on shared political values without requiring or expecting agreement on ultimate ends or a comprehensive set of philosophical values" (2000: 170). Accordingly, Macedo contends that his civil liberalism can "avoid directly confronting or denying the *Mozert* families' contention that the Bible's authority should be accepted uncritically" (2000: 174). Instead, civic liberalism recommends that we proceed by "simply leaving aside the religious question as such"; this "leaves the school door open to reasonable fundamentalists – that is, to those willing to acknowledge *for civic purposes* the authority of public reasonableness" (2000: 175).

From the point of view of Macedo's civic liberalism, the fact that the Hawkins County public school reading curriculum promotes attitudes of toleration towards other religions and worldviews does *not* constitute a violation of the *Mozert* parents' right to the free exercise of their religion because the toleration that is promoted is, according to Macedo, strictly *civil* rather than comprehensive (2000: 175). That is, on Macedo's view, public schools are warranted in – in fact, are obligated to – engage in a "reasonable attempt to inculcate core liberal values" such as "toleration and other basic civil virtues" (2000: 201), because such values are necessary for citizenship in a modern democratic society. Macedo holds that, importantly, these values can be inculcated without taking a stand on larger questions of the good life or salvation; they are, again, the virtues appropriate to our role as *citizens*, not as persons as such. Thus, Macedo's civic liberalism is based in the claim that "the lives of liberal citizens are in a sense properly divided: we have a public and a private side, and the public (or political) side is guided by imperatives designed to make our shared life together civilized and respect-ful" (2000: 164).

However, Macedo recognizes that the civic virtues will inevitably "spill over into other spheres of life," and that these virtues are "far from neutral with respect to the forms of like that are likely to prosper and gain adherents" in a society governed by them (2000: 179). But this failure of neutrality of effect is of no concern, for Macedo contends that the relevant sense of neutrality is that of *justification* (2000: 179). As we've seen, Macedo holds that the values and virtues associated with his civic liberalism can be justified "independently of religious and other comprehensive claims" (2000: 179). Macedo holds that the justification for his civil liberalism derives from the "widespread (though not perfect) consensus on the sorts of basic guarantees that constitute the core of a political morality" that Americans enjoy; he holds that, despite deep disagreement, "there is never-theless a reasonable consensus on certain shared matters of urgent political concern, a consensus that is freestanding in the sense that we do not need to agree on any one comprehensive religious or philosophical grounding" (2000: 173).

But here is where the limits of Macedo's neutralism come to the fore. The *Mozert* case demonstrates that the reasonable consensus Macedo describes is not as widespread as he seems to think. More importantly, it could be the case that the *Mozert* parents indeed recognize the high value of the "basic guarantees" which constitute the "core of a political morality" that Macedo describes. This is suggested by the fact that the *Mozert* parents did not press an objection to the idea of secular education as such.[22] On a plausible reading of the case, part of what they objected to is the idea that this core political morality should *take priority over* the aims and values of their religious or comprehensive morality. What reason could Macedo give that

---

[22] As John Tomasi (2001: 92) notes, some of the parents objected not to the mere exposure of their children to the non-Christian stories, but to the fact that Christianity was not given equal represen-tation in the readers.

is consistent with his justificatory neutralism for prioritizing political morality over comprehensive morality in cases of direct conflict? His response to this kind of challenge is telling; in considering that certain religious believers may object to the very idea of partitioning their "private" and "political" morality in the way civic liberalism requires, Macedo writes:

At this point, there may be nothing more to say to such people, except to point out that their religious beliefs are, unfortunately, inconsistent with the demands of good citizenship in a religiously pluralistic society. (2000: 186)

This is an awkward reply because the aptness of Macedo's conception of the demands of good citizenship in a religiously pluralistic society is precisely what is in question. Elsewhere, he concedes that "civic education is bound to have the effect of favoring some ways of life or religious convictions over others"; but instead of offering a neutralist justification for his conception of civic education, he simply declares, "So be it" (Macedo 1995: 485). But this is not a justification of any sort, and, in any case, it is an odd stance given Macedo's commitment to the idea that "public institutions should operate based on mutually accessible reasons" (2000: 184).

The problem is that in order to avoid appealing to controversial moral claims in his justification of his civic liberalism, Macedo must appeal to "shared political values" (2000: 185). But *Mozert* shows that even if there were a suitably robust collection of such values, there would still be a question of how they are to be prioritized in cases of conflict. To simply declare that the political values override religious ones is to betray the very justificatory ideal that Macedo claims is central to his liberalism; however, to give a moral argument for the priority of the political to the religious is necessarily to invoke the kind of controversy Macedo most wants to avoid.

Epistemic perfectionism accepts the justificatory ideal of Macedo's liberalism, but can propose a justification for the idea that public schools must expose students to diverse worldviews. Such a justification would run along the lines of the folk epistemic arguments devised in Chapters 3 and 4. More specifically, the argument would first respond to Vicki Frost's claim that "the word of God as found in the Christian Bible is the totality of my beliefs" (quoted in Macedo 2000: 158) by pointing out that this claim cannot possibly be true, since the Bible does not contain the sentence:

The word of God as found in the Christian Bible is the totality of Vicki Frost's beliefs.

By her own admission, Vicki Frost has beliefs that are not contained in the Bible, and, therefore, she is committed to the idea that there are some truths that are not found there. The next move would be to present her with the vast Christian literature devoted to Biblical interpretation, laying bare all of the internal controversies among Christian scholars concerning the Bible's core moral teachings. The aim would be to follow Michael Perry in urging that:

Widespread transdenominational disagreement among Christians over whether the Bible teaches about morality what some claim that it teaches is not a new phenomenon. In the past, there was such disagreement over, for example, whether the Bible teaches that slavery can be morally permissible. Precisely because such disagreement is not a new thing, and because the historical experience of Christians discloses that Christians can be radically mistaken about whether in fact the Bible teaches about morality what some claim that it teaches, such disagreement – increasingly widespread disagreement among Christians, disagreement that is not interdenominational but transdenominational – should be an occasion for Christians to subject the traditional belief to careful, critical scrutiny. (2003: 63)

According to Perry, such "careful, critical scrutiny" will often require "dialogue with the other" (2003: 76), since such dialogue is frequently what is needed if we are to uncover the tacit assumptions and intuitions driving our own thinking. That is, Perry contends that religious beliefs should be "presented in public political argument *so that they can be tested there*" (2003: 39) (original emphasis). Now, it may seem that the injunction to engage in critical dialogue for the sake of testing one's religious commitments *itself* constitutes a violation of one's religious commitments, since it seems to call for some kind of skepticism or a willingness to doubt one's religious beliefs. However, Perry correctly emphasizes that the kind of scrutiny he calls for does *not* require religious believers to deny or doubt core commitments of their faith. The recognition that the Bible has in the past been wrongly interpreted, and thus that any proposed interpretation must be examined carefully, does not conflict with a commitment to the Bible's infallibility; it requires only an admission of one's own fallibility in interpreting the Bible, an admission that is perfectly fitting for Christians in light of their view of "the fallenness, the brokenness" of human beings as such (Perry 2003: 79).

Perry's point is crucial and obviously quite in line with the folk epistemic argument I have been developing. The folk epistemic view has it that, no matter what their moral comprehensive doctrines happen to be, citizens have, from their own epistemic perspective, compelling reasons to engage each other in critical, reasoned dialogue. Given that such engagement requires that participants exercise certain epistemic capabilities, all citizens have compelling reasons from their own epistemic perspective to support political institutions that aim to cultivate the requisite capabilities. Consequently, epistemic perfectionism supports Macedo's position that the *Mozert* parents should not be accommodated on the grounds that "We have every reason to take seriously the political project of educating future citizens with an eye to their responsibilities … as participants in a democratic project of reason giving and reason demanding" (2000: 165). But whereas Macedo's justification of this position necessarily invokes the kind of moral controversy he correctly aspires to avoid, epistemic perfectionism justifies this position on the grounds that Vicki Frost's positive epistemic commitments must *support* critical engagement with opposing doctrines *for the sake of* developing the epistemic capacities that enable her children to better apprehend and maintain belief in the truth. Again, the argument does not appeal to a supposedly "widespread consensus" on a shared "political morality" (Macedo 2000: 173), but rather draws from the epistemic commitments we already endorse by virtue of the fact that we have beliefs at all.

A *word about* Wisconsin v. Yoder

Before moving on, I should mention briefly that epistemic perfectionism can support Macedo's view concerning a case that is often thought to be closely related to *Mozert*, namely *Wisconsin* v. *Yoder*.[23] In *Yoder*, Amish parents brought a complaint against the state of Wisconsin, which mandated that all children attend school until the age of sixteen; thereby requiring at least ten years of schooling – eight years of primary education plus two years of secondary school. The Amish parents objected on the grounds that:

Secondary schooling, by exposing Amish children to worldly influences in terms of attitudes, goals, and values contrary to beliefs, and by substantially interfering with the religious development of the Amish child and his integration into the way of life of the Amish faith community at the crucial adolescent stage of development, contravenes the basic religious tenets and practice of the Amish faith, both as to parent and child. (quoted in Macedo 2000: 153)

The Supreme Court upheld the right of Amish parents to withdraw their children from school following completion of eighth grade.

Again, we cannot examine all of the philosophical issues that *Yoder* raises. The question is whether one can consistently support the decision not to accommodate the *Mozert* parents but accept the court's decision in *Yoder*. Macedo claims that we "cannot be entirely happy about accommodating the Amish," but we must adopt an attitude of "grudging tolerance" towards

---

[23] Like *Mozert*, *Yoder* has been the subject of extensive commentary. See Reidy 2001 for a nice overview of the issues.

them (1995: 488–489). The reason, Macedo holds, is that although the Amish "are not in important respects good liberal citizens," they nonetheless "do not wholly tyrannize over their children and they keep to themselves" (1995: 489).

But, in light of the commitments of Macedo's civic liberalism, the basis of our toleration of the Amish claims is not clear.[24] Macedo's view seems entirely prudential – he reasons that the state must choose its battles, and should not interfere with a religious community that seeks political isolation and is not internally wholly tyrannical. The epistemic perfectionist can share with Macedo the attitude of grudging toleration, but can offer the additional thought that the *state's* interest in cultivating the epistemic capabilities requisite to democratic citizenship weakens in the case of groups like the Amish whose religious convictions bid them to non-obstructively exit from democratic politics. We can see the desire to avoid exposure to non-Amish ideas and norms as an unfortunate abdication of one's responsibility as an epistemic agent, a kind of *epistemic shame*; but when combined with the renunciation of the role of citizen, there is not much the democratic state can do, except to ensure that a suitably viable exit option is available to those who wish to opt out of Amish society (Macedo 1995: 489).

The folk epistemic view is also able to support Macedo's way of drawing the distinction between the *Mozert* and *Yoder* cases. According to Macedo, the *Mozert* parents do not deserve accommodation because their fundamentalist Christianity does *not* involve a renunciation of the role of democratic citizen. In fact, as Macedo emphasizes, unlike the Amish, fundamentalist Christians "are not sectarians living apart, but are … increasingly politicized" (1995: 489). Insofar as they intend for their children to take up the role of democratic citizen, the *Mozert* parents cannot be permitted to shield their children from the training requisite to that task. As we have said, responsible democratic citizenship requires the exercise of certain epistemic capabilities, the cultivation of which requires exposure to a diversity of arguments and worldviews.

Before moving on to the concluding section of this chapter, I need to address a concern with the folk epistemic approach that is raised by the analysis of *Yoder* that I have just proposed. In light of what has just been said, it might seem that I have conceded that the Amish reject the folk epistemic commitments that I have claimed are intrinsic to the very concept of belief. I do not think that the analysis implies such a concession. To explain: the kind of social isolation that the Amish seek has more to do with

---

[24] Note that Brian Barry (2001: 242ff.) argues on liberal grounds for the reversal of *Yoder*.

a positive judgment about their substantive religious beliefs than with negative judgments about the non-Amish world. The Amish aspire to have *no beliefs* concerning the modern world. To be sure, they *renounce* the ways of modern society, but they do so in a way that expresses the aspiration to be *unexposed* to it, to leave it behind, to *disregard* it, to be *ignorant* of it. Put in other words, they do not *object* to modern society in as much as they simply seek to *ignore* it. If one wanted a philosophical term to characterize this stance, one could say that the Amish endorse a *one-way Pyrrhonist* view: whereas the Amish wholeheartedly endorse their own religious, moral, and social commitments, they nonetheless withhold or suspend belief altogether with regard to nearly everything else.[25]

Whether Amish individuals succeed at actually suspending concern with the modern world is, of course, an issue worth examining. But the point here is that their desire for isolation is driven by a desire to be free of the modern world to the extent of being free of having beliefs about it. To check to see whether the Amish recognize the folk epistemic norms I have appealed to, one would need to begin with the beliefs that they actually hold. The claim is that *when* one believes, one takes oneself to have reasons sufficient for that belief, and so on. The folk epistemic view does not pronounce on the issue of when one should suspend belief or the related questions concerning on which matters one should seek to have beliefs at all.

IV CONCLUSION

The main argument of this book is now complete. By appealing only to the folk epistemic commitments that we – you and I – already endorse, I have made a case for a form of democracy that can respond to the problem of deep politics. Although this form of democracy involves some innovations – including most obviously the concept of epistemic perfectionism – it is nevertheless discernibly liberal and, I hope, attractive for that reason. By way of conclusion, I want to engage a position recently advanced by Ronald Dworkin that is in many ways similar to the position I have been developing. More specifically, I want to punctuate some contrasts between the folk epistemic position and Dworkin's, but then articulate the substantial points of agreement.

---

[25] I thank Jeffrey Tlumak for the term and for helpful discussion on this point.

Is democracy possible here?

Ronald Dworkin's recent book, *Is Democracy Possible Here?* (2006), is infused with a deep concern for the future of democracy. According to Dworkin, we are in the midst of "a period of special political danger for the United States" (2006: xi). Diagnosing this danger, Dworkin writes:

American politics are in an appalling state. We disagree, fiercely, about almost everything. We disagree about terror and security, social justice, religion in politics, who is fit to be a judge, and what democracy is. These are not civil disagreements: each side has no respect for the other. We are no longer partners in self-government; our politics are rather a form of war.[26] (2006: 1)

As should be obvious, I share Dworkin's concerns for our modes of political disagreement and for our democracy at large. In many ways, Dworkin's analysis is similar to the one I have offered in this book. Dworkin rejects the politics of omission, arguing that democrats "will not succeed if they ask people of faith to set aside their religious convictions when they take up the role of citizens" (2006: 65). Furthermore, he agrees that we must seek to give an account of democracy that follows from the norms we already endorse. Finally, he proposes a series of policies concerning education, elections, and the courts designed to repair our democratic practice (2006: 148).

Yet Dworkin's approach differs from the one I have proposed here in significant respects. Dworkin endeavors to show that underlying all of our moral and religious disagreement, there are two moral principles to which we all subscribe which constitute a common conception of human dignity. Dworkin writes:

These principles hold, first, that each human life is intrinsically and equally valuable and, second, that each person has an inalienable personal responsibility for identifying and realizing value in his or her own life. (2006: 160)

Dworkin's strategy of seeking shared commitments that run deeper than those commitments over which we are divided strikes me as correct. However, that Dworkin attempts to identify *moral* commitments that fill this role seems to me misguided for all of the later Rawlsian reasons concerning the fact of reasonable pluralism that we canvassed in Chapter 2.

---

[26] *Cf.* Gore (2007: 2–3), "The truth is that American democracy is now in danger – not from any one set of ideas, but from unprecedented changes in the environment within which ideas either live and spread, or wither and die. I do not mean the physical environment; I mean what is called the public sphere, or the marketplace of ideas."

Briefly, the problem is this: Dworkin's principles of equal value and responsibility are not only subject to a variety of different interpretations, but there are also other deep values – including liberty, autonomy, utility, membership, loyalty, devotion, and community – that are widely held and not taken to be reducible to Dworkin's conception of dignity. But Dworkin never once considers the possibility that some may take dignity to be a very important, but nonetheless ultimately derivative value. He offers his principles on a "take it or leave it" basis, envisioning only two paths of resistance to his call for a new public debate, namely, rejecting the moral principles he proposes in favor simply of conservative policies (rather than in favor of different and competing moral principles), or ignoring altogether his challenge (2006: 162). Both of these paths come to the same thing: a disregard for principles. Hence, according to Dworkin, his opponents must accept his premises and argue that his conclusions do not follow from them, or else they do not argue at all. But this is overly simplistic. Surely the most sophisticated conservatives would want to offer arguments *against* Dworkin's premises; they would want to argue either that Dworkin has the wrong conception of dignity or that dignity is not the most important value in a free society. In any case, this is not a promising way to begin a reasoned argument.[27]

Importantly, Dworkin's analyses of such crucial topics as torture, terrorism, and economic justice, as well as his conception of democracy itself (2006: 144) and his policy suggestions for improving democracy (2006: 147), all proceed on the assumption of his own conception of human dignity, a conception which, according to Dworkin, forms "the best understanding of liberalism now" (2006: 161). Perhaps Dworkin is right about this; however, as a constantly growing mountain of academic literature demonstrates, there is considerable disagreement among political theorists about the "best understanding of liberalism." If Dworkin's assessment of the state of our current mode of democratic politics is correct – and I believe it is – the worry arises that we *cannot even begin* to try to reach reasoned agreement about our most fundamental moral commitments until we shore up our commitment to argumentation itself. Put otherwise, insofar as his strategies for recovering democracy and democratic political argument presuppose his account of human dignity, Dworkin's position amounts to just one more reasonably rejectable comprehensive moral doctrine. And if Dworkin is correct – again, I think he is – that our current modes of public political discourse "fails the standards of even a decent junior high school

---

[27] See Berkowitz 2007 for a similar criticism.

debate" (2006: 127), his call for a new political debate across deep ideological divides (2006: 160) cannot be met.

Dworkin recognizes his predicament. Having devoted a large part of his book to lamenting the debasement of democratic discourse and the absence of reasoned argument in response to disagreement, he sets out a substantive moral position and then calls for an argument in response (2006: 160). But those who "delight in cartoons of a simian President Bush dragging his hands on the ground or in books with titles like *How to Talk to a Liberal (If You Must)*" (2006: 162) are not able to or interested in proffering a reasoned response. In the end, he admits that he may have "fallen back only on faith" in his fellow citizens (2006: 164).

There is nothing wrong with having faith in one's fellow democratic citizens, and Dworkin is surely correct to say that "argument is pointless without faith in those with whom you argue" (2006: 164). But the position I have developed provides a basis for this faith because it provides reasons, drawn from epistemic commitments citizens already accept, for engaging in the kind of public debate Dworkin rightly calls for. If democracy is possible here, it cannot depend upon widespread agreement on a manifestly controversial moral conception of human dignity. As I have argued in the early chapters of this book, citizens deeply divided over fundamental moral commitments, nonetheless, share a common set of epistemic principles which can form the basis of our plea for reasoned argument.

Dworkin's policy proposals

More importantly, Dworkin's concrete policy suggestions can be supported from the folk epistemic view, independently of his moral conception of human dignity. Dworkin calls for innovations in education, elections, and the courts. Although I endorse all of Dworkin's proposals, I would like to discuss briefly only the first two.

Recounting an encounter with a fellow citizen who claimed that because the political issues surrounding the 2004 election – torture in Guantanamo, tax reductions, and so on – were too complicated, he would be voting for Bush simply on the grounds that Bush is religious, Dworkin laments the state of our public education system. He insists that "we must no longer tolerate secondary school education that puts so many thoughtful voters in that impossible and undemocratic position," and calls for the addition of a "Contemporary Politics" course to every high school curriculum (2006: 148). Explaining that the course is not to be fashioned on the model of a civics lesson, Dworkin writes:

The dominant pedagogical aim must be to instill some sense of the complexity of these issues, some understanding of positions different from those the students are likely to find at home or among friends, and some idea of what a conscientious and respectful argument over these issues might be like. (2006: 149)

The folk epistemic conception of democracy we have developed can endorse this suggestion, noting, with Dworkin, the inherent difficulties such a proposal raises concerning textbooks and content (2006: 150). Yet the folk epistemic view perhaps can provide some guidance in navigating such difficulties. Since, on the folk epistemic view, the justification for this kind of course lies in the development of the epistemic capabilities requisite for democratic engagement rather than a moral conception of human dignity, the specifics of such a course should be selected with a view toward maximizing exposure to clear, careful, and forceful argumentation on behalf of, as Dworkin says, views the students are not likely to have already considered. Again, the aim is not to win converts to unfamiliar viewpoints, but to help students sharpen their thinking by exposing them to examples of reasoned argument.

The second policy propose of Dworkin's that we will discuss concerns the way we presently conduct elections. Here, Dworkin's concern is with the increasing respects in which our elections are conducted like marketing campaigns, where candidates are treated as brands to be sold to a consuming public. His proposal has three components. First, he proposes that "Congress should create and fund two special public broadcasting channels to offer continuous election coverage during each presidential election period"; these channels, Dworkin recommends, should be "subject to severe equal-time and fairness coverage restrictions" (2006: 51). Second, Dworkin recommends that:

Political commercials in the familiar form should be forbidden on all networks except subject to the following regulations: the advertisement must run for a minimum of three minutes, of which at least two minutes must consist in a candidate for office or an officer of an organization that has paid for the advertisements speaking directly to the camera. (2006: 151)

Finally, Dworkin proposes that during the presidential election period, each major network "should be required to set aside a prime-time slot of half an hour each week" for the purpose of allowing "each of the major parties to correct what it takes to be errors or bias in that network's reporting and political opinion broadcasts during that proceeding week" (2006: 152).

Of course, Dworkin makes these recommendations as part of his general mission to begin a proper debate about what democracy requires; they are not offered as proposals to be considered rather than policies to be adopted. Moreover, Dworkin recognizes that his proposal concerning the content of political advertisements raises substantial First Amendment issues (2006: 152). From the folk epistemic view, we can applaud the spirit of Dworkin's proposal, while adding that these innovations find considerable support in the folk epistemic approach, for these measures share with Sunstein's suggestions mentioned above the aim of creating a republic of reasons. But the virtue of the kind of approach I have been advocating is that it can supply the justification for such policies without asserting the priority of some contestable moral value; it instead proffers a collection reasons, drawn from the *epistemic* commitment we already share, for thinking that democratic elections should be conducted differently from marketing campaigns.

Summary

The argument of this book can be summarized as follows: the folk epistemic norms to which we – you and I – are already committed simply by virtue of being epistemic agents provide compelling reasons to endorse a democratic political order, even in cases where democratically generated collective decisions seem from our own points of view drastically wrong, even intolerable. In this way, the folk epistemic argument provides a response to the problem of deep politics as described in Chapter 1. Due to the fact that the folk epistemic commitments underlying even one's deepest moral convictions can be satisfied only within a democratic politics, citizens who find themselves on the losing end of a democratic decision that involved fundamental moral principles, nonetheless, have reason to engage in *petition* and (in certain cases) *civil disobedience* rather than *rebellion*; that is, folk epistemology gives us reason to exercise *voice* rather than *exit*.

According to the argument I have been developing, proper democratic dialogue requires not only legal and institutional protections for deliberating individuals, but also certain cultural and civic institutions that foster the habits and capabilities necessary for proper deliberation. Certainly, the formal and legal arrangements associated with democracy – freedom of speech, assembly, the press, and the like – are not in themselves sufficient to promote the epistemic benefits of a democratic society, since these very institutions allow individuals to epistemically detach themselves from the wider society in which their view might be challenged and criticized. Hence, we find that the Internet, arguably an ideal institution for democratic deliberation, is frequently used as a filtering mechanism that epistemically insulates individuals from potential critics. A similar story can be told about the current state of news media. Empirical work shows the dangers of doxastically homogenous and epistemically insular groups and the need for open public spaces in which dissent and contestation are encouraged. Hence, a dialogical democracy must countenance a state that actively *promotes* a politics of engagement by cultivating certain epistemic habits among citizens and creating and maintaining civic and political institutions within which proper deliberation can commence. Consequently, dialogical democracy is mildly *perfectionist* in its account of legitimate state action; that is, it requires the state to pursue the *cultivation* of certain epistemic capabilities among its citizens. Drawing on recent work by Sunstein and Dworkin, we sketched some general proposals.

In November of 2004, the United States conducted a Presidential election with an unusually high degree of participation. This is a good thing, no matter what you may think of the results of that particular election. But consider again the findings of the study conducted by the University of Maryland's Program on International Policy Attitudes (PIPA): misperceptions concerning the Iraq war "vary significantly according to individuals' primary source of news" such that "those who primarily watch Fox News are significantly more likely to have misperceptions, while those who listen to NPR or watch PBS are significantly less likely."[28] A more recent PIPA study, "The Separate Realities of Bush and Kerry Supporters," shows that, in the final run-up to the 2004 presidential election, a significant majority of George W. Bush's supporters held demonstrably false beliefs about his policies and their international reception.[29] The same study shows that most of these supporters based their support for Bush on these false beliefs.

Again, no matter what you may think of the election, or of George W. Bush's presidency, or of the war in Iraq, you, as a democratic citizen, must find these results highly disturbing. Government of the people, by the people, and for the people cannot exist except where the people are well-informed, or at least not thoroughly deluded. If you are indeed disturbed by these findings, you have already accepted the core of folk epistemic conception of democracy that I have proposed in these pages: democratic self-government is crucially an epistemic enterprise. The bare existence of such findings completes the picture: in order for democracy to endure in a healthy condition, a social epistemic system must be maintained by a state that takes positive steps to cultivate and enable proper epistemic

---

[28] www.pipa.org/OnlineReports/Iraq/Media_10_02_03_Report.pdf.
[29] www.pipa.org/OnlineReports/Pres_Election_04/Report10_21_04.pdf.

practice. Although it is not clear what the future has in store for the United States, or what domestic or international policies are best, the democratic commitments we hold dear despite disagreements over our deepest moral doctrines – commitments to believing on the basis of evidence and reasons, rational debate and argumentation, respectful even if heated disagreement, and intelligent collective decision – are undeniably in jeopardy. I have tried in this book to indicate a way in which we can, despite our considerable differences over our deepest moral commitments, reach reasoned agreement about what our shared and underlying commitment to democracy amounts to.

Works cited

Ackerly, Brooke 2000. *Political Theory and Feminist Social Criticism*. Cambridge University Press.

Ackerman, Bruce 1989. "Why Dialogue?," *Journal of Philosophy* 86: 16–27.

Ackerman, Bruce and James Fishkin 2003. "Deliberation Day," in James S. Fishkin, and Peter Laslett (eds.), *Debating Deliberative Democracy*. Oxford: Blackwell.

2004. *Deliberation Day*. New Haven, CT: Yale University Press.

Adler, Jonathan 2002. *Belief's Own Ethics*. Cambridge, MA: MIT Press.

Anderson, Elizabeth 2006. "The Epistemology of Democracy," *Episteme* 3.1–2: 8–22.

Apel, Karl-Otto 1980. "The *A Priori* of the Communication Community and the Foundations of Ethics," in *Towards a Transformation of Philosophy*. London: Routledge.

Aristotle. *Metaphysics*. 1952. Richard Hope, trans. Ann Arbor, MI: University of Michigan Press.

Arneson, Richard J. 2003. "Liberal Neutrality on the Good: An Autopsy," in *Perfectionism and Neutrality*, Steven Wall and George Klosko (eds.), Lanham, MD: Rowman & Littlefield.

Axtell, Guy 2006. "Blind Man's Bluff: The 'Basic Belief Apologetic'," *Philosophical Studies* 130: 131–152.

Barber, Benjamin 2004. *Strong Democracy*. Berkeley, CA: University of California Press.

Barry, Brian 1995. *Justice as Impartiality*. New York: Oxford University Press.

2001. *Culture and Equality*. Cambridge, MA: Harvard University Press.

Bates, Stephen 1993. *Battleground: One Mother's Crusade, the Religious Right, and the Struggle for Control of our Classrooms*. New York: Poseidon Press.

Beatty, Jack 2007. "Cognitive Dissonance," *The Atlantic*, July 24 at: www.theatlantic.com/doc/200707u/beatty-bush (accessed August 2, 2008).

Benedict XVI 2005. "Homily at the Mass for the Election of the Roman Pontiff," April 18, 2005 at: www.vatican.va /gpII /documents/ homily-pro-eligendo-pontifice_ 20050418_ en.html.

Benhabib, Seyla 1992. *Situating the Self*. New York: Routledge.

1996. "Towards a Deliberative Model of Democratic Legitimacy," in Benhabib (ed.), *Democracy and Difference*. New Jersey: Princeton University Press.

Berkowitz, Peter 2007. "Illiberal Liberalism," *First Things* 172: 50–54.

Boghossian, Paul 2006. *Fear of Knowledge*. New York: Oxford University Press.

Bohman, James 1996. *Public Deliberation*. Cambridge, MA: MIT Press.

Bozell, L. Brent 2004. *Weapons of Mass Distortion*. New York: Crown.

Brock, David 2004. *The Republican Noise Machine*. New York: Crown.

Buchanan, Allen 2004. "Political Liberalism and Social Epistemology," *Philosophy & Public Affairs* 32.2: 95–130.

Buchanan, Patrick 1990. "This is the Battle for America's Soul," *L. A. Times*, March 25, M5.

  1992. "Republican National Convention Speech," at: www.buchanan.org/pa-92-0817-rnc.html.

  2001. *The Death of the West*. New York: Thomas Dunne Books.

Callan, Eamonn 1997. *Creating Citizens*. New York: Oxford University Press.

Carter, Stephen 1998. *Civility*. New York: Basic Books.

Chambers, Simone and Anne Costain (eds.), 2000. *Deliberation, Democracy, and the Media*. Lanham, MD: Rowman & Littlefield.

Charen, Mona 2003. *Useful Idiots*. New York: Regnery Publishing.

Christiano, Thomas 2001. "Is There Any Basis for Rawls' Duty of Civility?," *The Modern Schoolman* 78: 151–161.

Churchland, Paul 1981. "Eliminative Materialism and the Propositional Attitudes," *Journal of Philosophy* LXXVIII.2: 67–90.

  1984. *Matter and Consciousness*. Cambridge, MA: MIT Press.

  1994. "Folk Psychology," *A Companion to the Philosophy of Mind*, Samuel Guttenplan (ed.), Oxford: Blackwell.

Clancy, Susan A. 2005. *Abducted: How People Come to Believe They Were Kidnapped by Aliens*. Cambridge, MA: Harvard University Press.

Clifford, W. K. 1999. *The Ethics of Belief and Other Essays*. Amherst, NY: Prometheus Books.

Cohen, Joshua 1997. "Procedure and Substance in Deliberative Democracy," *Deliberative Democracy*, James Bohman and William Rehg (eds.), Cambridge, MA: MIT Press.

  1998. "Democracy and Liberty", in *Deliberative Demcoracy*, Jon Elster (ed.), Cambridge University Press.

Conason, Joe 2003. *Big Lies*. New York: Thomas Dunne.

Coulter, Ann 2003. *Treason: Liberal Treachery from the Cold War to the War on Terrorism*. New York: Crown Forum.

  2004. *How to Talk to a Liberal (If You Must)*. New York: Crown Forum.

  2006. *Godless: the Church of Liberalism*. New York: Crown Forum.

  2007. *If Democrats Had Any Brains, They'd be Republicans*. New York: Crown Forum.

Dean, John 2004. *Worse Than Watergate: The Secret Presidency of George W. Bush*. New York: Little, Brown.

Dennett, Daniel 1987. *The Intentional Stance*. Cambridge, MA: MIT Press.

  1996. *Kinds of Minds*. New York: Basic Books.

Dewey, John 1935. *Liberalism and Social Action*. New York: Putnam.

Dietrich, Franz 2008. "The Premises of Condorcet's Jury Theorem Are not Simultaneously Justified," *Episteme* 5.1: 56–73.

Dryzek, John 1996. *Democracy in Capitalist Times*. New York: Oxford University Press.

Dworkin, Ronald 1985. *A Matter of Principle*. Cambridge, MA: Harvard University Press.

2006. *Is Democracy Possible Here?* New Jersey: Princeton University Press.

Eberle, Christopher 2002. *Religious Conviction in Liberal Politics*. Cambridge University Press.

Estlund, David 1997. "Beyond Fairness and Deliberation," *Deliberative Democracy*, James Bohman and William Rehg (eds.), Cambridge, MA: MIT Press.

1998. "The Insularity of the Reasonable," *Ethics* 108: 252–275.

2008. *Democratic Authority*. Princeton University Press.

Etzioni, Amitai 2001. *Next*. New York: Basic Books.

Fish, Stanley 1999. "Mutual Respect as a Device of Exclusion," *Deliberative Politics*, Steven Macedo (ed.), New York: Oxford University Press.

Fishkin, James 1993. *Democracy and Deliberation*. New Haven, CT: Yale University Press.

Frank, Thomas 2004. *What's The Matter with Kansas?* New York: Metropolitan Books.

Franken, Al 1996. *Rush Limbaugh is a Big Fat Idiot*. New York: Delacorte Press.

2003. *Lies and the Lying Liars who Tell Them*. New York: Dutton.

2005. *The Truth (with Jokes)*. New York: Dutton.

Frazer, Nancy 1992. "Rethinking the Public Sphere," in Calhoun, Craig (ed.), *Habermans and the Public Sphere*. Cambridge, MA: MIT Press.

Freeman, Samuel 2007. *Rawls*. New York: Routledge.

Friedman, Jeffrey 2005. "Popper, Weber, and Hayek: The Epistemology and Politics of Ignorance," *Critical Review* 17, nos. 1–2: i–lviii.

Fritz, Ben, Bryan Keefer, and Brendan Nyhan 2004. *All the President's Spin*. New York: Touchstone.

Gallagher, Mike 2005. *Surrounded by Idiots*. New York: William Morrow.

Galston, William 1999. "Diversity, Toleration, and Deliberative Democracy," in *Deliberative Politics*, Stephen Macado (ed.), New York: Oxford University Press.

2002. *Liberal Pluralism*. Cambridge University Press.

2005. *Public Matters*. Lanham, MD: Rowman & Littlefield.

Gastil, John 2000. *By Popular Demand*. Berkeley, CA: University of California Press.

Gaus, Gerald 1997. "Does Democracy Reveal the Voice of the People," *Australasian Journal of Philosophy* 75.2: 141–162.

2003a. *Contemporary Theories of Liberalism*. London: Sage.

2003b. "Liberal Neutrality: A Compelling and Radical Principle," in *Perfectionism and Neutrality*, Steven Wall and George Klosko (eds.), Lanham, MD: Rowman & Littlefield.

George, Robert and Christopher Wolfe 2000. "Introduction," in *Natural Law and Public Reason*. Washington, Georgetown University Press.

Gingrich, Newt 2005. *Winning the Future*. New York: Regnery.

Goldberg, Bernard 2003. *Bias*. New York: Harper.

Goldman, Alvin 1986. *Epistemology and Cognition*. Cambridge, MA: Harvard University Press.

1999. *Knowledge in a Social World*. New York: Oxford University Press.

Goodin, Robert 2003. *Reflective Democracy*. New York: Oxford University Press.

Gore, Al 2007. *The Assault on Reason*. New York: Penguin.

Gray, John 2000. *Two Faces of Liberalism*. New York: New Press.

Gutmann, Amy and Dennis Thompson 1996. *Democracy and Disagreement*. Cambridge, MA: Harvard University Press.

2004. *Why Deliberative Democracy?* New Jersey: Princeton University Press.

Habermas, Jürgen 1990. "Discourse Ethics," *Moral Consciousness and Communicative Action*. Cambridge, MA: MIT Press.

1996. *Between Facts and Norms*. Cambridge, MA: MIT Press.

2006. "Religion in the Public Sphere," *European Journal of Philosophy* 14.1: 1–25.

Hampshire, Stuart 1999. *Justice Is Conflict*. New Jersey: Princeton University Press.

Hannity, Sean 2004. *Let Freedom Ring*. New York: Regan Books.

Hardin, Russell 2002. "The Crippled Epistemology of Extremism," in Albert, Breton (ed.), *Political Extremism and Rationality*. Cambridge University Press.

Harpine, William D. 2004. "Is Modernism Really Modern? Uncovering a Fallacy in Postmodernism," *Argumentation* 18: 349–358.

Hirschman, Albert 1970. *Exit, Voice, and Loyalty*. Cambridge, MA: Harvard University Press.

Holmes, Stephen 1995. *Passions and Constraint*. University of Chicago Press.

Hookway, Christopher 2000. *Truth, Rationality, and Pragmatism*, New York: Oxford University Press.

Huffington, Arianna 2004. *Fanatics and Fools*. New York: Miramax Books.

Jacoby, Susan 2008. *The Age of American Unreason*. New York: Pantheon Books.

James, William 1977. *The Writings of William James*, John McDermott (ed.), University of Chicago Press.

Kingwell, Mark 1995. *A Civil Tongue*. College Station, PA: Penn State University Press.

Klosko, George 2003. "Reasonable Rejection and Neutrality of Justification," in *Perfectionism and Neutrality*, Steven Wall and George Klosko (eds.), Lanham, MD: Rowman & Littlefield.

Kukathas, Chandran 2003. *The Liberal Archipelago*. New York: Oxford University Press.

Lakoff, George 2002. *Moral Politics*. University of Chicago Press.

2004. *Don't Think of an Elephant!* New York: Chelsea Green Press.

2006. *Whose Freedom?* New York: Farrar, Straus, and Giroux.

2008. *The Political Mind*. New York: Viking Adult.

Larmore, Charles 1987. *Patterns of Moral Complexity*. Cambridge University Press.

1996. *The Morals of Modernity*. Cambridge University Press.

2003. "Public Reason," in Samuel Freeman (ed.), *The Cambridge Companion to Rawls*. Cambridge University Press.

Lefort, Claude 1988. *Democracy and Political Theory*. Minneapolis: University of Minnesota Press.

Leib, Ethan 2004. *Deliberative Democracy in America*. Pennsylvania: Penn State University Press.

List, Christian and Robert Goodin 2001. "Epistemic Democracy: Generalizing the Condorcet Jury Theorem," *Journal of Political Philosophy* 9: 277–306.

Lynch, Michael 2004. *True to Life*. Cambridge, MA: MIT Press.

Macedo, Stephen 1990. *Liberal Virtues*. New York: Oxford University Press.

   1995. "Liberal Civic Education and Religious Fundamentalism: The Case of God v. John Rawls?," *Ethics* 105: 468–496.

   2000. *Diversity and Distrust*. Cambridge, MA: Harvard University Press.

MacIntyre, Alasdair 1984. *After Virtue*. Chicago, IL: University of Notre Dame Press.

Mackie, Gerald 2003. *Democracy Defended*. Cambridge University Press.

Mansbridge, Jane 1983. *Beyond Adversary Democracy*. University of Chicago Press.

Mill, John Stuart 1991 [1861]. *On Liberty and Other Essays*. New York: Oxford University Press.

Misak, Cheryl 2004a. *Truth and the End of Inquiry*. New York: Oxford University Press.

   2004b. "Making Disagreement Matter," *Journal of Speculative Philosophy* 18.1: 9–22.

   2007. "Pragmatism and Deflationism," *New Pragmatists*, Cheryl Misak (ed.), New York: Oxford University Press.

Moore, Michael 2002. *Stupid White Men*. New York: Regan Books.

Mouffe, Chantal 2000. *The Democratic Paradox*. New York: Verso.

Mulhall, Stephen and Adam Swift 1996. *Liberals and Communitarians*, 2nd edn. Oxford: Blackwell.

Nagel, Thomas 1987. "Moral Conflict and Political Legitimacy," *Philosophy & Public Affairs* 16: 215–240.

   1991. *Equality and Partiality*. New York: Oxford University Press.

Nozick, Robert 1974. *Anarchy, State, and Utopia*. New York: Free Press.

Nussbaum, Martha 2000. *Women and Human Development*. Cambridge University Press.

   2006. *Frontiers of Justice*. Cambridge, MA: Harvard University Press.

   2007. *Frontiers of Justice*. Cambridge, MA: Harvard University Press.

   2008. *Liberty of Conscience*. New York: Basic Books.

O'Neill, John and Jerome Corsi 2004. *Unfit for Command*. New York: Regnery Publishing.

Orwell, George 1968. *In Front of Your Nose*. New York: Harcourt.

Page, Benjamin 1996. *Who Deliberates? Mass Media in Modern Democracy*. University of Chicago Press.

Peirce, Charles Sanders 1878. "How to Make Our Ideas Clear," in *Peirce: Philoosphical Writings*, Justus Buchler (ed.), New York: Dover.

Perry, Michael 2003. *Under God?* Cambridge University Press.

Pettit, Philip 2001. *A Theory of Freedom*. New York: Oxford University Press.

Phillips, Anne 1991. *Engendering Democracy*. College Park: Pennsylvania State University Press.

Pincone, Guido and Fernando R. Teson 2006. *Rational Choice and Democratic Deliberation*. Cambridge University Press.

Popper, Karl 1971. *The Open Society and Its Enemies*. Princeton University Press.

Posner, Richard 2002. "Dewey and Democracy: A Critique," *Transactional Viewpoints* 1, no. 3: 1–4.

    2003. *Law, Pragmatism, and Democracy*. Cambridge, MA: Harvard University Press.

    2004. "Smooth Sailing," *Legal Affairs* January/February 2004: 41–42.

Price, Huw 1998. "Three Norms of Assertibility, or How the Moa Became Extinct," *Philosophical Perspectives* 12: 241–254.

    2003. "Truth as Convenient Friction," *Journal of Philosophy* 100: 167–190.

Quine, W. V. O. 1985. "States of Mind," *Journal of Philosophy* LXXXII: 5–8.

Rawls, John 1985. "Justice as Fairness: Political Not Metaphysical," *John Rawls: Collected Papers*, Samuel Freeman (ed.), Cambridge, MA: Harvard University Press, 2001.

    1999. *A Theory of Justice*, revised edn. Cambridge, MA: Harvard University Press.

    2005. *Political Liberalism*, paperback edn. New York: Columbia University Press.

Raz, Joseph 1990. "Facing Diversity: The Case of Epistemic Abstinence," *Philosophy & Public Affairs* 19: 3–46.

Reidy, David 2000. "Rawls's Wide View of Public Reason: Not Wide Enough," *Res Publica* 6: 49–72.

    2001. "Pluralism, Liberal Democracy, and Compulsory Education," *Journal of Social Philosophy* 32.4: 585–609.

Riker, William 1988. *Liberalism Against Populism*. London: Waveland Press.

Rodin, Judith and Stephen Steinberg 2003. "Incivility and Public Discourse," in *Public Discourse in America*, Judith Rodin and Steinberg (eds.), Philadelphia, PA: University of Pennsylvania Press.

Rorty, Richard 1979. *Philosophy and the Mirror of Nature*. New Jersey: Princeton University Press.

    1995. "Is Truth a Goal of Inquiry?," *Philosophical Quarterly* 45: 281–300.

Rorty, Richard and Pascal Engel 2007. *What's the Use of Truth?* New York: Columbia University Press.

Ross, Lee, Lepper, Mark R., and Hubbard, Michael 1975. "Perseverance in Self-Perception and Social Perception: Biased Attributional Processes in the Debriefing Paradigm," *Journal of Personality and Social Psychology* 32.5: 880–892.

Rousseau, Jean-Jacques 1988. *On the Social Contract*. Donald Cress, trans. Indianapolis, IN: Hackett Publishing.

Russell, Bertrand 1949. *Authority and the Individual*. London: George Allen & Unwin.

Sandel, Michael 1996. *Democracy's Discontent*. Cambridge, MA: Harvard University Press.

1998a. *Liberalism and the Limits of Justice*, 2nd edn. Cambridge University Press.

1998b. "What Money Can't Buy," Tanner Lectures.

Sanders, Lynn 1997. "Against Deliberation," *Political Theory* 25.3: 347–376.

Savage, Michael 2005. *Liberalism is a Mental Disorder*. New York: Thomas Nelson.

Schultz, Ed. 2004. *Straight Talk from the Heartland: Tough Talk, Common Sense and Hope from a Former Conservative*. New York: Regan Books.

Schumpeter, Joseph 1942. *Capitalism, Socialism, and Democracy*. New York: Harper & Row.

Schweizer, Peter 2005. *Do as I say (Not as I do): Profiles in Liberal Hypocrisy*. New York: Doubleday.

Sellars, Wilfrid 1997. *Empiricism and the Philosophy of Mind*. Cambridge, MA: Harvard University Press.

Sen, Amartya 1975. *On Economic Inequality*. Oxford University Press.

1999. *Development as Freedom*. New York: Knopf.

Shapiro, Ian 2003. *The State of Democratic Theory*. New Jersey: Princeton University Press.

Sher, George 1997. *Beyond Neutrality*. New York: Cambridge University Press.

Smith, Glenn W. 2004. *Unfit Commander: Texans for Truth Take on George W. Bush*. New York: Regan Books.

Somin, Ilya 1998. "Voter Ignorance and the Democratic Ideal," *Critical Review* 12, no. 4: 413–458.

2004. "Richard Posner's Democratic Pragmatism and the Problem of Public Ignorance," *Critical Review* 16, no. 1: 1–22.

Stossel, John 2006. *Myths, Lies, and Downright Stupidity*. New York: Hyperion.

Stout, Jeffrey 2004. *Democracy and Tradition*. New Jersey: Princeton University Press.

2007. "On Our Interest in Getting Things Right," *New Pragmatists*, Cheryl Misak (ed.), New York: Oxford University Press.

Sunstein, Cass 1996. *Democracy and the Problem of Free Speech*. New York: Free Press.

2001a. *Republic.com*. New Jersey: Princeton University Press.

2001b. *Designing Democracy*. New York: Oxford University Press.

2003a. "The Law of Group Polarization," in *Debating Deliberative Democracy*, James Fishkin and Peter Laslett, (eds.), Oxford: Blackwell.

2003b. *Why Societies Need Dissent*. Cambridge, MA: Harvard University Press.

2006. *Infotopia*. New York: Oxford University Press.

Swain, Carol 2002. *The New White Nationalism in America*. Cambridge University Press.

Swain, Carol and Russ Nieli (eds.) 2003. *Contemporary Voices of White Nationalism in America*. Cambridge University Press.

Talisse, Robert 2002. "Two Faced Liberalism," *Critical Review* 14.4: 441–458.

2004. "Can Value Pluralists be Comprehensive Liberals?," *Contemporary Political Theory* 3.2: 127–139.

2005. *Democracy After Liberalism*. New York: Routledge.

Talisse, Robert and Scott Aikin 2006. "Two Forms of the Straw Man," *Argumentation* 20.3: 345–352.

2008. "Modus Tonens," *Argumentation*. 22.4: 521–529.

Tomasi, John 2001. *Liberalism Beyond Justice*. New Jersey: Princeton University Press.

Von Hoffman, Nicholas 2004. *Hoax*. New York: Nation Books.

Waldron, Jeremy 1993. *Liberal Rights*. Cambridge University Press.

Wall, Steven 1998. *Liberalism, Perfectionism, and Restraint*. Cambridge University Press.

Wall, Steven and George Klosko 2003. "Introduction," in *Perfectionism and Neutrality*, Wall and Klosko (eds.), Lanham, MD: Rowman & Littlefield.

Walzer, Michael 2004. *Politics and Passion*. New Haven, CT: Yale University Press.

Wiggins, David 1987. *Needs, Values, Truth*. Oxford: Basil Blackwell.

1998. "C. S. Peirce: Belief, Truth, and Going From the Known to the Unknown," *Pragmatism*, Cheryl Misak (ed.), *Canadian Journal of Philosophy*, supp. vol.

Williams, Bernard 1973. "Deciding to Believe," in *Problems of the Self*. Cambridge University Press.

1995. *Making Sense of Humanity*. Cambridge University Press.

2005. *In the Beginning was the Deed*. New Jersey: Princeton University Press.

Wolf, Susan 1995. "Commentary on Martha Nussbaum's 'Human Capabilities, Female Human Beings,'" in Martha Nussbaum and Jonathan Glover (eds.), *Women, Culture and Development*. New York: Oxford University Press.

Wolterstorff, Nicholas 1997. "The Role of Religion in Decision and Discussion of Political Issues," in *Religion in the Public Square*. (Lanham, MD: Rowman & Littlefield).

Young, Iris Marion 2000. *Inclusion and Democracy*. New York: Oxford University Press.

2003. "Activist Challenges to Deliberative Democracy," in *Debating Deliberative Democracy* James Fishkin and Peter Laslett (eds.), Oxford: Blackwell.

Index

abortion 18, 19, 20–21, 33, 34, 36, 49, 53, 55, 109, 135
accountability 124, 125
Ackerly, Brooke 174
Ackerman, Bruce 50–51, 76, 160, 171
Ackerman, Bruce and James Fishkin 138, 160, 161, 163
Adler, Jonathan 86, 96, 100
affirming the consequent 166
agent ignorance/belief ignorance 158, 159, 161, 162
agonism 107
Aikin, Scott 168
Amish 183, 184
anarchism 45
Anderson, Elizabeth 135
anti-democrats 126, 130, 132, 133
Apel, Karl-Otto 129
argument 5, 6
Aristotle 90, 91
Arneson, Richard J. 171
assertion 101, 102
authenticity 125
authority 11
autonomy 3, 7
Axtell, Guy 118

Barber, Benjamin 26
Barry, Brian 50, 51, 171, 184
Bates, Stephen 177
belief 5, 6, 83, 84, 85, 88, 89
    de facto 132
    de jure 132
    full 90
    genuine 131
    religious 100, 101
    untenable 94, 105
Benedict XVI, Pope 110
Benhabib, Seyla 52, 129
Berkowitz, Peter 187
Berlin, Isaiah 23, 28
Bible 16, 18, 182
Boghossian, Paul 111

Bohman, James 60, 71
Bozell, L. Brent 112
Brock, David 112
Buchanan, Allen 141
Buchanan, Patrick 64
burdens of judgment (Rawls) 146
Bush, George W. 7, 110, 112, 113, 169, 188, 191

Cahn, Steven 168
Callan, Eamonn 177
capabilities approach 173, 174
Carter, Stephen 107
Chambers, Simone and Anne Costain, 160
Charen, Mona 113
Christiano, Thomas 77
Churchill, Ward 168
Churchill, Winston 25, 28
Churchland, Paul 83, 85
citizen juries 138
civic liberalism (Macedo) 179
civil disobedience 37, 39, 190
civil war 28, 42
civility 29, 107
Clancy, Susan 97
Clifford, W. K. 99, 100
coercion 45
Cohen, Joshua 55, 93, 128
Cold War 1
commitments
    basic 12
    moral 12, 35, 36, 42, 49, 69, 78
    religious 27, 30
communication 130, 131
communitarianism 25, 69
comprehensive doctrine 46, 53
compromise 3, 19, 20, 22, 23–24, 36
Conason, Joe 112
concept/conception 85
Condorcet Jury Theorem 135
conscientious engagement 151
conspiracy 40

constitution 11, 24
content 89, 91
conversation stoppers 110
Coulter, Ann 8, 9, 65, 103, 112
culture war 64

Dean, John 113
deciding to believe (Williams) 97
deep politics 35, 37, 39
    problem of 41, 42, 46, 50, 60, 69, 71, 77, 78, 79,
        114, 121, 139, 149, 152, 190
deliberative enclaves 59
deliberative polling 138, 160
demagoguery 127
democracy 14, 42, 44
    adversary 25
    constitutional 14, 44
    deficit 2
    deliberative 128, 129, 133, 136, 157, 159
    dialogical 139, 154, 155, 156, 170, 172, 177, 191
    as procedure 23
Dennett, Daniel 83
Dewey, John 6, 77
dictatorship of relativism 110
Dietrich, Franz 135
dignity 3, 35, 44, 186, 187, 188, 189
disagreement 8, 9, 13, 109, 115, 148, 149, 176
discourse failure 162, 165, 167
division of epistemic labor 125, 141
Dobson, James 20–21
doxastically homogenous groups 58
Dryzek, John 125
Dworkin, Ronald 4, 6, 53, 59, 156, 168, 171,
    185–190, 191

Eberle, Christopher 59, 151–152
elections 11, 189
eliminativism 85
Ellison, Ralph 77
emergency contraception 17
emotivism 110
enclave deliberation 57
"end of inquiry" conception of truth 92
Engel, Pascal 101, 116
Enlightenment 114, 116–119
epistemic
    action 5, 92, 104
    agency 121, 124, 126, 133, 140, 190
    akrasia 86
    bad faith 105
    capacities 176
    commitments 5, 6, 8, 78, 79, 80, 87, 145, 152
    deference 141
    deliberativism 133, 134
    dependency 141, 143

egalitarianism 143
elitism 136
etiquette 106
exclusion 60
failure 102, 105
peers 124
perfectionism 170, 172, 177, 179, 181
practices 108
principles 4
proceduralism 135, 136, 137
reasons 4, 7
self-control 99
shame 184
epistemic capabilities 157, 173–176, 191
    communicative capabilities 175
    formal capabilities 175
    informational capabilities 175
    methodological capabilities 175
    interpersonal capabilities 175
epistemic character 109
    three components of 105
epistemically closed system 52
epistemically excluded groups 60
epistemic perfectionism 156
epistemology 9
    crippled 57, 58, 60, 64
    everyday 5
    first-personal 4
    folk 5, 6, 78, 79, 80, 82, 85, 86, 87, 98, 113,
        121, 189
    reformed 118, 119
    self-insulation 68
    social 6
epistocracy 137
equality 3, 7, 35, 36, 124
Estlund, David 55, 133, 135, 137
Etzioni, Amitai 26
evidence 5, 6, 85
evidentialism 99, 117
    extrinsic/intrinsic 100
evolution, theory of 15, 30–31
exclusion objection 52
exit 38–39, 41, 42, 47, 190
    obstructive 39, 40–41
    non-obstructive 39, 41
externalism 98
extreme views 58
extremist groups 62

fact of reasonable pluralism 46, 56, 145, 148, 149
fairness 3, 25, 29
fanatics 14, 19
fantastical beliefs 97
feminism 114
fideists 98, 99

First Amendment 190
first-personal (epistemic) perspective 87
Fish, Stanley 129
Fishkin, James 138, 160
Frazer, Nancy, 52
Focus on the Family 20–21
folk epistemology 5, 6, 78, 79, 80, 82, 85, 86, 87,
 98, 113, 121, 189
 as actional 105
 as internalist 98
 commitments of 7, 102, 127
 defined 88
 five principles 87
 inclusion in 105
 justification 127
 norms 7
 principles 8
 vs. professional 105
folk theories 82
folk psychology 5, 82, 83–84
frames 66, 67, 68
franchise 125
Frank, Thomas 32–35
Franken, Al 8, 65, 103, 112, 167
freedom 3
 of assembly 123
 of conscience 6, 123
 of the press 6, 123
 of speech 6, 123, 190
 of thought 122
Freeman, Samuel 43
freestandingness (Rawls) 47, 55, 62, 71, 79
Friedman, Jeffrey 162
Fritz, Ben, Bryan Keefer, and Brendan Nyhan 112
Frost, Vicki 177, 181, 183
fundamental commitments 2, 3, 14, 15,
 18, 42

Gallagher, Mike 65, 112
Galston, William 2, 53, 55, 72
Gastil, John 138
Gaus, Gerald 25, 55, 134, 135, 171
gay marriage 16, 31–32, 33
George, Robert 53, 72
Gingrich, Newt 29
Goldberg, Bernard 112
Goldman, Alvin 6, 96
Goodin, Robert 56
Gore, Al 7, 112, 113, 186
Gray, John 46, 55
group polarization 56–59, 62, 143–144,
 167, 177
Gutmann, Amy 168
Gutmann, Amy and Dennis Thompson 128,
 129, 136

Habermas, Jürgen 106, 129, 130, 131
Hampshire, Stuart 46
Hannity, Sean 167
Hardin, Russell 57, 58, 60
Harpine, William D. 115
Hauerwas, Stanley 73
Heston, Charlton 168
higher rationality (Lakoff) 66, 68
Hirschman, Albert 38, 41, 42
Hobbes, Thomas 3, 11, 22, 38, 42, 46, 47, 79
Holmes, Stephen 48, 69
homosexuality 16, 19, 32
Hookway, Christopher 93
Horowitz, David 168
Hubbard, Michael 96
Huffington, Arianna 112
Hume, David 44
Hussein, Saddam 164

immanent criticism (Stout) 75, 76, 150
inclusion 124, 125
instability 59, 60
intelligent design 15
interests 2, 27, 29, 31, 32, 34
intolerance 2, 12, 18
Iraq 169, 191
Iraq War 164

Jacoby, Susan 112
James, William 100, 146
Jefferson, Thomas 44
Jesus (of Nazareth) 77
Joyce, James 90
justice 3, 12, 16, 17, 19, 35, 43, 44

Kansas Board of Education 30
Kant, Immanuel 44
Kantianism 148
Kerry, John 113
King, Jr., Martin Luther 54
Kingwell, Mark 107
Klosko, George 173
Kukathas, Chandran 173

Lakoff, George 65–68, 167
Larmore, Charles 50–51, 54, 56, 70, 71, 76, 128,
 145, 171, 173
Lefort, Claude 71
legitimacy 11, 22, 41, 42, 47
Leib, Ethan 138
Lepper, Mark R. 96
liar paradox 90
liberalism 43, 44, 46
liberties/liberty 3, 7, 11, 35, 36
List, Christian and Robert Goodin 135

Locke, John 44, 77, 116, 119
loyalty 38, 39
Lynch, Michael 111

Macedo, Stephen 177–181, 183, 184
MacIntyre, Alasdair 28, 73
Machiavelli, Niccolo 44
Mackie, Gerald 25
Madison, James 77, 125
majority rule 24
Mansbridge, Jane 25
Mao 123
McVeigh, Timothy 61
Milbank, John 73
Mill, John Stuart 6, 44, 136, 171
Millian standard of toleration 13
minimal plausibility 13
Misak, Cheryl 93, 109, 116
modus ponens 166
modus tolens 166
modus vivendi 23, 47, 60
monarchy 23
Montesquieu, Charles de Secondat 44
Moore, Michael 8, 65, 112, 168
moral
    argument 109
    cognitivism 110
    pluralism 3, 11, 13–14, 26, 32, 34, 35, 41, 55, 59,
        73, 139, 144, 145, 147, 148
    relativism 13, 111, 146
moral/religious commitments 12, 13, 22,
        27, 149
Mouffe, Chantal 46
Mozert v. *Hawkins* 139, 177
Mulhall, Stephen and Adam Swift 146

Nagel, Thomas 51, 69, 171
National Alliance 61
natural law 53
natural rights 44
naturalism 80
Nazi 3, 20–21
Nieli, Russ 61, 63
no spin zone 8, 111, 127
norm of rational dialogue (Larmore) 51
Nozick, Robert 45, 171
Nussbaum, Martha 70, 168, 173, 174

O'Neill, John and Jerome Corsi 113
O'Reilly, Bill 8
oligarchy 24
one-way Pyrrhonism 185
Operation Rescue 20–21
oppression 14, 41, 60

Orwell, George 95
overlapping consensus 47, 60, 145

Page, Benjamin 160
paradox of democratic justification 11, 15, 18, 19,
        20, 21, 22, 23, 25, 26, 27, 31, 32, 35, 36
participatory democrats 25
peace 25, 29, 42
peaceful co-existence 3, 42
Peirce, Charles 92, 93
perfectionism 171–172, 174
performative contradiction 130
Perry, Michael 182
petition 37, 39, 190
Pettit, Philip 125
Phillips, Anne 41
Philosopher Kings 137
Pierce, William 61
Pincione, Guido and Frenando Teson 163
Plato 136, 162
pluralism 3, 11, 13–14, 26, 32, 34, 35, 41, 55, 59, 73,
        139, 144, 145, 147, 148
plutocracy 24
political
    agenda 49, 51, 52
    deliberation 49
    discourse 111
    equality 6
political liberalism (Rawls) 43, 46, 79
political realism 22, 23
politics
    of engagement 71, 150, 154
    of omission 49, 51, 60, 72, 150, 154
Popper, Karl 6
Posner, Richard 27, 157, 159, 161, 163
Postmodernism 114
pragmatism 74, 80, 114
preferences 2, 27, 29, 42
Price, Huw 116
principle of neutrality 171–172
proceduralism 24–36, 112
propaganda 123
proposition 88
proviso, the (Rawls) 54, 55, 131
pseudo-deliberation 165, 169, 170
psychics 96
public displays of religious symbols 18
public education 176
public ignorance 156, 157, 158
public reason 43, 49, 51, 52, 53, 54, 55, 72, 128, 131,
        152, 153
Public Ignorance Objection 158, 159, 161, 163

al-Qaeda 164
Quine, W. V. O. 85

rationality 99, 100
Rawls, John 14, 23, 41, 43, 45, 47–48, 53, 54, 56, 60,
    62, 73, 74, 78, 116, 128, 131, 144–146, 148, 153,
    171, 173, 174
Raz, Joseph 55
reason-responsiveness 94, 97, 98, 102, 104, 105,
    123, 126, 127
reason exchange 104, 105
reasons 5, 6, 92
    moral 7
    motivating 7
    religious 49
rebellion 37, 38, 190
Reidy, David 153, 183
relocation 37, 38
Republican (Party) 33–34, 65
revolution 40
rights 11, 12, 24, 35, 44
Riker, William 25
Rodin, Judith 107
Roe v. *Wade* 37
Rorty, Richard 85, 115, 116
Rorty, Richard and Pascal Engel 116
Ross, Lee 96
Rousseau, Jean-Jacques 44, 134, 135
Russell, Bertrand 4, 6

same-sex couples 16
Sandel, Michael 27, 53, 68, 70, 172
Sanders, Lynn 41
Savage, Michael 65, 103, 112, 167
Schumpeter, Joseph 27
Schultz, Ed 112
Schweizer, Peter 112
self-deception 86, 95, 133
self-preservation 29
Sellars, Wilfrid 104
Sen, Amartya 173
Shapiro, Ian 26, 140
Sher, George 171
skepticism 13, 50, 146, 147
Smith, Anna Nicole 162
Smith, Glenn 44
social epistemic system 142, 143, 172, 176
Somin, Ilya 157, 159, 161
sophists or sophistry 110, 127

Southern Poverty Law Center 62
stability 22, 25, 47, 56
Stalin, Joseph 123
Steinberg, Stephen 107
Stossel, John 112
Stout, Jeffrey 43, 71–77, 116, 129, 150–152
Straw, Jack 3
Straw-man fallacy 104, 168
Sunstein, Cass 56, 58, 60, 61–64, 68, 138, 160,
    176, 191
Swain, Carol 61–64
Swift Boat Veterans for Truth 113

theocracy 24
third-personal knowledge attribution 87
Tlumak, Jeffrey 185
toleration 12, 19, 20, 21, 23, 30, 124, 148, 179
Tomasi, John 180
truth 5, 6, 85, 88, 90, 92, 127
truth-possessors 139
truth-seekers or truth-seeking 105, 139, 140
Turner, Lisa 61

United States Constitution 32, 123
utilitarianism 146, 148

Vigil, John E. (Judge) 16
voice 38, 39, 41, 190
Von Hoffman, Nicholas 112

Waldron, Jeremy 45, 171
Wall, Steven 171
Wall, Steven and George Klosko 171
Walzer, Michael 138
Weak-man fallacy 168, 169, 170
Whitman, Walt 77
Wiggins, David 109
Williams, Bernard 97, 170, 174
Wisconsin v. Yoder 183
wishful thinking 86
Wolf, Susan 174
Wolfe, Christopher 53, 72
Wolterstorff, Nicholas 59, 116–119
World Church of the Creator 61

Young, Iris 41, 52